The Trauma-Sensitive School

The Trauma-Sensitive School

Transforming Education to Heal
Social and Emotional Wounds

GERALD W. NEAL

McFarland & Company, Inc., Publishers
Jefferson, North Carolina

This book has undergone peer review.

Library of Congress Cataloguing-in-Publication Data

Names: Neal, Gerald Wade, author.
Title: The trauma-sensitive school : transforming education to heal social
and emotional wounds / Gerald W. Neal.
Description: Jefferson : McFarland & Company, Inc., Publishers, 2021 |
Includes bibliographical references and index.
Identifiers: LCCN 2020045118 | ISBN 9781476681238 (paperback : acid free paper) ∞
ISBN 9781476640990 (ebook) ∞
Subjects: LCSH: Students with social disabilities. | Psychic trauma in children. |
Post-traumatic stress disorder in children. | Affective education.
Classification: LCC LC4065 .N343 2020 | DDC 371.826/94—dc23
LC record available at https://lccn.loc.gov/2020045118

British Library cataloguing data are available

ISBN (print) 978-1-4766-8123-8
ISBN (ebook) 978-1-4766-4099-0

Front cover images © 2021 Shutterstock/focal point

Printed in the United States of America

*McFarland & Company, Inc., Publishers
Box 611, Jefferson, North Carolina 28640
www.mcfarlandpub.com*

To my little brother
Freddie

Acknowledgments

Thank you to Dr. Camille Goins, my colleague and friend at the University of North Carolina at Pembroke, for involving me in her research on cultural sensitivity and relevance. She expanded my understanding of culture, including the significance of its role in trauma and how cultural awareness can solidify and enrich relationships so critically important to social-emotional learning strategies.

I would also like to express my appreciation for the insights and direction of Dr. Gary Mauk of the Department of Counseling at the University of North Carolina at Pembroke. Lengthy conversations with Dr. Mauk and his willingness to share related materials had a profound impact on the book's intended contribution to education and school leadership.

Finally, I would like to express appreciation for the pioneering and substantive contributions of Collaborative for Academic, Social, and Emotional Learning (CASEL), the "gold standard" for social and emotional learning, which serves as a foundation for nearly all credible, contemporary educational transformational efforts. The CASEL competencies, standards, and theory undoubtedly influence the aspects of this book that require social and emotional learning concepts and suggested frameworks. The application of CASEL's framework suggested in the text has been done independently. CASEL is merely a reference and has not endorsed or approved the content or suggestions herein at this time.

Table of Contents

PART I

"Children of an Idle Brain"
Understanding Trauma

"I talk of dreams,
Which are the children of an idle brain"
—*Romeo and Juliet*, 1.4.103–104

Introduction:
The Author's Voice

"The wheel is come full circle; I am here."—*King Lear*, 5.3.173

My path from a violent childhood into the world of higher education has revealed many disturbing norms that continue to plague the children I now represent and the adults with whom I team. Seeing my experiences reflected in those of my students has been frustrating, but as a survivor of childhood trauma, I feel a sense of duty to bear witness, and to use my voice to advocate for those without one. It is a calling that grows louder and more insistent as time passes, as if the remaining days of my life should be dedicated to this purpose. To campaign against widespread, misguided ideas about child development, I must convince adults how horrifyingly wrong they have been about raising and educating children. It would be cowardice to depersonalize this message with third-person distance, so I will take a brief opportunity to share pain and sacrifice secrets, in the hope that it imparts a sense of realism to the pages that follow.

The story I tell is the product of constructive reflection and moral outrage, and there is as much damaged child behind these words as there is college professor. It is a synthesis of family, community, and institutional malpractice triangulated into a massive detriment to this nation's youth. This work approaches the problematic, shared assumptions as a whole by piecing together the child's world to expose erroneous suppositions and faulty practices. The fact that we formulaically accept the failure of students with a formal, irresponsible distancing from our roles in the process is at the core of this book. This is not a radical idea that challenges common sense; it is common sense to challenge the radical ideas that underlie a deformed normalcy. All statements lead to hope and the actions needed to turn that hope into realistic, reachable goals. First, however, we must understand. It is important that the reader question his or her practices and tolerances, analyzing the superficial reasons these life incompetencies persevere. We have been tragically guided by concepts we accept without question and entranced by old customs that are easily dispelled, despite what is too often our unwillingness to deviate from them. "Idle brains," in other words, cultishly performing ancient rituals of sacrifice on children without reflection or remorse.

I will not assume that the reader understands the severity and scope of these atrocities at this point, but an open mind will help the light shine in more quickly. To fully appreciate the hold these critical assumptions have on American culture, we need to peel back the tapestries of denial and bias and reveal truths about families, churches, schools, and laws. Despite what the reader has been conditioned to believe, facing the truth is better than living the lies, but it is not my intention to discredit the overall benefit of these institutional pillars. We need empathy to lead children, not blindness. If truth makes the reader defensive, it simply illustrates the points being made. To combat falsehoods or misinterpretations, educators need honesty, even if it runs contrary to what they believed to be real but were forbidden to question. Educators are creatures of this culture, so to lead, they must display courage and understanding because our schools are full of traumatized children. By being honest with ourselves, we have taken the first and most important step.

This book is intended to honor the lives we have been too willing to sacrifice. It is also to save the lives of those who are yet to enter the nightmarish arena, like the defenseless victims of Roman times who were prodded into the Colosseum's deadly center. It is time we stopped supporting the lions. We will attack the pillars of inherited wisdom by explaining how the cancerous notions were allowed to become unquestioned "common sense." Extracting myth will not be without pain or awkwardness. In a sense, we are gullible, naive creatures of habit, applying repetitious, fixed, archaic answers to ever-changing, complex questions.

Everything within these pages matters. The introductory quotations, the sources, the candor, the metaphors—they are words carefully selected by a man who feels it is his duty and obligation to serve those who still attempt to navigate through the darkness of recurring horrors. This book will not only expose the enemies within the institutions who feed on the vulnerabilities of those they are charged to serve; it will provide strategic empowerment for educators to effectively address problems that have plagued schools for decades. Things once considered beyond the educator's control can now be managed at school. There is a need for awareness of what trauma is capable of doing to a child—and to the adult that child becomes. In many cases, this will pull the readers from the comfortable distance they prefer because it will not dance around sensitive issues that are usually considered to be off limits, especially in education. It will teach the reader what he or she already knows but has been unwilling to confront.

I do not wish to dishonor my mother and father, and my siblings probably do not (or would not) appreciate the full disclosure of our particular shared situation, so I will avoid details about my brother and sister and how they navigated through the tempest that battered our sails. Our outcomes were different. The demons caught up with my brother a few months ago when he died prematurely, another statistic to prove the seriousness of this cause; a painful reminder that everyone in my violent, trauma-plagued family has failed to survive his fifties. I share the demons that claimed the life he was trying to salvage, and I wonder how closely behind they follow my sister and me. Losing a brother, when you know his ordeal better than anyone because, as children, you shared everything—a room, stories, belt whippings, emotional abuse, and so many secrets—is gut-wrenching. Essentially, I knew his baggage, saw the signs, and watched him die while naively expecting an unrealistic outcome. As an adult, he was probably not going to save himself or be saved, but I wonder if I could have helped him as his big brother and childhood roommate. There were times when I reached out to him, and there were times when I was simply too broken to fix anyone. Only regret remains when a person becomes aware of a gap between what he could have done and what he actually did to save a lost child. An educator's worth is best measured by the narrowness of that gap. Character can be measured by what someone does in the shadows of anonymity when given freedom of choice. It is what someone sacrifices to improve a world that he or she may never know. It is the focus on the others over the self, a concern for breaths yet to be taken over judgmental gasps. I will always carry the burden of lost opportunity, haunted by the ghosts of what might have been. If only I had listened more deeply to Freddie's stories as we talked at night from our twin beds in the blackness of our small room. If only I shouldered more of his pain and assumed the role that he hoped I would, his days might have been brighter and his life longer.

When Freddie was in second grade, we started drifting apart. Mom and Dad made me supervise my siblings after school until they got home, probably to save the expense of daycare. It was a long three hours every day. I was blamed if something went wrong, and that happened quite regularly. I was spanked for things my siblings did, and they hated me because I was a mean boss, one that strongly opposed being beaten for the things they did. I felt alone in my middle management position. I lost my midnight chats and Freddie lost his big brother because I started reporting him to save myself. My choices were limited to being a protective brother or a trustworthy son. So I was either beaten with a belt for protecting him or forced to watch him being beaten, and at my seeming instigation. I am not sure which I hated more.

That was about 50 years ago, when the world seemed to be falling apart—when school children were trained to crawl under desks to avoid radioactive fallout from a Soviet nuclear blast, when Apollo 13 failed to land on the moon and hobbled back to an indifferent Earth, and when the shootings at Kent State embodied the frustrations of a torn nation at war in Vietnam. It was that fall when Jimi and Janis fell, just 16 days apart, behind a spring when the Beatles decided to let it be. Closer to home, the school board gerrymandered attendance districts to eliminate segregated schools. It was a year when my classmates and I were asked to function socially in a manner our parents could not, alongside different-looking kids from the other side of the city. These black children between the ages of six and ten endured two hours on buses each day in the name of equity. After a decade in which we lost two Kennedys and one King to assassins' bullets, my first memories were back-dropped by public peace rallies and hidden hate crimes. I saw teenage neighbors leave town as smiling soldiers and return emotionless, derided as "baby killers." I had no idea the world was in such disarray because I was eight at the time. Yet as young as I was, I thought that my life would hopelessly evolve from the popping of Dad's belt in my bedroom to the popping of assault rifles in the killing fields of Southeast Asia, where boys who aged out were sent to become men, or die.

When we are born, the people closest to us hold our tiny, vulnerable bodies in their hands like open books and prophesy greatness in the years ahead. It may be the only time in our lives when we are pure potential. No failures to hinder us; no regrets to pause ambition, and no doctrines to control us. We are the first words of a fairy tale that ends with "happily ever after." I never lived by codes developed by others, and never thought the meaning of life could be marketed to the masses via refrigerator magnets and bumper stickers. Purpose always comes from within, and anyone telling others what to think is either hiding or selling something. Honest self-assessment is the only way to escape the cultural trappings that lead to routine habits. As I matured, I analyzed my beliefs to determine whether they were my own or someone else's that had been pounded into my head since birth. I concluded that I was falling into error by trying to apply another's logic to my blueprint. As I lost the security of having others think for me, the world certainly became more challenging. By questioning the chains of traditional thought, I clumsily found creative freedom and intellectual curiosity. I did not know what life had in store, but the adults around me were not convincing enough to inspire me to follow their advice.

My father grew up in a world where ambition was related to becoming the first shift slubber doffer or bobbin turner at the cotton mill. Poverty was considered "middle class" because the people of that community knew little else. Life was what happened between shifts. Cultural norms were developed by people who knew only what their parents taught them or what the "fire and brimstone" preacher spewed into the fearful faces on Sundays. Their values became traditional wisdom to be handed down to me, without scrutiny, something I was to accept as common sense. Customs, habits, language, beliefs, and morals were things that I inherited from these people because they had nothing else to give. I decided not to be them because I was not sure what happened to them, why they seemed to surrender so early and easily, instead of betting on themselves and taking that life-changing gamble. They were born, sold their lives by the hour, and faded into old age without ever seeking more.

I was brought into the world by a teenager who married into that uneducated labor force in the midlife of American industrialism, the newest member of a family caught in the cycle of life broken into eight-hour blocks and accentuated by hammering time clocks and brown-bagged lunches. While my parents were not employed at the local textile plant, many of my extended family members resided in the tiny frame houses surrounding it, packed together like white, wooden Monopoly pieces lining the cheapest properties beside the railroads. Most were born and buried in an area everyone called "Mill Hill," where next-door neighbors could shake hands from their respective kitchen windows. Each morning, lines of workers would pour in and out of the huge smoke-stacked edifice like black ants marching in and out of a red mound of clay. They were non-union workers, bought for minimum wage by the man who drives the Cadillac and puffs the stinky cigar—fatigued and frustrated creatures of commissary shopping and frequent infirmary visits. Laboring only to acquire the means to afford junk food and a sheltered bed, occasionally breaking away for a few days with family where they would blast cigarette smoke toward stained ceilings, guzzle cheap beer, and talk about things they knew nothing about. I am so thankful that my father was not one of these steel-toe-boot-wearing front porch philosophers, slurring out pearls of wisdom to all within earshot. My step-grandfather and most of my uncles, the men I was destined to become, were Vitalis-soaked racists with foul mouths and mounting alimony debt—drugstore cowboys of yesteryear who, without shame, grossly disappointed the promise of their births.

The fact that my father overcame that fate by catching footballs on Friday nights in high school well enough to earn a scholarship to a big university is very significant to my siblings and me; it broke the cycle. The fact that he would later beat me as he was beaten demonstrated that some cycles would remain intact. Dad challenged me to venture beyond his limitations.

Although money was scarce at times, he gave me the skill and enough coaching to catch a football well enough to earn a scholarship too. I was issued a helmet to minimize the chance of permanent brain injury so that I could bounce off of oversized, muscle-bound strangers in numbered jerseys, all in the name of higher education. Dad and Mom often credited their good parenting skills, characterized by the beatings and shamings, as the secret to my success. I now understand. Each generation must learn from the mistakes of the previous. I am much more interested in facilitating growth than assigning blame, but I am also honest with myself: Mom and Dad were afraid of losing me to the real world's vultures sitting on the power lines across from the house, waiting for a fresh carcass to pluck to the bone. They thought a weak parent is one who neglects disciplinary actions. Physical punishment was thought to be the legal, Biblical, and ethical way to raise a child in those days, and in many ways, these days too. This book is intended to educate and facilitate school reform, but first it will challenge cultural norms.

We live in a world where we polarize life's characters to better understand them. I remember watching old westerns on television with my father, who explained to me that Hollywood often provided the good guys with white hats and the bad guys with black ones. When movies were black and white, it made it easier for the viewer to follow the action. If only life were that simple. Movies have heroes and villains, our books have protagonists and antagonists, law has its cops and robbers, and faith has its angels and demons. Everyone else, it seems, has many hues and layers. Our hats are gray and change from time to time. We are unreliable and inconsistent beings, moved to act by things like conformity, personal experiences, and social pressure. My father was a great man in many ways, and Mom, raised in a very verbally abusive family, would make bold sacrifices for her children. They both bore the burdens of abuse that became magnified when they became parents at a very young age. Times change, people grow, and the context of sin fades quicker than the memory of the act itself. The point is not to condemn the actions of others, and it sure is not to condone them. It is, however, to examine ways to systemically help children overcome cultural and historical challenges that prevent them from reaching their full potential.

William Shakespeare is the most poetic and quoted ambassador of Renaissance humanism, a philosophical movement characterized by a transformational celebration of the human condition in the aftermath of the Middle Ages. The Bard empowers the reader by challenging antiquated chains of practice and custom, opening rusted gates that lead toward self-discovery. He encourages non-conformity and demonstrates the heavy costs of perfunctory adherence to social codes or norms. It was

Shakespeare who showed me the way when my path seemed darkest, as if the faint light of a flickering star nearly 500 years away landed on my cheek during my darkest moment, directing me toward the person I never knew that I could be. Education has never needed a breath of hope from the Renaissance more than right now. My hope is that the influence of Shakespeare within this text will provide it.

As Shakespeare so aptly wrote, "I would my father looked but with my eyes" (*A Midsummer Night's Dream* 1.1.58). As a child, I made promises to my adult self, as if floating distress balloons into future skies, hoping they would somehow land in the hands of the man I would become. There were teachers and coaches who gave me the courage to challenge the creeds and codes that formed the cyclical blindness of my family's self-destructive traditions. These educators are almost mythical characters in my memories now, ingrained into everything that is good about me. I am very proud of the child who had the maturity and presence of mind to launch those balloons a half century ago. I am so grateful to my child self for choosing the most untraveled roads, the lonely, dark streets that led him back to me.

1

Maslow and Bronfenbrenner

Their understanding
Begins to swell, and the approaching tide
Will shortly fill the reasonable shore
That now lies foul and muddy
—*The Tempest*, 5.1.89–91

Maslow's "Deficiency Needs"

Most problems in education that have been effectively resolved have a rather unremarkable commonality. Beneath the politics and the drama, the red tape and the boxes of expiring reformation snake oils lies a solution that is usually directly linked back to the quintessential reason schools are built and educators are hired. Educational success is based on the ability of the school to meet the needs of the students. Today, the role of the school is gradually expanding to meet those needs. People are realizing that when needs are met, students prosper; when they are not met, students struggle. New efforts to meet needs are not always directly aligned with the initial mission of a school, so there need to be deliberate practices aligned with the support structures essential to maximal child development.

Too often, political and educational leaders attack recurring symptoms without identifying or understanding the central problem. A cyclical pattern of reactions to reactions has become the norm. Perhaps this is why schools are toiling to meet growth needs while ignoring the more fundamental deficiency needs. Providing free lunches and evacuation procedures is a step in the right direction, but the majority of the attention is dedicated to academic growth that is measured in terms of content acquisition and application. It is as if a gardener is watering a seed in the sunshine, expecting a beautiful plant to emerge without realizing that the soil is barren. Just the right amount of water, a perfect dose of light and temperature,

9

but the plants struggle and wilt. Perhaps the gardener did not know how to nurture the part of the plant that is hidden from view. Maybe he or she was not in charge of the soil and did not see it as his or her responsibility. More than likely, the gardener will eventually assume that the seeds are bad and throw them away. Fortunately, the central problem, one that has been hiding in plain sight for some time, is not complex. When students' needs are met, the chance for success increases dramatically. The most essential needs are in the soil—the foundation that supports growth and leads to the quality of life all humans deserve.

Abraham Maslow's hierarchy of needs is an established theory of psychological health that escalates from the most basic requirements, or the deficiency needs, to the growth needs, culminating with self-actualization, in which cognitive and aesthetic needs are met and the individual reaches his or her full potential. Maslow's model has undergone changes over the past several decades, so to eliminate confusion, this book will refer to the original model, with self-actualization representing all growth needs. Each level of the hierarchy requires fulfillment of the need below. Maslow estimated that two percent of all people reach self-actualization, which is to suggest that the gaps in the foundation below that level become increasingly difficult to overcome.[1] That is not to suggest that they *cannot* be overcome. Part II of this book will demonstrate how the curriculum can increase student academic achievement by at least 11 percent.[2] A focus on deficiency-needs development in a trauma-informed classroom is effective because it supports the foundation beneath cognitive development; too often schools focus on the growth needs and consider some critical deficiency needs to be beyond the scope of an educator's responsibilities. In fact, because satisfying deficiency needs leads to fewer teen pregnancies, incarcerations, dropouts, and mental health issues, every dollar invested in the trauma-informed, social-emotional approach to education saves 11 dollars.[3] A program that builds systems of support, develops non-academic social and emotional skills, and prepares students to become productive members of the community (and in a manner that saves that community money a no-brainer. It all begins with an understanding of Abraham Maslow's hierarchy of needs, and specifically with the deficiency needs, or the basic and psychological needs that one must possess to achieve self-actualization.

Physiological Needs

The first and most basic needs are physiological (biological). Without air, food, shelter, warmth, and water, for example, other developmental needs are inconsequential. Over the years, the school has played an increased role in helping students meet these needs. Consider the provision of food: Schools did not serve lunch until 1946, when Harry Truman signed the National School Lunch Act.[4] Since then, there have been programs to serve students and families breakfast and provide snacks during the school day.

Schools are heated, but recent concerns about the impact of heat on learning in school districts without air conditioning is now getting attention. Jisung Park, in a recent Harvard University study, claims that students measurably underperform in hot conditions: "Taking an exam on a 90° F day relative to a 72° F day results in a reduction in exam performance that is equivalent to a quarter of the Black-White achievement gap, and meaningfully affects longer-run educational outcomes as well, leading to a 12.3 percent higher likelihood of failing a subject exam and a 2.5 percent lower likelihood of on-time high school graduation."[5] This study has helped school leaders understand the relationship between growth and one of the most essential needs. In New York, for instance, where a quarter of city school classrooms were not air-conditioned as of 2017, it was announced that the city would spend nearly $29 million to air-condition every classroom by 2022.[6] When these basic needs are not met, the brain will devalue things unrelated to survival. Since both heat and cold are threats to human survival in extreme conditions, the brain becomes more aware of external conditions when they cause any degree of discomfort.

Safety Needs

Safety is the second most prioritized need, and this is an area that has seen dramatic change over the past several decades, usually motivated by a reaction to tragedy. In 1851, following the deaths of 40 children, the first fire-drill training was established.[7] About a century later, schools implemented "duck and cover" drills to offset the impact of nuclear bombs during the Cold War. Later, metal detectors and police officers would be added to schools. There is now debate over arming teachers and fortifying lockdown procedures. While the motives for these changes are usually reactions to tragedy and political pressure instead of some vision of proactive, whole-child development, the responsibility of the school to provide a safe environment is critically important. Aside from protection from external threats, policies on bullying, violence, crowd protocols, bus procedures, and transitions, for example, demonstrate a strong commitment to safety. Teachers trained to be first responders or to administer epinephrine or diabetes injections are now more common. In terms of protecting students in the community and at home, the school is rather powerless, save the creation of an inviting, protective school culture that fosters strategies to minimize the impact of threats to children by training them how to protect themselves if necessary.

Belongingness and Love Needs

While schools can accommodate many physiological needs and mandate safety procedures to protect children from internal and external threats, there are no consistently applied mandates for the next level in Maslow's hierarchy, belonging and love. Frankly, many schools are built on an antiquated model that packs as many children into a classroom as possible and encourages teachers to become authoritarian figures to preserve order. This traditional model has created occupational stereotypes that need to be challenged, and it concerns an area of Maslow's hierarchy in which great schools excel and poor schools fail. Belongingness is family, unconditional love, and acceptance, where the individual's contributions are considered necessary parts of the whole. Belongingness is attitudinal, and the school culture and classroom climate shapes the mindset of the student. There must be a uniform philosophy that builds a school culture sensitive to the impact of trauma caused by the home, community, and social networks that victimize children. The severity of the problem must be understood by the adults in the school. The school needs to be a safe haven focused on active participation and collaboration, and there should be protocols and training to assure that it perpetuates this condition. Failure needs to be encouraged as part of a process, not a brand sent to parents and colleges that measure worth on one rather insignificant scale. Social interaction and relationship building, often discouraged or minimized in a school setting in favor of directives aligned with curricular competencies, need to be a huge part of the process. Many schools feel coerced into the structures that lead to something that facilitates a form of "overcrowded isolation," something that is basically the opposite of belongingness. Rows of desks, hand raising, lectures, objective tests, extensive homework, and strict rules that minimize social behavior often hinder the meeting of this need. Instead, practices such as restorative justice, culturally responsive pedagogy, and collaborative projects and activities are key fibers in the fabric of a culture of belongingness, as is the trauma-informed classroom and the social-emotional learning culture.

Educational leaders are still learning about the impact of trauma on children, and they now understand that a failure to adequately address belongingness and love creates a huge foundational gap. This understanding brings with it an awareness of how a lack of love and belong-ingness may have contributed to failures of the past. So focused on con-cepts that trivialize the relationship between emotion and cognition, many educational practices have long neglected the developmental skills that support the measured brand of intelligence. Instead, students find belong-ingness in other places, never making it to the levels where they value cog-nitive and aesthetic development, key parts of Maslow's self-actualization process. Progressive school leaders value leadership over obedience, origi-nality over standardization, trial and error over correctness, and creativity over repetition. They are aware of the investments needed to facilitate the whole-child developmental culture.

Self-Esteem Needs

The fourth level of Maslow's hierarchy of needs is reached only when the student's physiological, safety, and emotional (love and belonging) needs are met. Once a student feels a sense of trust and purpose through inclusion and support, that student gradually develops the self-esteem needed to accept challenges and take educational risks. A belief in the self replaces the fear of failure. Self-esteem is not confidence; it is a love of the self that creates a duty to that self to become fulfilled as a human. It is the final block in the foundation, the one most difficult to establish. It provides the mental preparedness required to advance into the growth needs, which give students the curiosity and courage to seek truths in a variety of set-tings. Self-esteem contributes to leadership and problem-solving skills, a trust in the student's ability to find and value meaning in educational tasks. It is the absence of isolation and insignificance and it not only fosters a desire to contribute to the greater good but develops competencies and

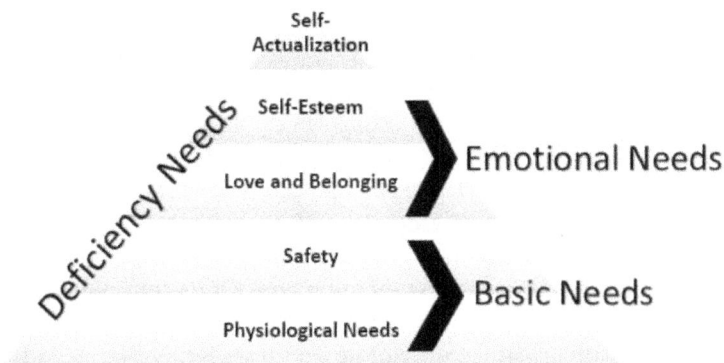

Figure 1. Maslow's Hierarchy of Needs

dispositions that relate to lifelong successes. It is the resiliency to recover from trauma without suffering a significant emotional setback. Educators that help students fulfill the four deficiency needs—physiological, safety, love and belonging, and self-esteem—have a tremendously potent effect on learning, and this help should supplement all attempts to develop measurable academic aptitudes.

Then, and only then, can students learn to value the lessons of history, see the beauty of poetry and art, hypothesize about a scientific experiment, or value the sequential and formulaic thinking in mathematics. Only after the needs detailed in the first four levels of Maslow's hierarchy have been met can students realize their potential. It is only then that the student is able to flourish in Maslow's cognitive and aesthetic stages. Yet the focus is rarely on the deficiency needs, because they are not easily measured. In fact, unmet deficiency needs are often revealed in poor grades and behavior issues, but they are rarely addressed by re-evaluating the extent to which a student's basic or emotional needs are being satisfied. Instead, educators have historically been prone to punish, stigmatize, and assign negative scores when exposed to the symptoms of under-developed deficiency needs, intensifying the degradation of the child. Alternatives to these negative actions will be recommended in Part II of this book, and they include ways to assess students while minimizing the impact of grading on the student's self-esteem.

While educators are not solely responsible for meeting deficiency needs, they should not assume that the needs are being satisfied elsewhere. It does not matter whether educators perfectly understand the nature of a child's trauma; the remedy is a blanket that nurtures everyone in the building, students and employees. Maslow's hierarchy of needs provides the map for nurturing schools to follow. Using it to create the institutional culture that school reformists have sought is not that complicated or expensive— certainly not as complicated or expensive as it is to ignore students' needs and development. The right approach requires awareness, skill, expertise, patience, and systems thinking.

The reader should understand that the intention is not to point fingers at parents, politicians, preachers, or principals, but to alert them to the new facts. The change needed to transform schools is a cultural matter, not one that requires legislation or approvals from policy-makers far removed from the classroom. Most desire change, and the habit has been to change for the sake of it, but nobody seems to understand or agree on what change will produce the desired effect. Many do not understand the complexity of the problem, because often it includes something they overlook. Since many politicians do not fully understand the process of learning or how to sustain academic growth, they can be manipulated by doom-and-gloom theories or by someone trying to sell them a magic potion that will cure all ills. For this reason, any change must produce data that show the degree to which students are learning. While high test scores are not significant to the intended consequences of this book, it is reasonable to assume that academic growth will be enhanced and sustained. Maslow's model has demonstrated this concept for more than 75 years, but there has been some confusion about what it means or how to apply it effectively. Hopefully, this book will help identify some of the cultural problems that cripple educational reform. These unchallenged, erroneous concepts, accepted as truths and contaminating our schools, are based on numeric evaluation, discipline, structure, competition, and content acquisition void of personal relevance. These methods and practices are characterized by a disregard for our ability to develop the needs of a child so they can be taught the material and skills society has deemed to be essential. Once focused on a basic, rather one-dimensional curriculum, the modern school now must develop an environment for personalized learning as a part of whole-child development, and must help heal the effects of things beyond the control of the school. This will require that educators stop seeing children through the eyes of adults and start seeing themselves through the eyes of students.

Maslow has never been proven wrong. His ideas are common sense, and his hierarchy of needs is just that—a hierarchy. Children and educators alike need to understand that diversity is not a condition, it is an opportunity. English may be the language that dominates the community, but it is not the dominant language for many who are equally entitled to learn. Educators must understand that there are unseen obstacles that effect learning and behavior, things like hunger, poverty, and domestic trauma. Some students live in fear or unsafe situations; some are overcoming a family death or bullying. Regardless of the reason, a healthy, informed culture and strategic pedagogy can heal most children. The remedy is rarely found in the teacher's grade book or principal's code of conduct. Educators cannot consistently teach children who do not feel as if they belong or work with parents who do not feel welcome in the building. They cannot teach children who mistrust the adults charged with their development. Fear is not an effective motivator; it is a warning of a threat. Educators must teach children who are safe and know it, who belong and know it, and who are confident and show it. The trauma-sensitive, social-emotional learning school culture is built on trust, belongingness, and ambitious expectations.

Bronfenbrenner

Russian-American developmental psychologist Urie Bronfenbrenner conceptualized four ecological systems that expand from the immediate family to cultural influences, specifically, the influence of religion on the laws and parenting values that are so essential to the well-being of the child. His bioecological model is one of the primary influences of the American Headstart prekindergarten programs.[8] Listed below from the inside out, each of the four inter-connected, ecological systems has some form of impact on the child. It is strongly suggested that these systems of support serve as the framework for the principal's community- and parental-involvement strategies and are evidenced in the school marketing plan (to be detailed in chapter 13). They are listed below, starting with the system most immediately and directly associated with the child and proceeding to the most distant or global:

1. The **microsystem** exerts the most direct and powerful influence on the child. It consists of human relationships, social interactions, and surroundings. An example of this system would be the circle of humans directly around the child, such as the parents, siblings, or school relationships. Friends, including those on social media, are also considered part of a child's microsystem.

2. The **mesosystem**, or second layer surrounding the child, involves the combination of elements of the microsystem. For example, parents and school leaders can forge a connection that contributes to the development of the child, creating a network of support. Of course, the school should take an active part in facilitating such relationships, providing events, resources, communicative opportunities, and guidance, should that be needed. School leaders can share a marketing plan that introduces the new social-emotional learning program, for instance, while a professional learning community hosts a hot dog dinner to inform and connect with parents.

3. The third layer, or **exosystem**, consists of external factors or events that impact members of the child's microsystem. Parents lose jobs, get divorced, and experience setbacks that create stress—all of it has an impact on the child. Friends could turn on each other, putting the child in a difficult situation, or a tornado could ravage the school. The trauma-sensitive school helps overcome threats to the child's exosystem by developing networks and providing information to external stakeholders.

4. The **macrosystem** includes societal beliefs, cultural norms, and laws, all of which are extremely powerful elements of the child's community and to some extent characterize the broader culture. If the elements of the macrosystem are found to threaten children in any way, or if there is new information that calls accepted customs and routines into question, the trauma-sensitive school must take the lead.

Using strategies such as topical town halls or roundtable discussions with community leaders, the successful school becomes the leading advocate for the child by injecting knowledge and empowerment into the bloodstream that ties family, community, and the wider culture together.[9]

If the school does not take the lead in understanding the spheres of influence around a child, it will be tasked with answering to those that do. Not all influences are direct, such as those exerted on a child by the parent; the educator must be aware of the influences that trickle down to the child, as when a work supervisor cuts back on the parent's hours, making life more stressful for both parent and child. This book addresses all of Bronfenbrenner's systems in multiple ways because the trauma-sensitive school supports children on every level, without apology to supporting adults or fear of intrusion into topics that some may consider off limits. These dynamics empower those directly associated with children.

2

Child Trauma

For we will fetters put about this fear
Which now goes too free-footed
—*Hamlet*, 3.3.26–27

Institutional Blindness

In the United States in 2014, there were about 73.6 million children at or below 17 years of age.[1] That same year, an estimated 702,000 victims of child maltreatment were identified through investigations that followed reports to child protective agencies.[2] According to this data, fewer than one percent (0.0095) of all children were identified as abused and neglected by the current process of identification, reporting, and investigating. Since recent studies suggest that there is a much larger population of abused or neglected children that is never identified, reported, or investigated, it stands to reason that many children are not being served. Mounting evidence supports the supposition that certain forms of child maltreatment may be tolerated in the United States; in fact, there are violent acts against children that impair cognitive functioning and psychological development that are supported by laws, religious beliefs, and cultural traditions. Some Christians, for instance, support the practice of spanking by referring to the Old Testament, where at Proverbs 13:24 they find the original version of the "spare the rod, spoil the child" cliché. Lawmakers, even those bound to a commitment to separate church and state, rely on personal morality that is deeply rooted in the soil of their personal spiritual doctrines. Most are products of families that used spirituality as the foundation for ethics and morality to determine right from wrong. Inevitably, this results in a triangulation of morality, ethics, and family values spawned by religious doctrine. Violent acts against children that would be crimes if the perpetrators were not their parents are tolerated because they are supported by the institutions that give a society civility and order. These adverse childhood experiences have a profound effect on the child's ability to learn, interact in society, and build loving relationships. In other words, child maltreatment adversely affects the long-term quality of life for the individual. Many adults ignore this data-supported logic and cling to erroneous, self-serving justifications for exercising tyrannical and violent control over those they are actually charged to nurture. Political leaders fund treatments of the symptoms of the central problem without attempting to identify the actual problem. They fail to accept that acts of aggression against children, which are in some instances legal and deemed moral by many, could have such a permanent, negative outcome.

This lack of understanding is why many educational reform efforts are neither lasting nor effective. It is probably also the biggest reason that our schools struggle to meet expectations. And because the problem is so twisted into the fabric of what many consider normal, monies flow over and around the actual problem, into the pockets of those treating recurring symptoms. Educators are blamed by society for not repairing the issues that same society creates and supports. To avoid all of the negative publicity unfairly attributed to them, schools resort to marketing and branding campaigns that often do little more than propagandize and glorify mediocrity because they lack a strategy to combat what threatens them. In essence, the effort to create an antiseptic, cost-effective process of elimination is under way. Churches, the core of morality and values for many, convert ancient biblical passages into dogma that supports a process negatively impacting children. Schools must dress the wounds without the ability to question those traditions or identify the severity of the damage, all while assuming the blame for traumatized children's inability to pass tests. If someone questions the laws that give parents the legal right to strike their children, adults fear their constitutional right to do so might be removed by the government. If someone questions a few Biblical verses that are interpreted to condone the cruel and destructive treatment of children, these challenges are ridiculed as heresy or blasphemy, often without reasonable counterpoints. This is the society that inadvertently damages children without objective reflection while issuing ratings to schools to measure their effectiveness. Most things that cause children to struggle in the school setting do not happen within the school setting; they happen at home and in the community. The nation is losing its children to cyclical patterns that perpetuate problems from generation to generation. The nation is losing its children to diseases and suicides because it fails to protect them from the adults in their support systems. The United States of America seems unaware that it is complicit, watching those who die prematurely from diseases because many do not see the link between sickness and adversity. We have accepted lunacy as common sense because that is how many have been trained to think. There is information available that should shock this nation into action, but it seems that the nation, as a whole, refuses to see what the rest of the world has come to realize.

Preventable domestic trauma is the primary cause for much of what inhibits schools from reaching maximal results. Many children bring dark secrets through the doors each day, hidden experiences that erode any sense of belonging or feelings of self-esteem. Parents and educators cannot expect children to learn when their deficiency needs are not being met. These guilt-ridden, frustrated children are demeaned and targeted in schools that prioritize obedience and order. In many cases, these battered kids develop unbalanced social skills that can result in suspensions, verbal humiliation, failing assessments, and exclusions from social and extra-curricular activities. They become withdrawn or rebellious as they struggle to fit in. Frankly, schools have focused on these reactive behaviors instead of focusing on proactive methods that might modify them. Any acts that disrupt the cognitive development plan of the majority are addressed by punitive measures. In an effort to coerce children to behave, schools punish improper behaviors as deviant acts against the social norms of the mainstream. The child's behaviors are often rather obvious cries for help, but those cries are lost in the chaos generated by the horrors of the home and the punitive consequences of the school. The source of the problem is ignored while the symptoms beget punishment. There is no place for children to satisfy needs or heal. Education has yet to develop effective strategies to meet needs, focusing instead on content curricula and disciplinary codes to develop children. Some of this is attributable to a lack of funding, which is rooted in a lack of awareness.

It is safe to assume that the number of children who suffer from a form of traumatizing maltreatment in the home is higher than 50 percent, the percentage of parents in America that spank their children.[3] It will be detailed later how spanking is proven to have the same neurological impact on the brain as physical abuse or neglect, so any attempt to excuse the practice of corporal punishment is based on suppositions unrelated to the developmental needs of the child. It is probably a safe assumption, although this data is not yet available, that the total number of children who suffer from trauma capable of causing neurological dysfunctionality is seven in every ten children in a school. It is also safe to assume that the percentage is higher in school districts characterized by high poverty. Since there are no definitive studies that gauge the total range of all forms of trauma, calculated speculation is necessary. Many children experience multiple forms of adversity, so the estimation of children enduring domestic trauma is not exact. Since the only identified difference between spanking and child abuse is the degree of physical damage or the name adults decide to attribute to the disciplinary action, and since long-term, psychological and emotional impact are not identifiers in most cases, the distinction between physical abuse and corporal punishment will be thoroughly analyzed throughout this book—because understanding the sources of trauma is critically important. This analysis will not endorse adult perspectives that are incongruous with valid research conclusions, even if supported by law or religious beliefs. Neither will it support any justification for hitting, shaming, or neglecting children. Perhaps the threat of physical violence forces people to conform to ideologies that run contrary to their beliefs, but we now know that those of us who were hit probably found it much more challenging to "turn out just fine." The focus of this text is to expose misconceptions, not embrace or validate them by accepting excuses or testimonies unsupported by data.

This is why the emotional and psychological needs (the third and fourth deficiency needs) of Maslow's hierarchy are so critical to learning and growth. By creating a culture that prioritizes the skills and dispositions needed to establish resiliency in all children, schools will immediately become more successful. This book provides a framework for teachers and leaders to develop trauma-informed teaching and social-emotional learning as a key component of a transformational, trauma-sensitive school culture. Since ownership and individualization are essential, this is not a recipe or cookie-cutter approach to program development. There are no quick fixes; we cannot undo centuries of bad practices and flawed logic in a few workshops or memos. Plan development requires awareness of the problem, a proper collective attitude, open minds, and a willingness to challenge sacred or established norms. It is hoped that the statistics and narratives contained in these pages will provide the motivation and blueprint to commit to save and effectively educate children.

Adverse Childhood Experiences (ACEs)

It is one thing to have a problem, but it is another to assume that it does not exist. To opine that the problem belongs to someone else, to consider it a "necessary evil" and feel powerless to address it, to be misled into thinking that the problem is much smaller than it actually is—all are disabling habits of mind. It is hard to believe that these forms of ignorance cloud such a critically important issue. In the United States, these faulty perspectives unite to cast attention away from what might be the most significant threat to its children. These elements of the culture form a perfect storm, a dangerous combination of outdated laws, misguided family values, and inadequate funding. To make matters worse, its powerless victims have no voice. Doing nothing eventually costs taxpayers 11 times more than programs that foster social-emotional learning, yet the nation continually writes checks to address the aftermath of this epidemic instead of focusing on prevention.[4] As a result, money that could be spent helping children overcome the ill effects of their circumstances is spent on services aligned with adult rehabilitation programs.

The lack of awareness, which the federal government does little to address, is breathtaking, and frustrating. The problem begins with the available data concerning *child maltreatment*, the term used to refer to both abused and neglected children. It is important to understand that the federal government relies on states to provide information that factors into this national statistic, which suggests that less than one percent of all children are maltreated. There are variations in funding, protocols, and laws from state to state that have muddied the waters for those attempting to grasp the problem. Most cases of abuse and neglect, for example, go unreported, yet they are among the few traumatizing actions that are illegal. While there are other factors that cause domestic trauma, these two forms are the most prevalent. Frankly, the severity of the situation is often hidden beneath other factors that either trivialize or condone the behavior. How many people who approve of spanking, for instance, know when a spanking becomes physical abuse? Even if they know, do they consider an accidental "crossing the line" to be a crime if they consider spanking moral and just? In other words, besides teachers, who interacts with children enough to identify patterns and develop communicative relationships that might reveal what goes on in the home? Teachers are obligated to report abuses to social services, but are they trained to detect them? Policies may clear institutions of legal responsibilities, but they do not concern the training needed to identify abuse, so this book will proceed with insights and strategies that heal abused children without identifying specifically who they are. It maintains a focus on the psychological, emotional, and cognitive impairments that tend to create unseen challenges for educators seeking to help all children become self-actualized adults.

The number of abused children reported by states influences funding, and any group constituting less than a single percent of the overall population of children is not going to generate much attention amid a sea of needs and causes. In 1995, for example, the funding for all government programs concerning child maltreatment was substantially higher than it was in 2014. A Princeton study claims that the large majority of the funding for child protection is applied to out-of-home care, not investigations or prevention programs.[5] So if the percentage of children found to be physically abused is less than one percent, and funding is based on demand, and most of the money invested is applied to treatments and other forms of "out-of-home" care, how are maltreated children actually being supported?

The financial costs for victims and the overall society are substantial. A journal article in *Child Abuse & Neglect* entitled "The Economic Burden of Child Maltreatment in the United States and Implications for Prevention" found the total lifetime estimated financial costs associated with just one year of confirmed cases of child maltreatment (physical abuse, sexual abuse, psychological abuse and neglect) is approximately $124 billion. "The lifetime cost for each victim of child maltreatment who lived was $210,012.... The cost includes discounted present values of $32,648 in childhood health care costs, $10,530 in adulthood medical costs, $144,360 in productivity losses, $7,728 in child welfare costs, $6,747 in criminal justice costs, and $7,999 in special education costs."[6] The burden on the taxpayer is substantial, indicating the importance of prevention efforts on all levels. Considering these data are based on "substantiated or indicated" cases as reported to Child Protective Services, there are a few variables that need to be considered to put this into perspective. First, the statistics are based on data that concludes the percentage of maltreated children represents less than 1 percent of the entire population of children.[7] For cases to be considered for "substantiated or indicated" screening, they must first be reported. By far, most cases go unreported.

Before we revise the number of children identified as traumatized by maltreatment and other stressors not directly identified by the federal government, we should understand that efforts to reform school culture need to target a much larger population of children. While the school administrator may be more focused on how academic achievement improves in a trauma-sensitive school culture, the societal impact is tremendous, something that may interest the politicians that fund school systems. As previously mentioned, the report published by the Center on Great Teachers and Leaders indicates that every dollar invested in social-emotional learning programs that lead to whole-child development saves the taxpayer $11 over the long term. Early interventions that can be proven to save money are more likely to be funded. Specifically, most of the adverse experiences that trigger life-long aberrant reactions such as alcoholism, drug addiction, violent and aggressive behaviors, smoking, unemployment, and various psychological disorders cost the American taxpayers billions of dollars. These are evidence of the emotional devastation abuse and corporal punishment causes, and our laws determine abuse by physical scarring alone. While the physical abuse is extremely disturbing, the long-term costs are attributed mostly to psychological damage, which seems to be of little interest to the courts, probably because it is not immediately noticeable and is nearly impossible to prove.

In many ways, it is disappointing that any suggestion to improve school culture so that it meets all students' needs must involve a discussion of economic feasibility. Programs that support maltreated children are being cut as awareness of these youngsters increases. In 2001, federal assistance to states for child care was cut by $200 million—"[slicing] 18 percent off federal funds to help states prevent and investigate child abuse and neglect"[8] It did not stop there. From 2005 to 2009, "Congress cut federal funding to states to treat and protect abused and neglected children by 17 percent."[9] Since then, even as the stock market has reached new highs and unemployment has approached all-time lows—both signs of economic prosperity—the funding to provide early interventions for needy children on the state and federal levels is disappearing. Many politicians consider these programs to be "entitlements," or funding "black holes," that provide no visible or expeditious return on the investment; so instead they give preferential treatment to popular programs that tend to show results more quickly and help get them re-elected. In light of that preference, it seems misguided to count on politicians or lawmakers to help the voiceless, non-voting population of our nation. But that is not to suggest persistence will not pay dividends.

If governmental support programs have seemed ineffective, it may be due to the fact that they were underfunded to begin with, with that funding based on misrepresentative data. The problem cannot be addressed unless the full shape of the iceberg is identified. By funding programs equipped to serve only a small number of reported cases—a mere fraction of the actual number of maltreated children—they set up the process to fail. The problem, then, is hidden by skewed data. Unfortunately, the purse strings are often controlled by people who do not understand the value of investing in children, perhaps because many leaders are the products of privilege. Or perhaps it is because children cannot vote. Whatever the reason, the system is set up to inhibit societal and cultural empathy, which makes the lack of investment no great surprise.

So what percentages of children are actually traumatized by maltreatment and how does one identify these children in order to help them? It is highly unlikely that parents, usually the abusers and the individuals responsible for the child's care, will consent to be interviewed on the topic or to provide detailed accounts of domestic violence or neglect to surveyors. Nor will they allow their children to be surveyed about such sensitive matters. As suggested in my previous book, *Quiet Desperation: The Effects of Competition in School on Abused and Neglected Children* (2008), perhaps the only way determine the severity of the problem is to survey adults willing to honestly reflect on their childhoods. This immediately dates the feedback, but nobody should be operating under the illusion that this problem is a new one or that it has improved over time. While there are people who might have blocked out traumatic memories, and while others may be unwilling to draw a distinction between physical abuse and corporal punishment to honor their parents or faiths, estimates based on these surveys are much closer to the truth than the government's estimate. In 1995, the Centers for Disease Control and Prevention (CDC) and Kaiser Permanente began surveying adults during physical examinations regarding childhood experiences and current health status and behaviors. Over 17,000 participants are still being monitored by this longitudinal study, which is expanding and garnering long overdue attention. It identifies domestic traumas called adverse childhood experiences (ACEs),[10] which are traumatic childhood events that could potentially have a lasting effect on a child's development, often negatively impacting that individual's entire life. While it should be understood that the ACE study is a fluid, expanding process, the early returns on the data reveal alarming realities. Abuse and neglect are examples, but so might be witnessing domestic violence, enduring a death in the family, or having a parent incarcerated. It is noteworthy that the ACE study covers 10 familial forms of trauma, while not clearly considering corporal punishment, which has recently been determined to have similar psychological and emotional stressors for children. While it defines physical abuse in a way that should include spanking, there is no indication that those surveyed made that distinction when compared to other data collected in a similar fashion about spanking. In addition, the ACE study does not include trauma experienced in the community or school, such as bullying or natural disasters. While the ACE study is the best of its kind to date, it does not examine all potential sources of trauma to a child. The number of ACEs and the frequency of them increase the likelihood for long-term complications that foster dysfunctionality, which in turn leads to poor choices (smoking, drug addiction, alcoholism, and so forth) and potential mental disorders. Until recently, few made the connection. Ultimately, the study shows a relationship between the number of ACEs and a shorter life expectancy. It does not make distinctions between simple or complex trauma, nor does it weigh traumas based on severity, but the study reveals the magnitude of the underestimations previously discussed.

According to the ACE data presented in table 1, of the 17,337 participants, approximately two of every three experienced a traumatic event during their childhoods. Nearly four in ten experienced multiple forms of trauma. It is relatively accurate to assume that at least one third of all children are victims of violent abuse and that a fourth of all girls are sexually abused. Since the ACE data does not factor recurrences or severity, it is difficult to break down the data beyond the report on the table, but it is not difficult to see how severely disjointed the federal government data are when aligned with the actual problem.[11] There are a number of probable reasons for this—most cases go unreported, evidence is often inconspicuous or nonphysical, programs have been cut and underfunded—and they undoubtedly combine to throw off the number of cases.

Table 1.
Prevalence of ACEs by Category, CDC–Kaiser Study

ACE Category	Women Percent (N = 9,367)	Men Percent (N = 7,970)	Total Percent (N = 17,337)
ABUSE			
Emotional Abuse	13.1%	7.6%	10.6%
Physical Abuse	27%	29.9%	28.3%
Sexual Abuse	24.7%	16%	20.7%
HOUSEHOLD CHALLENGES			
Mother Treated Violently	13.7%	11.5%	12.7%
Household Substance Abuse	29.5%	23.8%	26.9%
Household Mental Illness	23.3%	14.8%	19.4%
Parental Separation or Divorce	24.5%	21.8%	23.3%
Incarcerated Household Member	5.2%	4.1%	4.7%
NEGLECT			
Emotional Neglect*	16.7%	12.4%	14.8%
Physical Neglect*	9.2%	10.7%	9.9%

*Note: Collected during Wave 2 only (N = 8,629).
Source: "Adverse Childhood Experiences (ACEs)." Centers for Disease Control and Prevention. April 1, 2016. Accessed March 8, 2019. https://www.cdc.gov/violenceprevention/child abuseandneglect/ acestudy/index.html? CDC_AA_refVal=https://www.cdc .gov/violenceprevention/acestudy/index.html.

In short, the understanding of the problem has been horribly underestimated by those in power, and every dollar that was cut from programs to help children cost taxpayers more than tenfold later. If investments in children are not a priority, what is? This lack of vision, responsibility, empathy, and common sense reflects a corresponding lack of leadership. It demonstrates thinking that is both fiscally and morally bankrupt. While citizens should be outraged by this, it has become so commonplace that they seem to accept it as a fact of life. Yes, we scratch our heads at town halls and school board meetings, wondering what to do about these gaps and underperformance, yet we cut funds to protect children, refuse to pay teachers what they are worth, and buy every quick fix or cookie-cutter program proposed, failing to address the central problem.

Death

Disease and
Disabilitties

Adaptation of health
risk behaviors

Social, emotional, cognitive
impairment

Disrupted Neurodevelopment

Adverse Childhood Experiences (ACEs)

"The ACE Pyramid," Centers for Disease Control and Prevention, June 14, 2016, accessed March 5, 2019, https://www.cdc.gov/violenceprevention/childabuseandneglect/acestudy/about.html.

Figure 2. The ACE Pyramid: From Birth Until Death

As with Maslow's hierarchy of needs (fig. 1), where the progress toward self-actualization is represented by levels in a pyramid, the ACE pyramid (fig. 2) represents a progression, in this case from birth to death. At the foundation of the ACE pyramid are any and all adverse childhood experiences. Obviously, the number of ACEs and their severity may be reasonably expected to determine the individual's quality of life, since ACEs often lead to disrupted neurodevelopment. There are severe trauma-related afflictions to brain functioning that create life-long neurological disabilities. The ACEs and their impact on the brain during its development lead to the third level of the pyramid: social, emotional, and cognitive impairment. While the educator may not be aware of the first two levels because they are not visible or easily known, it is quite certain that he or she is familiar with this third level. Learning, in its quintessential state, is emotional. In children, it is reasonable to argue that most learning is also social. It is short step from there to conclude that adverse childhood experiences distort children's abilities to regulate emotions and socialize. It is devastating to realize that these children are often disciplined and flunked without any awareness of their conditions or any attempt to modify their environments to support them.

In relation to Maslow's pyramid, educators would become involved primarily during the students' belonging and love need, which intersects with the social and emotional impairments level of the ACE pyramid. Like ships passing in the night, one headed toward a welcoming port, the other headed out into the blackness of a turbulent sea, it marks the point at which the child must be either saved or lost. Yet this extremely important junction of two forces in the child's social, emotional, and psychological development generally garners little attention in public schools. It is the sweet spot, the moment of truth, and the point of no return all wrapped into one teachable, rescuable opportunity; yet many schools do not have a deliberate, effective plan to establish a sense of love and belonging that leads to the establishment of self-esteem. Again, this is the most critical point in a child's development, where he or she could be lost to the destructive forces described in the ACE study or redirected toward an inclusive embrace that leads to self-actualization and a lifetime of personal success and happiness. What does the school do? Too often, it suspends the child for reacting to the traumas that unaware adults or volatile peers often trigger. It evaluates the child and issues scores based on their cognitive abilities, even though adverse experiences lead to impaired cognitive functioning. It calls the parents, often the source of the trauma, to discuss the child's outrageous behavior, often in a manner that enrages the parent. Meanwhile, at central office, heads are being scratched over unimpressive data that indicates the degree to which funding is financing underperformance.

Social-emotional development, for the most part, is assumed to be ingrained into the curriculum and extra-curricular offerings or else to be a natural byproduct of teacher-student relationships—but not something that is (in most cases) a deliberate or measured component of the school culture. It is far from obvious that the school is engaged in a battle for the child's future, one that requires the staff to overcome the threats that haunt the child when he or she is not at school. Can the school pull the child into its supportive network that features love and a sense of belonging, or will it fail, allowing the child to drift out of its harbor into that turbulent sea? How ironic that the institutions designed to educate children so that they might become productive adults have such a huge blind spot at this incredibly critical juncture. The significance of the parallels between Maslow's pyramid and the ACE lifespan pyramid cannot be overstated. Meeting deficiency needs is the most effective way to offset or ease the impact of dysfunctional neurodevelopment. Schools and teachers have the ability to create nurturing, supportive, social environments that can offset the devastation of ACEs. Part II of this book will provide much more detail concerning how that can be done, with perspectives for both teachers, staffers, and school administrators.

As children age, according to the ACE study, they go through a process of "adoption of health-risk behaviors" that leads to increased risk for disease and disabilities. This could involve finding acceptance in gangs, for instance, or with other outcasts who may resort to drugs or alcohol as a means of self-medication. Many of the risk factors are associated with depression, so there are concerns that range from obesity to suicide, depending on the number of ACEs. Often these behaviors are dictated by the group that adopts the child, since the search for acceptance and belongingness leads the child to those who are willing to affirm bad decisions— that is, decisions more aligned with escaping than developing. When the individual gets to this stage, it is difficult to make a significant impact in the school, but there is little doubt educators in middle and secondary schools are quite familiar with the symptoms. Essentially, the window to reach the child has nearly or fully closed, and short of some cataclysmic event in the child's life, it is difficult to make the necessary connection; however, it is a mistake to assume that educators cannot save a child from more severe consequences and that they should not try. These children are lost in a confused state of rebellious coping or retaliation. Later, the hospital model of therapeutic interventions will be introduced, and the metaphor is applicable here. The higher the child ascends the ACE pyramid, the more critical his or her condition becomes and the likelihood for a cure is reduced.

What do these children look like? They might be the quiet, shy, withdrawn children who want to be ignored. They might be the children who dress and act like someone they admire, such as a popular musician or athlete, attempting to escape their identity. They might be the gang members or the bullies. Understand that these children are in search of a way to ease their pain but trust few adults. There is no one-size-fits-all profile for these children, but their behaviors can be life threatening because they often lead to poor choices. They are all self-medicating in some way. They all have needs, and the most challenging students are likely to have the biggest gaps in their deficiency needs. Establishing trust is the first step in the process of reaching out to these children effectively, and it is no small accomplishment.

These behaviors are often associated with increased potential for long-term illnesses that are attributed to premature death when compared to the control group. The ACE study reveals that the number of ACEs is directly related to an increased likelihood to contract a chronic or life-threatening disease. Participants in the study who suffered from four or more ACEs were:

- 2.2 times more likely to develop heart disease
- 1.9 times more likely to develop cancer
- 2.4 times more likely to suffer a stroke
- 3.9 times more likely to develop chronic bronchitis or emphysema
- 1.6 times more likely to develop diabetes[12]

This is how childhood trauma costs $24 billion each year. This is the price our nation pays for hitting and abusing children or exposing them to other forms of maltreatment. This is why some traumatized children's lifespans are 20 years shorter than those who have no adverse experiences.

It is statistically evident that participants in the ACE study were unable to avoid some degree of personal bias and did not apply the ACE's operational definition of "physical abuse" when responding to that question. Instead, they seem to have made a distinction between corporal punishment and physical abuse because the percentage of physically abused children in the study is approximately half the number exposed in surveys about spanking. In the ACE study, physical abuse is said to occur when "a parent, stepparent, or adult living in your home pushed, grabbed, slapped, threw something at you, or hit you so hard that you had marks or were injured."[13] While this description certainly describes physical abuse, it could also be applied to practices that are legally and ethically accepted as parental discipline. Since the term *physical abuse* is not generally thought to include what most categorize as corporal punishment, it is unlikely that a person who believes in spanking will consider it traumatic, even when belts or boards are used, or entertain the possibility that it might result in a negative outcome. In addition, it is doubtful participants engaged in spanking as parents (it can be cyclical) would decide that anything they do to discipline their children is physical abuse. Finally, some may be unwilling to identify their parents as abusive at the time of the survey. For this reason, much of this book is dedicated to the premise that all forms of violence are traumatic, regardless of how they are supported by religion, law, or tradition. Since educators focus on learning and behavior, it is imperative that educational leaders and teachers understand that physical abuse is psychological or emotional abuse; there is no way to have physical abuse without the child paying an emotional toll as well. It is akin to the "pound of flesh, but not one drop of blood" distinction central to the *Merchant of Venice* plot. In fact, the hypocrisy of religion and the law, these cornerstones of human morality and ethics, should be diplomatically challenged by school leaders, and without apology. This issue will be analyzed in more detail in chapter 3 so that the reader grasps the full range of things that traumatize children, developing an understanding that most children are victims and their behavior is nothing more than an immature reaction to the "idle brain" that governs them.

3

Other Common Sources
of Trauma

'Tis the eye of childhood
That fears a painted devil
—*Macbeth*, 2.2.70–71

Spanking

As discussed in the previous chapter, an area that seems problematic in the adverse childhood experiences (ACE) study is how corporal punishment (domestic and institutional spanking) is addressed. The ACE study seems to address corporal punishment data in the area of physical abuse, but there is reason for concern that personal bias may have clouded the participants' abilities to literally and operationally define the term. Specifically, the ACE study defines physical abuse using terminology that is applicable, in part, to practices that are also aligned with common views of corporal punishment. It fails to draw the line between the two, something that could skew data in this area, assuming it is important to make the distinction. Again, the ACE study defines physical abuse this way: "A parent, stepparent, or adult living in your home pushed, grabbed, slapped, threw something at you, or hit you so hard that you had marks or were injured."[1] It is curious that hitting without leaving marks seems to fall short of meeting the standards, a fact that makes this definition somewhat confusing. It seems that being grabbed is abuse, but hitting someone with a paddle without leaving a mark is not. Since other studies conclude that the number of adults who were spanked as children ranges between half to nearly two thirds, there seems to be a disconnect between this data and that which includes all forms of physical discipline. The ACE study indicates that the percentage of adults who experienced being "pushed, grabbed, slapped … or hit" is between one fourth and one third of the population. It seems unlikely that anyone could have experienced corporal punishment in a manner that doesn't meet the study's operational definition for physical abuse, but it is possible that the survey takers failed to consider spanking as a form of the latter, despite the study's operational definition, because the ACE definition is not exhaustive. Many individuals might feel that physical child abuse is bad and spanking is good, yet struggle to define the line between the two. Many of those surveyed may feel that their parents' intention was not malicious or uncontrolled and that, therefore, they were not abused. Yet there is very little or nothing that separates spanking and physical abuse in the area of emotional harm. According to a recent Rasmussen Reports survey, only 18 percent of Americans favor laws that prohibit corporal punishment, or spanking, by parents.[2] If most survey takers likewise consider spanking acceptable, it is problematic that the survey asks them to include corporal punishment under the "physical abuse" heading. This is not an attempt to discredit the ACE study, but it is interesting to note that it features data illustrating a key societal flaw, and one that will be challenged later in this book.

Frankly, the line between physical abuse and spanking is blurry or even nonexistent until a social worker or judge applies an interpretation of the facts. The addition of an eleventh ACE, corporal punishment, would remove bias and ambiguity from being applied to a very direct operational definition. Since the ACE study seems to focus on emotions, attitudes, and behaviors associated with trauma and not the pain or physical harm attributed to the stressor, it stands to reason that any act of domestic trauma with psychological implications should be clearly represented, regardless of intention or adult ideologies. The only real difference is the adults' perception of the act, not the results. Classifying spanking as physical abuse would necessitate a rather disturbing admission—that something so long believed to be correct, moral action is in fact traumatizing children. In that case, if spanking had been afforded its own category as an ACE, there is little doubt the results of the study would have been different. The survey invites descriptions, not perceptions. Most people would agree that our cultural norms and laws have created a tolerance for spanking. Before that dynamic is analyzed, however, the issue must be examined through the statistical data that aligns certain adverse childhood experiences to symptoms of adult trauma. According a study conducted over a 20-year period, "Spanking may reduce the brain's grey matter.... It includes areas of the brain involved in sensory perception, speech, muscular control, emotions and memory.... Children ... subjected to child abuse and neglect have less grey matter than children who have not been ill-treated."[3] To summarize, there is evidence to suggest that spanking and physical child abuse have nearly identical impact on child development and long-term trauma.

A recent study published in *Child Abuse & Neglect*, "Spanking and Adult Mental Health Impairment: The Case for the Designation of Spanking as an Adverse Childhood Experience," confirms the preponderance of evidence concerning the long-term impact of spanking. These findings provide strong support that spanking should be considered yet another form of early domestic adversity. The relationship between reports of being spanked in childhood and mental and behavioral health impairment in adulthood is similar in direction to the association between physical or emotional abuse and adult suicide attempts, moderate to heavy drinking, and street drug use. Since the long-term effects of spanking are consistent with an ACE, yet corporal punishment is not specifically defined within any of the 10 categories identified by researchers, it seems fair to say that the study does not include all forms of domestic trauma. Researchers have noted that expanding the types of ACEs included in research could increase the public understanding of poor outcomes and strengthen ACE studies in general.[4]

In the *Child Abuse & Neglect* study, nearly 55 percent of adults surveyed reported having been spanked on a fairly routine basis when they were children. Since the ACE study seems to have defined the term *physical abuse* in a way that could exclude some forms of corporal punishment, such as spanking, the percentage of ACEs reported (28.3) seems likely to have been driven down by bias or ambiguity. The *Child Abuse & Neglect* study, in contrast, focused only on spanking, and the survey, consistent with other surveys about spanking, nearly doubled the ACE results. It seems logical then to assume that the participants in the ACE study did not include spanking or corporal punishment in their responses in the "physical abuse" category. It should be noted that the ACE results are consistent with comparable studies that focus specifically on physical abuse not tolerated by law or social norms. The *Child Abuse & Neglect* study also came to a rather common and unsurprising finding: males were spanked more than females, which is more evidence that bias and social norms affect parental decisions.[5]

It is hard to imagine that any society would willingly beat its children if its citizenry is made aware that it causes long-term suffering. Could parents justify doing something that is shown to decrease intelligence quotient (I.Q.) scores by causing cognitive impairments, social and emotional difficulties, and psychological abnormalities? Are they willing to replace the love between a parent and child with fear? The erroneous assumptions adults have made for centuries in justifying the use of violence to motivate positive behavior in children need to be discussed with parents and influential members of the community. It is time for reflection and application of the new findings about disciplinary action. This will require a re-evaluation of sacred beliefs and legal rights for the long-term health of children. It may surprise many adults that the research on spanking suggests that it leads their children down a trail littered with poor life choices. They will have to realize that while the courts may afford them the right to physically discipline children, they have the option of speaking to children instead. There is no broken rule or inappropriate act that justifies an adult hitting a child with a belt, board, or hand. Children make mistakes, but those mistakes never make it reasonable to rob them of dignity, love, belongingness, self-esteem, and cognitive ability. Yes, many faiths in American culture seem to endorse a belief that tolerates spanking as a means of discipline. And yes, laws establish the parents' right to spank children without fear of prosecution, unless kids are physically and severely harmed. But our families, faiths, and laws have attached themselves to ideas about corporal punishment that are at odds with the research. Instead, they have normalized the acceptance of a practice that causes long-term emotional, psychological, and social impairment of the children those same adults are entrusted to protect and develop. Children would have brighter futures if adults inspired the desired behavior through non-threatening communication and demonstrated an awareness of the impact of adversity on children.

Educators might feel compelled to devise ways to facilitate partnerships with parents to expose them to the recent discoveries about spanking children. Information, collaboration, and open-mindedness will unlock these toxic chains and lead these adults away from practices that traumatize children in the home. Since churches and governments have failed children in this regard, the school must assume the lead and use solid networks and relations to advocate for children by strengthening the relationship with parents. Leaders need to inform teachers, preachers, law makers, and parents and seek alliances with them to transition from destructive approaches to child development to a more nurturing strategy. In doing so, fewer children will make ill-advised life choices trying to cope with domestic traumas. Laws can be reformed to protect children from physical aggression, as they do all other citizens, instead of classifying children as if they are the property of the parents. However, it should be noted that a movement does not need politicians and lawmakers to effect change. Teachers and school administrators can meet needs and strengthen the foundation being dismantled by parents and others. Since educators are products of the same society that reinforces these destructive values, they must inquire into that which is forbidden to question, challenge that which is no longer discussed, and confront the illogical habits that are deemed by many to be common sense. It is called advocacy, and there has never been a better time or cause.

While the ACE study should shock us into an understanding of the horrible effects that domestic trauma has on children, it is not a conclusive report. There are extensions and other factors that cause trauma as well. Because the ACE study does not specifically identify traumas such as spanking (specifically), bullying, or natural disasters, it demonstrates the extent of domestic trauma without allowing complex and controversial entanglements to cloud its findings. That explains why there is such a discrepancy in the data between its operational definition of child abuse and research that focuses on the impact of spanking on child development. While a general description of spanking could easily fall within the parameters of the ACE definition of child abuse, the data suggests there was no attempt to interfere with personal biases on the topic, beyond how they might have interpreted the ACE description of abuse. That being said, the findings are minimal because the ACE study deliberately ignores forms of trauma that are not domestic in nature. Cultural, environmental, and social traumas also impact child development, and must also be considered in an attempt to understand the full scope of unseen toxins to which our children are routinely exposed.

Bullying

As mentioned, another cultural norm that causes children and adults complex traumas profoundly expands upon the foundation established by the study. For the first time, the trauma is caused, in most cases, by individuals outside the student's home, often occurring at school. Bullying is a symptom of socialization because there is a darker, Darwinistic side of human existence that has yet to be replaced with civility in many settings. In some ways it could be a product of domestic trauma, caused by children seeking redemption or validity by the same means that it was taken from them at home. While there have been recent campaigns for awareness of bullying and cyberbullying, the school culture that supports the traumatized child needs to be more than merely aware. Bullying is experienced by 77 percent of all children in some form or another, whether physical, emotional, or verbal; and it has a long-term impact that runs parallel to adverse child experiences.[6] According to the National Bullying Prevention Center, "Experts have begun to identify a second definition for Post-traumatic Stress Disorder (PTSD) that allows for the victims of repeated traumatizing incidents. Bullying falls into this category. This is often referred to as 'complex PTSD.'"[7] Coincidentally, children suffering from abuse and neglect are prime targets for bullying, and while "only 10 U.S. studies have been conducted on the connection between bullying and developmental disabilities, … all of these studies found that children with disabilities were two to three times more likely to be bullied than their nondisabled peers."[8] Bullies attack children based on things like race and sexual orientation. Bullies have even been known to attack children whose parents are divorcing or to mock the bullied child's pain after a death in the family. Essentially, bullies are predators that find their victims' most glaring vulnerability and seize it for some expected form of self-gratification.

Lesbian, gay, bisexual, and transgender (LGBT) students are perhaps the most obvious targets. Recent studies indicate that 70.1 percent of LGBT students have been verbally bullied over the past year, and a disturbing 28.9 percent have been physically bullied. Fully 59.5 percent feel unsafe at school. It is perhaps unsurprising, then, that a third (34.8 percent) of LGBT students missed at least one day of school per month, while 10.5 percent miss four or more days of school each month.[9] The bullying of LGBT students is rooted not in childish antics but in the communal values of adults. Until recently, for example, there were states that refused to recognize same-sex marriages. While it is unlikely that most school-aged children are hearing wedding bells, bullying that mirrors the attitudes behind the law suggests that it is spawned by cultural values. When laws and the Constitution conflict, it tends to boil down to a need to change laws. Are these laws based on religious beliefs and personal interpretations? Lawmakers' sense of morality is often grounded in some form of religious dogma and shared by the communities they represent; for that reason, it can be difficult to separate laws from religious influence. Laws that fail to protect children will stand until awareness increases and attitudes change on many levels.

The term "bullying" is not meant to imply that only one party suffers. It is very similar to child abuse in that it is cyclical in many cases. Often the bullied become the bullies. In a recent study featured in *Parents* magazine, the long-term impact of being victimized by bullying was measured, with those who were not bullied forming a control group. The bully victims were subdivided into groups that included victims on the one hand and those victims who became bullies (bully/victims) on the other: "Victims were four times as likely to develop an anxiety disorder in adulthood compared with kids who were uninvolved in bullying. Bully/victims had a 500 percent greater risk of depression than uninvolved kids, as well as 10 times the likelihood of suicidal thoughts ... and 15 times the likelihood of developing a panic disorder."[10] This sentiment is supported by a recent megastudy conducted at Yale University that examined 37 studies about bullying from around the globe. Five of these studies revealed that bullying victims are more likely to have suicidal thoughts, at frequencies two to nine times greater relative to other children.[11] This finding is supported by the Centers for Disease Control and Prevention (CDC), the federal agency that conducted the ACE research, which insists that "any involvement with bullying behavior is one stressor which may significantly contribute to feelings of helplessness and hopelessness that raise the risk of suicide."[12]

Like other childhood traumas, bullying has long-term consequences. Years after being bullied, according to Kate Baggaley of *Medical Examiner*, victims "commonly struggle with trust and self-esteem, and develop psychiatric problems…. Some become people-pleasers, or rely on food, alcohol, or drugs to cope."[13] More specifically, there are links to specific anti-social and self-destructive behaviors. Bullies often display the symptoms found within the ACE pyramid, adopting the same health risk behaviors when belongingness and love seem beyond their social and emotional abilities. Bullies suffer from depression, anxiety disorders, and emotional complications. They often self-medicate to temporarily ease their anxiety and guilt with drugs and alcohol. Bullies, then, are more than cruel children struggling with social skills; their behavior is often a response to trauma. Yet they are undeniably also serious threats to the natural process of human development. Are schools doing enough to stop bullying? That would be rather difficult under the current structure because the content of the curriculum is prioritized over social development. It is probably considered more of a discipline problem to be punished than a behavior problem to be treated. Educators must understand that this is an environment that can be controlled and monitored, the one setting that can help children overcome the adverse conditions they face in the home and community. Educators cannot begin to heal things happening in the home without first addressing the traumatic things happening in the school. While there has been increasing awareness, many programs to address bullying are created without a full understanding of the dynamic complexity of the problem.

Trauma can affect children in ways that resemble the post-traumatic stress disorder (PTSD) developed by soldiers. It is interesting to note that in a recent study published in *Clinical Psychological Science,* a journal of the Association for Psychological Science, PTSD was determined to be caused by three factors: combat exposure, prewar vulnerability, and involvement in harming civilians or prisoners. The study examined Vietnam veterans to determine the degree to which long-term PTSD exists. While the severity of the combat correlated with the degree of long-term trauma, 97 percent of those who possessed all three factors suffered from PTSD.[14] "Prewar vulnerability" refers to trauma, like child abuse, experienced before joining the military. Many bullies also suffer from these vulnerabilities. It is the last characteristic, however, "involvement in harming civilians or prisoners," that suggests the degree to which the soldier has become a victim of his environment, having seized the opportunity of war to rebel against the demons of the past. In other words, the oppressed becomes the oppressor. That is not surprising, but the fact that these oppressors experience trauma as a result of the guilt they feel for perpetuating what afflicts them is interesting. Thus the bully is not merely abusing others but is also self-inflicting trauma that will lead to probable PTSD. Since the three factors that lead to almost certain long-term PTSD are not concurrent, there is little doubt that the bully reacts to the conditions of his or her circumstances when bullying, as the soldier does when acting cruelly to civilians or prisoners. Guilt, combined with the stressors that necessitated the bullying, intensifies the social-emotional impairment beyond that already underlying the antagonism. In *Scientific American,* a recent study concluded, "The consequences of isolating or ostracizing another person may include heightened feelings of anger, shame, and guilt, as well as a sense of social disconnection."[15]

Bullying contains all of the ingredients of an adverse childhood experience (ACE), with a few exceptions. What makes the category unique are the facts that (1) the bully (abuser) is usually another child, (2) the bully generally suffers long-term effects that equal or surpass those of his victim, and (3) the bully is generally not someone related to the family (it is called "abuse" in the home). The intention here is not to criticize perceptual limitations of the ACE study; it is to build on its breakthroughs for a purpose perhaps beyond the spectrum of intended or projected uses of the data. The focus of the ACE study was never global or societal, but my interest is more in examining all possible threats that traumatize the child. So to understand the full scope of trauma from the school leader's perspective, any attempt to understand and treat childhood trauma through school culture must also consider the biggest threats to the child within the school culture. Eliminating all forms of bullying must be the first step in developing a school culture that accommodates traumatized children and minimizes the impact of their wounds and scars.

We distinguish between bullying and child abuse, but that doesn't mean that the two are unrelated. Abused children often react to the abuse, and parents teach children to react with violence and aggression if frustrated or angry. Violence becomes a normal, accepted form of communication. If children are abused by those who have control over them, they often seek redemption by seeking control over another. These are natural, if not instinctive, reactions. "Children who were exposed to violence in the home engaged in higher levels of physical bullying than youngsters who were not witnesses to such behavior," researchers from the University of Washington and Indiana University reported. "We know that bullying leads to further antisocial behavior and this study shows how family violence leads to bullying."[16]

Bullying takes on many forms and occurs in nearly every setting, including social media. It is insecurity that spawns the bully, a person who finds some temporary solace in mocking others to elevate his or her self-image. Bullying can seem to be the cost of growing up in a competitive culture, where those who are weak or different are preyed upon. But that's not always the case. Sometimes bullies target those who are admired by others, attempting to discredit their victims' reputations in a bid to elevate their own status. The bully attempts to redeem his self-worth in the same manner in which it was taken, in other words.

The Teacher Bully

Most schools boast that they have a no-bullying policy, but fewer have an effective no-bullying practice. Furthermore, many assume that any bullying policy or practice should target the students only, but that would reflect an unawareness of the adult bullies in the building. Transforming schools is a matter that must begin with the faculty. Some have histories that may influence their abilities to manage and lead vulnerable people without an overpowering managerial style. Many staff members were or are abused or bullied; others suffer from other forms of trauma. School leaders need to understand the complexity of the issues and commit to the habits of mind necessary to foster a culture focused on trauma sensitivity. Sometimes that means taking care of the adults. No adult with social, emotional, or psychological issues should be left to deal with the problem on his or her own, nor should that adult be entrusted to supervise children without supportive monitoring.

Bullying is a tremendous threat to schools' ability to establish a sense of belonging in all stakeholders. In fact, 25 percent of teachers do not see "why bullying is a problem and will only step in four percent of the time when seeing a bullying situation," while two of every three students "feel that the school doesn't hear their concerns about bullying and does nothing to stop it."[17] Among the faculty, complicity and a lack of awareness about bullying are issues that can be addressed through staff development. The teachers are the torch bearers of school culture, as are the counselors, psychologists, custodians, bus drivers, and office staff. They need to know that this source of trauma occurs at school, and that they have the opportunity to thwart bullying, unlike abuse, neglect, and other family-based stressors.

Unfortunately, eliminating school bullying starts with an examination of the tactics of some teachers. There are occasions when the teacher's style (or refusal to adapt) conflicts with the overall school culture and counters any attempt to reform. These teachers may share the vision but fail to see the adverse effects of their teaching styles. In other words, teachers who adhere to an authoritarian style of classroom management might not be the best fit for schools committed to the needs of traumatized students.

Frankly, some teachers and administrators are bullies. Teacher bullying can be defined as "a pattern of conduct, rooted in a power differential that threatens, harms, humiliates, induces fear in or causes students substantial emotional stress."[18] It is an abuse of power, one that has long been accepted and tolerated by most stakeholders. The bully teacher is, sadly, far too common in American schools. The leaders of the school must first address this problem before building the trauma-sensitive school culture, since having the right personnel is key.

Most teachers are not intentionally cruel. When both sides of the teacher-student relationship are triggered into defense mode, the outcome is rarely positive. A good teacher uses empathy, healthy routine, positive behavior reinforcement, monitoring, and many other techniques to minimize frustration, even when their instruction is not the source of that frustration. In many cases, teachers tend to apply a quick-fix approach to class discipline with no real long-range plan. They must have order and control of the classroom, out of concern that it might become chaotic and unproductive. This belief can lead to an authoritative approach to classroom management that actually runs counter to processes that in the trauma-sensitive classroom minimize behavioral issues. The teacher who loses the respect and cooperation of the class often resorts to bully-like tactics, which damage the child's trust for authority. Teachers are given a lot of discretion and are expected by parents and supervisors to act as an adult and in the best interest of every child, often without full knowledge of the child's world beyond the school day. Regardless, the child who enters the classroom bearing the baggage of traumas forged in the fires of poverty-stricken communities and ill-equipped parents has no chance in the bullying teacher's classroom. If a school does not meet their needs, children lose hope, and a frustrated, hopeless child tends to rebel against the system. According to Dr. Alan McEvoy of Wittenberg University, "Teachers who bully feel their abusive conduct is justified and will claim provocation by their targets.... They also disguise abuse as an appropriate disciplinary response to unacceptable behavior by the target. The target, however, is subjected to deliberate humiliation that can never serve a legitimate educational purpose."[19]

The bottom line is simple: engaged students are not behavior problems. A frustrated child who is called out in front of their social group, for example, will often challenge the teacher, unlike those whose indiscretions are addressed in a manner that does not shame the student. Many teachers use shaming to counter what they perceive to be challenges to their authority. The teacher feels compelled to respond to the student in a manner that re-establishes his or her authority in the classroom. Teachers should remove students from any social setting before targeting specific aspects of undesirable behavior. Public reprimand, especially if it personally embarrasses or humiliates a child, is inviting insubordinate behavior from all who witness it. To intentionally embarrass a child and then enforce rules that govern behavior after that child reacts is an abuse of power that is rarely dealt with properly by the school administrator. As McEvoy notes, "Bullying by teachers produces a hostile climate that is indefensible on academic grounds; it undermines learning and the ability of students to fulfill academic requirements."[20] There is no place for bullies in the classroom, especially at the front of it. We need leaders who foster positive affect—leaders who create trusting, supportive, encouraging environments where children are not afraid to take chances. Learning communities based on belongingness and social justice cannot tolerate anyone who fails to model the basic dispositional traits that are so critical to that environment.

Natural Disasters

A natural disaster, such as a tornado, wildfire, or hurricane, is very traumatic for adults and children. A violent storm can bring death, destruction, uncontrollable fury, loss of power, fear of harm, and a shaken sense of security. It is akin to the experiences of children living in European cities during World War II air raid blackouts, hiding in basements as enemies bombed the city. Recently, it seems children have been exposed to more natural disasters than in the past; the children in the eastern areas of North Carolina, for example, have experienced two hurricanes (followed by severe flooding and extended periods of time without power) within a three-year period. During a few visits to the region immediately following the most recent hurricane, I observed entire neighborhoods that were gutted, rows of half-submerged mobile homes lining the streets behind piles of ripped-out wall boards and insulation. I saw children's clothes, toys, and furniture stained by flooding and soaked in black mold following Hurricane Florence, the most recent intruder to shatter the community. The poor are often underinsured and without the ability to recover. Once is brutal, but to endure the destruction twice within approximately 700 days is devastation from which many families never recover. Imagine what it was like for a child to be hidden in a closet or under a bed in the pitch blackness of a hurricane as gusts of wind shake the home and rising flood waters begin to seep in through doors and battered windows. The sound of trees cracking in half and falling into homes and cars, as Mom and Dad's battery-powered AM radio picks up a static-ridden voice warning everyone to remain calm and safe. And then there is the morning after, when the daylight reveals the damage to the child's world through a window smeared with grime. Missing pets, the inability to contact family, and new threats of flood waters cresting several dozen feet above existing river banks become the new forms of anxiety as the searches and clean-ups begin. The sudden realization dawns that the entire family will have to vacate their home, but not until the flood waters recede. Trapped in darkness and humidity that makes it difficult to breathe, surrounded by undrinkable water as hunger and thirst set in, the feeling of powerlessness takes on multiple forms as every pillar of support in a child's life is battered and smothered by nature's rage.

Research reported by CNN found that even a year after Hurricane Andrew blew through, 20 percent of children demonstrated disrupted cognitive processing directly related to natural disaster trauma. In addition, a similar study following Hurricane Katrina concluded that 29 percent of children still displayed symptoms of cognitive impairment between one and two years following the storm. The article explains that even for those who "bounce back" (return to normal levels of cognition) within that two-year window, the impact often extends into adulthood.[21] While about three of four students are reported to have returned to normal functioning within two years, it should be noted that two years is 15 percent of the child's entire public school experience. Impaired cognition for such a length of time certainly creates gaps, especially for those living in poverty, the most vulnerable natural disaster victims. They live in substandard housing and cannot evacuate to hotels or drive to stay with relatives. They are often uninsured, and their homes contain all they own, assuming they have homes.

One of the goals of this book is to inspire empathy in educators by asking them to consider perspectives to which they may have trouble relating. Fires, tornadoes, hurricanes, floods, and earthquakes are much more frightening to children than adults, especially when children look up to parents who are noticeably shaken or panicked. The sense of safety, a basic need, is threatened when parents show fear amid the chaos of a storm. Alarming news coverage that features videos of these events, such as footage from a drone fly-over following a disaster can be traumatic. Teachers and schools, however, can offer some degree of comfort and security to students and their families through a simple process of awareness and preparation. It is an opportunity to reach out to the community and lead it through a time of danger and chaos. A community that comes together when tragedy hits is so critically important to children; compassion for one another and deep experiential resilience is inspiring. Most children do not have that support system. Details and strategies will be discussed later in this book that help schools serve students, families, and communities before, during, and after natural disasters.

4

Brain Research

Canst thou not minister to a mind diseased,
Pluck from the memory a rooted sorrow,
Raze out the written troubles of the brain
And with some sweet oblivious antidote
Cleanse the fraught bosom of that perilous stuff
Which weighs upon the heart?
—*Macbeth*, 5.3.50–55

First Responders

Trauma can be understood by considering the way the brain both develops and reacts to stressors that inhibit development as identified in Maslow's hierarchy of needs. The failure to meet children's physiological needs is called neglect. The absence of safety is danger, and intentional exposure to danger is abuse. The repeated failure to meet the most basic needs forms complex trauma, as opposed to the forms of trauma that occur only once. Since traumas adversely affect the brain development and functioning required for a sense of belongingness and to meet esteem needs, adverse child experiences (ACEs) impede or prohibit learning. Bruce Perry of the Child Trauma Academy explains it this way:

> All experiences change the brain, yet not all experiences have equal "impact" on the brain…. Traumatic experiences and therapeutic experiences impact the same brain and are limited by the same principles of neurophysiology. Traumatic events impact the multiple areas of the brain that respond to the threat. Use-dependent changes in these areas create altered neural systems that influence future functioning. In order to heal (i.e., alter or modify trauma), therapeutic interventions must activate those portions of the brain that have been altered by the trauma. Understanding the persistence of fear-related emotional, behavioral, cognitive and physiological patterns can lead to focused therapeutic experiences that modify those parts of the brain impacted by trauma.[1]

Individuals who offer therapeutic experiences or interventions function similarly to rescue workers who go into a region devastated by a tornado or flood. By showing strong support for the victims, these workers restore power, haul away fallen trees, bring food and water—they meet immediate and long term needs through this network of support. Communities rebound, return to their routines, and forget about the storm as quickly as possible. The difference? We cannot see the storm damage ravaging children's brains. There are no visible power outages or downed trees. There is no radar-reading meteorologist sounding alarms. Fire departments, emergency vehicles, first responders, Red Cross wagons—not one of them appears at the scene to help a child rebound. In children, the trauma often goes undetected until it reveals itself in the form of anxiety that leads to emotional outbursts, fighting, or some other disciplinary issue. Instead of responding to these outbursts with punishment such as in-school suspension, out-of-school suspension, or parent conferences (which might in some instances bring about parental anger and abuse), perhaps we should interpret them as signs of social-emotional deficiencies, for which therapeutic intervention is needed. The best way to help the traumatized child is to build trauma-informed classrooms inside a trauma-sensitive school. Staff are usually the first responders following a traumatic event; if educators do not sense and work to undo the unseen disarray within, then who will? Six hours each day is a lot of positive therapy and rehabilitation.

It is important to consider the relationship between memory and emotion, which is similar to the relationship between memory and learning. Teachers who focus on meeting needs and fostering social-emotional development improve so much more than a child's ability to learn. A great deal of research over many decades has indicated that learning is much more than the ability of the individual to retain content. Emotion is associated with interest that is related to experience, becoming the motivation used to create engagement, or the state in which the teacher can now do their job effectively. Engagement in turn creates experiences that the brain converts to short term memories temporarily stored in the hippocampus. If valued, these short-term memories are then sent to various regions of the brain on a wave of gray matter (condensed cell bodies), through synapses, until they are delivered to the part of the brain that functions in a manner associated with the experience. (It is much like a package finding the right address.) There, these short term memories are reinforced and layered into more complex, similar experiences that welcome the new memory into the fold. It is a process that increases the complexity of prior experiences and enhances understanding, stimulating growth in that area of the brain. Or something we call learning. Brains learn resiliency and intellectual, social, and emotional skills that empower the child to reach his or her full potential. It is a wonderful thing, but this is not a perfect world, which is why we need educators dedicated to whole-child development.

To summarize Dr. Perry's description of how trauma impedes this process, stressors associated with danger cause the distributor and filter of short term memories, the hippocampus, to shut down. When a child senses danger, the limbic system's amygdala, located just above the brain stem (the part of the brain that is associated with survival and defense), sends an "alarm" that temporarily halts normal functioning. The hippocampus goes into defense mode as well, something that manifests in a person as fear, anger, or anxiety. In that state, thinking is distorted because survival instincts take over. When people feel threatened with violence they react differently. Most react rather irrationally. This process protects humans, believe it or not, but prolonged or repeated amygdala warnings are unhealthy because stress inhibits short term memory distribution and synaptic stimulation in the various regions of the brain, which can cause atrophy in some cases, creating permanent inabilities. The left hemisphere cannot communicate with the right, critical thinking becomes distorted, and emotions become unpredictable because the intersection between the two hemispheres, the corpus callosum, actually erodes during extreme or prolonged traumas.[2] In fact, the hippocampus (the brain's FedEx for memory delivery) seems to be involved in severe mental illnesses. In both schizophrenia and some severe depressions, the hippocampus appears to be smaller.[3]

Needless to say, an atrophied, eroding brain leads to many other issues related to learning, relationships, and self-esteem. For example, in cases of extreme neglect, the brain is deprived of stimulation and nutrients. About 22 years ago, when the technology was relatively new, Dr. Perry demonstrated brain atrophy using magnetic resonance imaging (MRI) to compare the brain of a normal three-year-old to that of a three-year-old who had experienced severe neglect. The neglected brain was 30 percent smaller.[4] This causes an enlarged cavity in the corpus callosum, and when the right side of the brain cannot communicate effectively with the left side, the learner experiences difficulties with creativity, problem solving, emotional control, cause and effect thinking, social abilities, and communicating feelings. Communication between brain hemispheres also regulates eye movement and vision, maintaining the balance of arousal and attention, and tactile localization.[5] One might accurately assume that these skills and abilities are important tools for students to bring to the classroom each day, so when children become frustrated because they are unable to perform the tasks assigned them, they become frustrated and defensive. That, of course, leads to emotional reactions that have historically led to punitive consequences.

The levels of toxic stress, anxiety, and depression that students experience have increased significantly in the past 50 years. These stressors are applicable to all students, not merely to those directly affected by adverse childhood experiences. In other words, it is harder to grow up now than it was in 1970. In fact, as Peter Gray writes, "some assessments reveal a startling five to eight times as many high school and college students who meet the criteria for major depression and/or an anxiety disorder diagnosis, as was met half a century ago."[6] There are many theoretical assumptions for this, but knowing the specific reasons for the increase in anxiety (toxic stress, depression, or both) is not as important as understanding that today's children need more support than their grandparents needed.

Jean Twenge, a San Diego State University psychology professor who conducted a study that spanned 30 years, reports that "[c]ompared to their 1980s counterparts, teens in the 2010s are 38 percent more likely to have trouble remembering, 74 percent more likely to have trouble sleeping, and twice as likely to have seen a professional for mental health issues." She adds that restless sleep, a feeling of being overwhelmed, and a poor appetite in young adults were "classic psychosomatic symptoms of depression."[7]

These findings, consistent with the expected results, reflect the effects of trauma on the nucleus accumbens, an area of the brain associated with motivation, pleasure, and rewards and responsible for modulating levels of dopamine that regulate emotional responses and learning.[8] Dopamine is directly related to motivation involved with behaviors and rewards. Stressors associated with recurring and prolonged trauma have a profound effect on the nucleus accumbens, which actually communicates with the prefrontal cortex, the area of the brain attributed to impulse control and functions critical to learning.[9] It is also linked to the amygdala, which sounds the "code red" that sends the brain into survival mode by shutting down the hippocampus as previously described.

Referencing Greek neurosurgeon Ioannis N. Mavridis's research, one gains insight to the interconnectivity of the brain and how it affects motivation and learning. Together with the prefrontal cortex, hypothalamus (hormone balance), and amygdala, the nucleus accumbens consists of a part of the cerebral circuit which regulates functions associated with effort. It is anatomically located in a unique way to serve emotional and behavioral components of feelings serving as a neural interface between motivation and action, having a key-role in food intake, sexual behavior, reward-motivated behavior, stress-related behavior and substance-dependence. It is involved in several cognitive, emotional and psychomotor functions that, when its development is impaired, play an important role in psychiatric disorders (such as depression, schizophrenia, obsessive-compulsive disorder and other anxiety disorders) and addiction (including drug abuse, alcoholism and smoking). In addition, the nucleus accumbens plays a role in bipolar disorder, attention deficit/hyperactivity disorder and post-traumatic stress disorder. Because of its rich dopaminergic projections, this nucleus has been subject of many studies in animals as well as in humans, connecting its malfunction with the disturbed reward process observed in depression.[10]

In other words, trauma impacts a part of the brain that serves emotions and behaviors associated with motivation and pleasure. If development is stymied, affecting the production of dopamine, the individual is prone to adopt behaviors in an attempt to self-medicate or replicate the feeling of reward. These could involve addictions to things that satisfy the need for pleasure, such as over-indulgence in food or sex, or self-medicating health-risk behaviors such as alcohol or drug abuse. These addictions inhibit or distort motivation and lead to imbalances that become problems in schools. Individuals become bipolar and hyperactive, suffering from attention deficits and post-traumatic stress disorder. For decades, the educator's response to these children has been, "What is wrong with you?" Now we have an answer that explains why punishment has been ineffective and why children suffering from trauma act out, especially in schools run like police states. There are no bad kids; there are only kids in bad circumstances.

Poverty and Toxic Stress

For the first time in over 50 years, a majority of students in the United States live in poverty.[11] Poverty is stressful and has a profound effect on anxiety and depression. Students who live in poverty face more traumatic stressors, and more often, than those who do not. Crime-infested neighborhoods, malnutrition, lack of supervision, fewer resources, and other factors diminish hope for equity. Poverty is also more aligned with parents who lack education, which makes supporting the family more difficult, thus increasing levels of stress related to finances, which leads to frustrations that other families may not encounter as frequently. Socially, children of poverty miss opportunities to participate in extracurricular activities such as trips, local events, and organizations because these activities are not considered financial necessities. Clothes that do not fit correctly ("hand-me-downs") are often out of style or have stains or holes—things that can lead to bullying or self-esteem issues. Many children come from single-parent families, where the supporting parent is in many cases unavailable for active involvement in the child's education. Unfortunately, poverty is now a characteristic of the majority of public school students. Researchers from the National Center for Children in Poverty (NCCP) at Columbia University's Mailman School of Public Health have determined that "the number of poor children in the U.S. grew by 18 percent from 2008 to 2014 (the latest available data), and the number of children living in low-income households grew by 10 percent."[12]

Children without support systems, who cannot trust the system to serve their best interests and to encourage them to succeed without fear of failure, are more vulnerable now than ever before. The politics of the education culture are systematically eliminating the neediest students. Schools must resist the pressure to assume practices akin to test-driven training centers that label and rate children. They must resist focusing on measured outcomes by emphasizing content memorization and skills that prepare children for the standardized test results, bypassing intrinsic, aesthetic, and emotional development that cannot be easily measured. Schools have changed, but they have not reformed to reflect a full understanding of increasing demands and new data on brain research. To reform, education must understand the needs of the students and meet them. Content and subject matter really have little to do with student needs, but meeting needs and revising teaching strategies to include social-emotional learning improves academic growth. Unless taught properly, most students retain very little content that is (or seems) applicable to them. There is alignment of subject matter with 21st-century skills, but it is geared more toward developing adult professional competencies than toward building a child's self-esteem and confidence, which are difficult to measure and so are often deprioritized. Without measurement tied to specific causes and effects, feedback is limited and subjective while accountability is difficult or even impossible. Educators are, in most cases, unaware of the extent to which students are being traumatized at home. They are not there when the child defenselessly watches parents hit one another or mourns the loss of a grandparent. They do not see a drunk or high parent take a belt out of the closet and whip a child because he or she forgot a chore or left a toy out in the rain. Children rarely tell teachers about things like domestic drug abuse or incarcerated or deported family members. These are things once considered beyond the teacher's territory when planning lessons and assigning homework, but knowledge of the probabilities and impact helps when one is designing lessons and creating relationships that heal and empower children. The teacher can build resilience to overcome the cruel nature of students' conditions without knowing what they are so long as he or she is aware that they exist. What trauma-sensitive schools are asking from teachers is not more but different—that they work to convert reactive, negative energies into positive relationships built on strategic, informed classrooms and school cultures.

The first step in becoming a trauma-sensitive school is for staff to become trauma-informed school employees. This is why so much of this book deals with awareness, which is the primary focus of Part I. It is the *Why?* before the *How?* (Part II). Everyone in the building must fully understand the problem. It is not enough to be told that trauma is "bad" and this new program is "good"; the entire school staff must be motivated, knowledgeable advocates for children. Educators need to acknowledge the forms of trauma and how and why they lead to behavioral, emotional, and academic problems. Full understanding leads to empathy and strategic planning that converts directives into a calling; it facilitates a commitment to become more than simply an employee. The staff, from the principal to the most recently hired bus driver, must become the facilitators of social and emotional development. They must understand the common threats to the school's students and how these threats manifest themselves not only in the building but in the individual child. Educators who interact with large numbers of students on a daily basis without an understanding of those students' other worlds are flying blind.

Financial resource allotments, community and parental involvement, pedagogy, and school cultures all require an understanding of student needs, a fact that brings Maslow back to the stage. The best teachers and educational leaders are successful because they help meet deficiency needs, which must be satisfied before growth needs can be addressed. School districts, individual schools, and classrooms have goals that are directly linked to the growth needs, sometimes the only needs targeted in curricular and pedagogical planning. Too often the development of belonging and self-esteem seems left to chance. Teachers who develop deficiency needs do so with the time they used to spend on drill and practice, re-teaching, and discipline. Many successful programs that are hailed by educational reformists are expensively replicated across the nation, only to become yesterday's trend, the latest quick-fix strategy dumped on the heap of failed reform formulas. The reasons these programs fail are debatable, but there are things in every replicated program or set of findings that are unique to the setting in which success was first gained. If the school employees do not understand the full extent of the central problem, they will not be able to think critically and creatively about it; they will address the problem's symptoms and not the problem itself, usually creating a cyclical pattern of recurrences that consume large amounts of time and resources.

Any program, process, or practice that does not contribute to the development of needs in the student is a potential waste of time and money. Any program that does not reflect a deep understanding of the culture, community, and students is cursed from the outset. Educators must develop resiliency to help all overcome hidden traumas. It is easy to view education from the perspective of the educator—the trained, wise, experienced adult who is paid to oversee the process. It is easy to target most resources and focus on the growth needs, and specifically on cognitive development. This is the fundamental flaw that threatens the best laid plans of leaders. Most were "winners" in a competitive structure, so they value the same systemic, unquestioned practices that crippled the "losers." They are successful in some indirect or direct manner because they triumphed over those with weaker abilities to cope with adversity and setbacks. The people making educational decisions were often the victors, not the victims, of the scholastic process of elimination. Perhaps they are reluctant to change the system in which they were provided self-esteem and are revered. The things that they overcame—with the help of their support systems—are considered "character builders" or "obstacles." They were made stronger by these things, not defeated by them, so they may view them through a completely different lens. They endorse competition in school cultures because winning motivated them. Should educators not attempt to view their practice through the lens of the least fortunate children and strive to develop ways to make those students successful? We need more empathic leadership in education. In a system that historically denies children the opportunity to heal because those in control refused to see it as a priority, educators need to make sure that they are not credentialing students with support systems at the expense of those who need what schools can offer the most.

5

The Influence of Religion

Heaven hath infused them with these spirits
To make them instruments of fear and warning
—*Julius Caesar*, 1.3.72–73

Bronfenbrenner's bioecological model of development explains the various "nested" systems that surround each child. The first, called the microsystem, defines the relationship between the child and members of his or her immediate circle and how that relationship affects the child. The next layer of influence in the child's ecological network is called the mesosystem, and it is defined by the relationships between aspects of the microsystem—basically, how they influence one another to directly impact the child. The church's relationship with the family, for example, affects the manner in which both interact as part of the supportive nest. The third layer, the exosystem, is defined by the things that impact those members of the microsystem and, in turn, have an effect on the child. For example, parents are part of the microsystem; if one loses his or her job, it indirectly impacts the child. Finally, the macrosystem consists of the dominant societal beliefs and ideologies that define the child's culture.[1] Religion, therefore, with the part it plays in family values, ethics, law, and morality, has a tremendously significant influence on everyone. It is the source of many wholesome and righteous perspectives, but it is also at the core of many conflicts and perceived hypocrisies.

Romeo and Juliet provides an excellent example of how these spheres of influence, all with positive intentions to support the child, can result in tragedy. It serves as an extended metaphor to serve as an extended metaphor in an effort to depersonalize the message here and remove some of the defensive biases that close minds. In Verona, for example, Romeo and Juliet were directly and indirectly impacted by the elements of their ecological layers. Was the original conflict between the Capulets and Montagues based on

51

a religious disagreement? Perhaps it originated with a dispute over some aspect of faith, or perhaps it was based on some difference in ethics or values influenced by faith. That is unclear, but the fact that the conflict spread to include extended family members and intensified over time suggests that the families adopted the ethical and moral principles to sustain the feud, and attributed values to it that are often grounded in some form of spirituality, things such as honor and a sense of right and wrong. While there are no direct references to the cause of the conflict, it seems to have led to the development of traits validated by religious values. If true, then the faith practiced by both sides of the conflict develops noble character traits such as loyalty to family and a defiance of all that threatens the sanctity of those blood relationships. However, it also inspires hatred that leads to violence and six deaths. There is evidence that both families were religious, especially at the end, when the issue of burial rights is demonstrated, consistent with the practice of the Catholic Church, the most dominant religion in England during Shakespeare's life span. Shakespeare uses the ending of the play, set in Italy but performed in England and bound by Greek dramatic conventions, to horrify the audience by using spirituality and hypocrisy in sending a chilling message.

As Romeo, unaware that Friar Laurence (the adult religious figure) has given Juliet a deep-sleeping potion to fake her death, enters the sanctity of the Capulet family tomb, he kills Paris in a duel. In essence, the main character, confined by the chains of his destiny, enters a sacred place and extinguishes a rival whose name represents a city in yet another country, France, which here may symbolize love and light. The Catholic audience would have understood the spiritual consequences for spilling blood in the Capulet's burial vault. Ironically, after extinguishing the light and love in the sanctity of a sacred tomb, Romeo commits suicide, thereby sending his soul into the fires of hell for all of eternity. Juliet follows Romeo into hell, as she commits suicide moments later. The parents, the priest, and the peacekeeper (law) all appear moments later to see the results of their actions (or inaction). *Romeo and Juliet* is not about love; it is a play that demonstrates how a pair of innocent teenagers are devoured by the blindness of those who are supposed to love and protect them. It demonstrates that the most carefully designed ecological "nests" can become toxic if the elements of the microsystem are tainted, part of a hypocritical system of blind tradition and conflict. While the Capulets demonstrate a commitment to the teachings of the church, their hypocrisies overcome its intended influence. All four levels of Bronfenbrenner's system of protective nests collapse on Romeo and Juliet, just as the fates predicted. When one considers all of the variables, perhaps there was no escaping their destinies. The macrosystem (cultural influence) of the church, the law, and the family's reaction to established societal norms (feud) dooms Romeo and Juliet, something predicted in the opening prologue.

The "stars," a symbol invoked as a reminder of the concept of predetermination made popular in Greek tragedies, are mentioned early in the text. Specifically, in the midst of a community inspired by the church and its teachings, Romeo refers to "some consequence yet hanging in the stars," which he seems to think of as distant, controlling forces to defy. Why does Romeo's belief about the power of the stars have more in common with Greek mythology than with Christian faith? From the Bronfenbrennerian perspective, a toxic ecosystem has changed their meaning for Romeo. His fate is determined not by the stars but by elements in his microsystem.

Perhaps educators would better serve children by learning to read their "stars," because the school staff is one of the dominant elements of each student's systems of support. Too often in education reform efforts, the focus quickly moves to offering up a solution, with an assumption that the problem is universally understood. Regardless of the religion or the depth of the individual's faith, moral codes will always be subject to human fallibility. Children who are basically forced into a faith by parents or caretakers experience cognitive setbacks because they are not free to choose or develop their own values without fear of repercussion. Some refuse to accept that which is forced on them, even if it is believed to be "for their own good." Romeo does not choose his faith over his fate; to him, his life is charted by other forces, robbing him of happiness and freedom of thought. "Religion has the ability to blind (children's) perception to the point that they won't be able to think freely for themselves," notes Diane Franc. "There is also a huge tendency that they would be living in fear if the religion they have is something that was imposed and was not something they discovered on their own."[2] Many parents and faiths do just that. For "their own good," children are forced into systems of belief, without buy-in, and robbed of the epiphanies that inspire self-created morality.

In addition, the majority of people in America follow religions that either support spanking or corporal punishment or refuse to denounce it—embracing an essentially violent, punitive system for children who violate the morality of the church. As discussed earlier, there is little to no difference between physical child abuse and spanking in terms of emotional and cognitive development. In his book *Spare the Child*, Philip Greven writes, "Abusive parenting styles have been driven by mainstream religious beliefs for centuries. They are part of our Euro-American heritage, and if religion-related child abuse is not acknowledged now as a problem by our society, it will be our legacy to the future."[3]

Leaders must be willing to objectively challenge their own attitudes in a healthy manner. This is not heresy, as some may attempt to frame it; it is growth that requires a painfully critical examination of the bedrock of one's personal codes. Educators must also understand the foundation on which abuse is either excused in the name of religion or even promoted by other adults charged with the child's development, for the sake of achieving a "positive outcome." For example, sharing data with preachers, politicians, and parents might help them arrive at their own conclusions. A direct confrontation, on the other hand, might be misconstrued as provocation or accusation. As the trauma-sensitive school culture is developed, community and parental relationships must include sharing the vision and the data that supports it. This cannot be done before trust is established and these stakeholders feel a sense of belonging in the school. There are no quick fixes. There will eventually be results and long-term, sustained growth, however, if trauma-sensitive policies are implemented patiently and cooperatively.

Tradition and ritual are embedded in family values, cultural norms, and laws because when most people make decisions that involve ethics, they rely on their faith for guidance. Religion is the moral foundation that shapes the way parents raise children, how laws are created and enforced, and how cultures decide between what is tolerated and what is not. Corporal punishment is seemingly protected by this triangulation of support because it is an accepted and recommended practice in some families, courtrooms, and churches.

Educational leaders cannot ignore the role of religion in American laws and family values. This aspect of child development has been ignored, however, in an effort not to offend. This is not to suggest that the school has any business intervening in religious practice, but it wise for teachers to understand the microsystem and for school leaders to partner with the elements of the macrosystem. The purpose is to give the children a voice and not fall into the trap of focusing on the feelings and rights of the adults who unintentionally scar them, literally and metaphorically. As mentioned in the Introduction, the Capulets and Montagues were feuding (without knowledge of the reason) because they were born into the blindness of the culture. They failed to consider how the hate they fostered put their children at risk until they lost them. They were fulfilling a duty to the family and honoring a toxic code, victims of a bad idea that somehow had become immune to any form of logical reflection or sensible analysis. Families seem to have learned little from the Capulets and the Montagues, sadly enough. Shakespeare turns the stage into a giant mirror and nobody seems to recognize the images in the reflection. Traditions that hinder or hurt our children without question or reflection are often permanently cyclical.

Spanking is central to the impact of religion on cultural norms and law because it illustrates a supported perception that the national culture has not yet evolved beyond some rather archaic practices that are still embraced in the twenty-first century. While there are other ways to address inappropriate behavior, most adults still prefer the use of physical violence to discipline children. Now that it has been researched and determined to be the leading cause of complex trauma in children, and to impair cognition to such a profound degree that it has been proven to lower a child's I.Q. score, how much longer will religions and laws continue to support the practice? Most studies on the topic reveal that a majority of parents support corporal punishment, so educators can assume that most students are experiencing at least one form of trauma that impairs cognition. Considering the fact that most children experience at least one adverse childhood experience (ACE)—not counting spanking, which is not specifically categorized as one—and that bullying and natural disasters have the same impact, it is safe to assume that many children are afflicted by multiple forms of trauma. Since it seems that the majority of childhood trauma is domestic, how significant would it be if families re-examined their interpretations of child nurturing in light of these revelations in brain research?

Interestingly, there seems to be a movement to address the traditional practices accepted (tacitly or otherwise) by many contemporary churches and courtrooms. In a departure from the predictable patterns of previous generations, the latest batch of young adults born into their respective religions have initiated a rather significant deviation from the church. The cause is unclear, but there are theories that do not bode well for American Christianity in particular, and educators need to pay attention because this group is the next generation of parents. Have these young people decided to "defy their stars" and, riding a wave of social media, establish relationships to create their own support systems that are less violent and authoritative? If so, what can schools learn from them?

The Millennial Movement

A careful analysis of Pew Research results from 2017 reveals a surprising development among millennials, that segment of the population born between 1981 and 1996. A whopping 36 percent—or 13 percent higher than the rest of the United States population—indicate that they are unaffiliated with a religion.[4] Most are leaving families aligned with some form of Christianity, based on the Pew data. Only half of young millennials believe with certainty that God exists (compared to 69 percent with baby boomers) and one in six does not believe that God exists (a rate nearly three times higher than among baby boomers).[5] Incidentally, only 23 percent of millennials said that religion provided guidance on right and wrong, a full 10 percent below the average that included all ages of the population. It is noteworthy that twice as many millennials (46 percent) stated that common sense provided the most guidance in determining the difference between right and wrong.[6] "The so-called millennials are far more diverse, educated and tolerant than their predecessors," according to the study. "They're also the least religious generation in American history—they're even getting less religious as they get older, which is unprecedented—and the majority of them identify Christianity as synonymous with harsh political conservatism."[7]

That finding is consistent with the Pew research data that states that only 15 percent of millennials believe that the Holy Scripture is the literal word of God, compared to about one third of those between the ages of 30 and 64.[8] As mentioned, conservative Christians are more inclined to accept a literal interpretation of the scripture than others. This movement parallels the conservative to liberal political continuum:

> Millennial voters have had a Democratic tilt since they first entered adulthood; this advantage has only grown as they have aged.
> Democrats enjoy a 27-percentage-point advantage among Millennial voters (59 percent are Democrats or lean Democratic, 32 percent are Republican or lean Republican).
> In 2014, 53 percent of millennial voters were Democrats or leaned Democratic, 37 percent tilted toward the GOP (Republican Party).[9]

Perhaps millennials choose not to adopt a morality that denies equity and opportunity to those who find the concept of religious dogma less appealing than social justice. It seems that in spite of family tradition and Sunday school, this younger generation is more inclined to question the logic or meaning behind ancient words. Is it possible that millennials are influenced by their access to instant fact checking, or that they have been conditioned to reject the social injustices other generations of churchgoers have accepted? Do they seek understanding from sources other than parents? Is it possible that they are grabbing the wrist of the person holding the rod to stop the violence? Could they be walking away from the fire-and-brimstone sermons that shaped values passed down for generations? In *The Merchant of Venice*, Shakespeare seems to represent the millennial position when, in response to those who cite holy doctrine to defend violent practices, he writes, "The devil can cite Scripture for his purpose" (1.3.107). If you consider how technology has changed the macrosystems of this generation like none before, should such an ideological transformation really be that surprising? Millennials are educated, direct, and apparently resolute in their morality. As Romeo and Juliet demonstrate, there will be a time when youth rebel against the unquestioned habits of tradition. Transformation is coming, but it looks as if religious, school, or community leaders will not be at the front of the pack to embrace new attitudes. Maybe it is time that educators, lawmakers, and religious leaders become reacquainted with their clients.

6

The Law and
Child Maltreatment

Th' abuse of greatness is when it disjoins
Remorse from power
—*Julius Caesar*, 2.1.19–20

The First Amendment of the Constitution establishes the freedom of religion, meaning that the United States government does not favor one religion over another, nor does it restrict the reasonable and legal religious practice of any individual or group.[1] The separation of church and state is something the Founding Fathers wanted to preserve, and for the most part, the judges have done an admirable job. However, there are laws that mirror religious code almost directly, and there is strong and rather obvious evidence that some laws are grounded in religious morality. It is nearly impossible to extricate one from the other. Murder and thievery, for example, are rather obviously tied to religious doctrine—both, for instance, make an appearance in the Ten Commandments of the Old Testament—even if it is impossible to detect which religions were prioritized because they make similar pronouncements. And it gets more complicated. As recently as June 26, 2015, for example, the United States Supreme Court ruled in a 5–4 decision that states cannot ban same-sex marriages.[2] It is nearly impossible to make the argument against same-sex marriages without revealing values that are tied to religion's influence on family values and culture, yet four Supreme Court Justices voted to allow states to ban non-traditional marriages. While this topic has nothing to do with education, it illustrates the Court's biases, which tilt toward traditional values and morality that run parallel to religious practices. Those advocating for same-sex marriages are generally adults, who at least had a voice with which to speak out in this example. Unless educators speak for them, children will continue to be treated like the property of their parents, whether because of 10,000-year-old verses or laws enacted when slavery was legal and monarchies were the dominant form of government.

The laws pertaining to children protect the parent's right to *discipline* them—a word that seems to mean "beat" or "spank" to some authority figures—a fact demonstrating that society will tolerate adults hitting children. It also illustrates how elements of a microsystem are fixated within the cultural confines of a macrosystem, something that can be good if productive, bad if destructive. These politicians and lawmakers, all adults, tolerate the beating of the voiceless, defenseless child in an effort to establish some degree of justice for their adult constituents, parents. They find loopholes in the semantics to get around the 14th Amendment, which in essence states that all American citizens are entitled to equal protection under the law. It was established to protect freed slaves, but somehow the verbiage that protects all individuals is not applicable to children. And with the knowledge that children endure intense pain and suffering at the hands of someone much larger than they are, government officials defend the rights of adults to inflict that suffering. That is the culture in which our children must be supported. Educators cannot rely on the law to save children, and they cannot expect the wand of morality to zap lawmakers and parents with a dose of common sense. The cultural triangulation of spirituality, law, and family values embraces the sort of violence that is now known to traumatize children and impair learning. Since there is a direct link between corporal punishment and trauma, this is significant because the acceptance of a practice that is supported by religion, courtrooms, and families is likely to be taken as a positive, something that builds character and self-discipline. The data suggests very strongly that it does neither. Accepting corporal punishment as an adverse child experience identifies the actual number of children in the schools that fight trauma. Simply put, people need to learn that hitting children with straps of leather and boards with gripped handles is bad.

A line from Shakespeare's *The Merchant of Venice* states, "The sins of the father / Are to be laid upon the children" (3.5.1–2).[3] Laws are indicators of what society thinks is important. They are based on values, and in a nation born and raised on the concept of religious freedom, it is plausible to assume the morality of the laws were spawned in churches and tent revivals as often as they were in government buildings. Laws are often the result of conflicting currents where conservative spiritual ideologies clash with a liberal view of human freedoms. The unlikely juxtaposition of the freedom of religion and the freedom from oppression is evident in the debates that result in the rules by which we live. Changes to laws over time often reflect the shifts in the mindset of the culture. For example, some states have abolished the death penalty because it is inhumane and its courts are not always accurate. According to Davison Douglas, a professor of law at William and Mary Law School, "Many contemporary proponents of the death penalty cite its legitimacy in the Jewish law of the Hebrew Scriptures as justification for its retention, while opponents rely on Jesus' message of mercy and forgiveness."[4] This demonstrates that laws in our country are not influenced by Christianity alone, it is true; but the majority decides most laws, proposed by politicians promoting the values of its constituents.

While laws may enforce the spiritual morality of the lawmakers, they may create a sense of social injustice for those who do not share the embedded religious points of view or reflect the perspectives of the lawmakers. These beliefs influence values and ethics, codes by which the fragile line between right and wrong is determined. They are often the products of debate and compromise, but if a particular view is not on the table or is buried in the ideologies of the minority, it gets lost. That which is extremely positive for the individual becomes toxic if forced on the masses, which can result in bad laws based on imposed concepts of what is acceptable and desirable and what is not. In addition, as in the case of corporal punishment, laws are supported by a supposition that outcomes are positive because the practice is widely supported. True intelligence, however, as well a pure leadership, is the ability to clearly see any issue from all relevant points of view, especially the perspective of the weakest and most vulnerable stakeholders. "The test of a first rate intelligence," F. Scott Fitzgerald wrote, "is the ability to hold two opposed ideas in the mind at the same time, and still retain the ability to function."[5] Beliefs that belong to those in power, who were elected by the majority, become laws that in some cases seem not to reflect the values of the minority. To summarize, it is impossible to separate religion entirely from law because laws are extensions of societal values, and societal values are influenced to a greater or lesser degree by religious morality. Since this religious morality tends to be conservative, the legal system can be hostile toward progressive legislation. Are our children's "stars" defined by the morality of a majority that has weaponized spirituality to repress or control threats to their beliefs?

To become a parent, there is no training, no minimal education, no standardized tests, and no screening interviews. For the child, just who one's parents are is a matter entirely of chance. Having a baby is considered a basic right; no government based on the freedoms and protections of its people would restrict something as private and wholesome as family. With rights come responsibilities, however, and parents have obligations that begin before the child is born. Utah attorney Kristina Otterstrom summarizes them in this way: "A parent must serve a child's emotional and physical needs and protect the child from abuse from the other parent or another household member. Additionally, parents must meet their children's basic needs for food, clothing, housing, medical care, and education."[6] In one role the parent is a protector, in the other a caretaker, responsible for the essential needs of a child. The law reflects the mandates of society that can be enforced, with apparent disregard for the fact that the child's fate is often subject to the whims of unstable or ill-prepared adults. Yet parents that cannot afford to provide the things Otterstrom mentions are still allowed to maintain custodial rights to their children and even have more children if they choose to do so. Social workers with knowledge of domestic drug and alcohol abuse leave children in homes characterized by multiple ACEs without hesitation. Corporal punishment, according to the laws, is basically anything the parent does to physically discipline the child that does not cause permanent or lasting damage. But as Valerie Tarico points out, corporal punishment itself can harm the child, "including to the level of functional impairment," and it "should be identified as physical abuse."[7] It should be noted that the "functional impairment" in this description is not synonymous with "cognitive functional impairment"; only a lasting injury directly related to a physical act by the parent is illegal. Long-term emotional, psychological, or cognitive impaired functioning is not clearly identified in most current state laws.

When the law reflects a widely held assumption that is so deeply ingrained into the moral fabric of the society that its point of origin is no longer discussed, ethical correctness may be delayed until societal attitudes are willing to change. Sometimes it takes a highly publicized tragedy that happens to fall on a slow news day to inspire enough outrage to trigger change. So any attempt to understand the problems that confront children from unstable or violent homes will have to wait until there is an effort to draft legislation with a more realistic view of the limitations and capabilities of the parent. For the present, children's vulnerability goes unrecognized by those entranced by misinterpretation and blind tradition. Parents cannot literally beat the devil out of children, but the laws of the land allow them to try.

North Carolina laws in this area are more similar to those of other states than they are different, so here is an examination of that state's laws, which will be less confusing than attempting to create a legal mosaic. Consider this a microcosm that represents, in general, most other states' laws and, more important, exposes the unseen influences that can affect law. Under North Carolina law, child abuse is defined in the following ways:

- a non-accidental, serious physical injury inflicted upon a juvenile less than 18 years of age
- creating or allowing to be created a substantial risk of serious physical injury

- using or allowing to be used cruel or grossly inappropriate devices to modify behavior
- committing, permitting, or encouraging rape or sexual offenses with a juvenile[8]

A careful reading identifies an obvious slant through the use of subjective, ambiguous verbiage. For example, what is a "serious" physical injury? What is a "substantial" risk? What constitutes a "cruel" or "grossly inappropriate" device that can be used to modify inappropriate behavior? Could a lawyer argue that an object used to hit a child may have been inappropriate, but not "grossly" inappropriate? Do these laws allow for the use of objects to strike small children as long as there is no "serious" physical injury? The most significant word in the description is "physical," a word that disqualifies any attempt to protect the child from the related psychological, emotional, or neurological harm. These long-term injuries cannot be evaluated in an emergency room or by photographing bruises. It seems in this case that the courts only judge the visible proof. By this standard, it is legal for parents to cause psychological and emotional harm because lawmakers decided some time ago that it was acceptable to hit children in the name of discipline. The laws sidestep any lasting emotional trauma, except in the case of sexual abuse. It appears that the lawmakers know that proving lasting cognitive impairment would be a slippery slope, one where the burden of proof would be impossible to establish. So they decided to trust the parent until there are broken bones or scars that never heal. In that distinction, the line between physical abuse and corporal punishment is defined. The difference is not focused on the degree of the assault on the child but on the child's physical ability to recover from it.

In North Carolina law, assault with a deadly weapon is the most serious assault charge and it is a felony. Even hands or feet can be a deadly weapon, depending on how they are used.[9] Children, however, can be assaulted with these potentially deadly weapons by an angry adult and it is not necessarily a crime; it is called discipline unless it requires medical attention beyond that which can be treated using a standard first aid kit. Even then, it is usually not treated as a felony. Consequences commonly result in counseling or visits from Child Protective Services (CPS). If there are subsequent incidents, many children are removed from the home and placed in foster care, where there is reason to be even more concerned for the child's safety. There are no simple answers from a legal perspective, a fact that is of little consolation to a child in need of rescue.

In North Carolina, state law 14-360, the law against cruelty to animals, applies when "any person shall intentionally overdrive, overload, wound, injure, torment, kill, or deprive of necessary sustenance, any animal."[10] It is interesting that the laws protecting children are more closely aligned with those that prohibit animal cruelty than felonious assault. As is the case with children, maltreatment of animals is usually a misdemeanor and can result in the victims being removed from the caretakers. It is also noteworthy to point out that the North Carolina statute refers to physical abuse that is lasting ("wound" and "injure") and to neglect ("deprive of necessary sustenance"). Yet when challenged that these laws do not provide children with equal, constitutional protection, lawmakers refer to the landmark North Carolina Supreme Court ruling that defines the legality of corporal punishment. In 1994, the case of *Peterson v. Rogers* (337 N.C. 397) declared, "Parents have a constitutionally paramount right to care, custody, and control of their children."[11] Apparently, "control" includes beatings. This decision would be supported six years later when the United States Supreme Court issued a landmark opinion on parental rights after acknowledging the fact that their position contradicts the 14th Amendment: "The liberty interest at issue in this case—the interest of parents in the care, custody, and control of their children—is perhaps the oldest of the fundamental liberty interests recognized by this Court."[12] The United States Supreme Court basically pushed this matter back to the states, citing a vague phrase and its age as reasons for overriding the verbiage of the 14th Amendment. That is dizzying logic that encourages an adherence to antiquated ideologies forged in another place and time without considering the possibility that they could be flawed. It is interesting to note that North Carolina Assistant Attorney General Anne Middleton addressed "the oldest of the fundamental liberty interests" in 2018, with a different reverence for an allegiance to traditional freedoms for adults:

> The Supreme Court tackled the issue of how far white men could go in beating children, women or slaves behind closed doors as far back as 181 years ago and some of the legal principles decided then remain… (However), we've moved to a recognition for about the past half-century that there is a need in private situations to somehow protect people from the very people who are assumed to be acting in their best interest.[13]

It is noteworthy that the opinion of the United States Supreme Court describes parental rights to control their children as "*perhaps* the oldest of the fundamental liberty interests," suggesting some degree of uncertainty about a factor that should not be relevant.[14] The Supreme Court decided to override a constitutional amendment that was ratified to correct and modify issues inherent in the Constitution; should these amendments be nullified based on the verbiage of the document they are to improve? The 14th Amendment was not created to preserve traditions; it was created to combat the ills of tradition. It was to assure that freed slaves (like all other citizens) were guaranteed "equal protection of the laws."[15] How can the

Supreme Court rule against a constitutional amendment in order to preserve allegiance to blind tradition, even when that tradition was spawned a half-century after another rather significant tradition, the Bill of Rights, which serves as the foundation for the 14th Amendment?[16] Any rational observer might point out that the judges were operating on some fairly dated and biased assumptions. In 2000, the American family was much different than it was many decades prior, when child abuse was not investigated or reported. In fact, states were not required to report child abuse data until NASA was sending astronauts into space on Apollo missions and Lyndon Johnson was transferring control of the nation to Richard Nixon. And even though reported cases of child abuse rose 22 percent between 1990 and 2000, the Supreme Court seems to have ruled to elevate the "good ol' days" over the United States Constitution.[17]

Other countries seem to be more realistic about all forms of psychological and physical violence against children. At the 25th anniversary of the United Nations' Convention on the Rights of the Child, Somalia became the 182nd nation (out of what was then 183) to ratify an agreement to create social awareness, including extensive education, to accompany a legal commitment to protect kids.[18] Somalia and other countries interested in ending corporal punishment and other practices that cause child traumas developed strategies focused on Article 19 of the pledge:

> Parties shall take all appropriate legislative, administrative, social and educational measures to protect the child from all forms of physical or mental violence, injury or abuse, neglect or negligent treatment, maltreatment or exploitation, including sexual abuse, while in the care of parent(s), legal guardian(s) or any other person who has the care of the child.[19]

The agreement calls for legislative action to "protect the child from all forms of physical or mental violence ... while in the care of parents." The only country in the United Nations that did not embrace this form of justice for children, and still hasn't, is also the one country that has never even sent this proposal to the floor of its senate—the United States of America.[20]

In 1797, the United States Senate, half-filled with signers of the Constitution, ratified the Treaty of Tripoli unanimously. That document, initiated by George Washington and proposed by John Adams, indicates that "the Government of the United States of America is not, in any sense, founded on the Christian religion."[21] Yet despite the wishes of the Founding Fathers, Christianity has managed to become a discreet yet significant part of politics and government. Christian morality serves as the foundation for laws, business ethics, and family values; any attempt to understand modern American culture fails without understanding the impact of Christian ideals. While it was never the founders' intention to dedicate so much effort to extricating the influence of religion from the fabric of society, it seems inescapably linked to so many things people of this nation hold sacred. Religion is the silent and powerful force that influences every other component of a child's macrosystem, whether that child embraces the spiritual influences or not. The benefits, it can be argued, are numerous, but the attachment to religion makes analysis and calls for change a rather emotional process. Families are guided by religious values, whether they know where these values originated or not. Laws are based on the ethical and moral views of the lawmakers. Politicians are elected to represent the views of their constituents, and the issues they confront often involve interpretation of religious doctrine. Educators must understand this issue because it is at the core of awareness that feeds motivation, diplomacy, trauma sensitivity, parental communications, and many more strategies that can save children. Educators must take the lead and exhibit the patience and compassion to make a difference. They should not assume that children are protected by laws, government programs, or even society's concept of what is right and what is wrong. The general belief is that children belong to their parents, and unless physical violence toward them is visible, reported, and investigated, the government feels that physical aggression by parents to control their children is an adult's right. Despite new evidence that shows that children suffer from undetectable, long-term trauma as a result, the courts continue to ignore the 14th Amendment in favor of some antiquated, unquestioned traditional belief.

Life Without Corporal Punishment/Child Abuse

In 1971, a murder case in Sweden ripped the heart out of that nation. A 3-year-old girl was beaten to death by her stepfather. Until then, approximately 90 percent of all Swedish children were spanked at home. The case ignited public outcry and activism that resulted in the world's first spanking ban, implemented by parliament in 1979. Today, it is estimated that only five percent of Swedish children experience some form of violence at home.[22] Two generations have grown up in Sweden under the corporal punishment ban, nearly 40 years of children that were not spanked. According to the research, their brains should not reflect the impact of the repeated trauma that plagues children in the United States, where corporal punishment is a parental right based on tradition, according to the Supreme Court. Some interesting statistical comparisons tell a grim story for those in the United States, where a large part of the population feels that spared rods spoil children. In Sweden, citizens are 88 percent less likely to be incarcerated than in the United States, 56 percent less likely to be unemployed, and 82 percent less likely to be murdered. The Swedish also live 2.8

years longer on average.[23] Of course, there are many variables that contribute to the differences here, but a careful examination of the data presented earlier that shows the impact of trauma on the developing brain, so these numbers should not shock. Childhood trauma has life-long implications, as demonstrated by the fact that Swedes outlive US citizens. Referencing the adverse childhood experiences (ACE) study once again, we can see that there is a correlation between the number of ACEs and life expectancy. Could this imply that a nation that does not traumatize its children by facilitating and legalizing the practice of corporal punishment should expect its citizens to live longer? According to *Scientific American*, "Participants who were exposed to six or more different types of adverse childhood events (ACEs), such as physical or sexual abuse, were also 54 percent more likely to die during the 10-year period of the study." It is worth noting, too, that the ACE study control group (individuals with no ACEs) lived longer than the other participants with fewer than six ACEs: "People in the control group died on average at 79.1 years, whereas the average age of death for people who had had two ACEs was 76; for people with three to five ACEs it was 73.5."[24]

Lord Montague and his rival Lord Capulet each sacrificed a child on the altar of blind tradition, where hate lingered far beyond the memory of the conflict that triggered it. Their children struggled to escape their destinies to no avail. At some point, those who embrace antiquated myths and misinterpretations will decide that their misplaced certainties are not worth the cost. Like the people of Sweden and Shakespeare's Verona, there will be a significant death that triggers a movement and rearranges children's stars so that they can escape their tragic, traumatic fates and develop into self-actualized adults. While American families seem to hold firm to their faith and judges seem very proud of precedent, it is time to question such things, along with our other assumptions about the parents' and children's rights. Educators are perhaps the last hope for saving these branded children, the only adults capable of pulling them off the worn paths that lead to a statistically probable demise. Educators can repair the damages children lug into classrooms every day if they are willing to close the gap between what we can do and what we are willing to do. Small gestures and empathy based on a newly discovered awareness can make a huge difference in the lives of a child. It is called justice. It is also called social justice.

PART II

A Model for the Trauma-Sensitive, Social-Emotional Learning School

"To take arms against a sea of troubles,
and by opposing end them."
—*Hamlet*, 3.1.60–61

Introduction:
The Field of Dreams

"Dreams, indeed, are ambition; for the very substance of
the ambitious is merely the shadow of a dream."
—*Hamlet*, 2.2.241–243

What if there were a serum that could improve teacher morale, student attitudes, and positive parental involvement? What if a dose also contained energy boosters to increase standardized test scores, improve attendance, and decrease disciplinary referrals? In addition, imagine that this magic potion could decrease drug abuse, alcoholism, and other behaviors that rob society of its raw talents. And how would community leaders react if they knew that every dollar spent on this elixir would save taxpayers 11 dollars spent on treatment programs later? Of course, all side effects must be disclosed, so let it be known that in some cases this magic medicine has been attributed to decreased suicide attempts, fewer incarcerations, and longer life expectancy. It has also been attributed to healthier family and marital relationships, high levels of self-esteem, and the propensity to secure and maintain steady employment. If taken in the right dosage and administered and monitored carefully by trained professionals, this miracle tonic has the capability of turning lifelong trauma into resiliency and self-esteem that empowers a person to reach his or her full potential. What would that medicine be worth? What would society be willing to pay?

The disease that plagues education has a cure with the power to do all just mentioned if administered properly and prescribed by experts. Of course, it is not a drug made from some exotic herb that grows only in the most remote areas of the rainforest, or something synthetic mass produced by Pfizer, Merck, or Johnson & Johnson. It is not a substance or chemical; it is a pervading attitude of calculated positivity that defines a place in terms of its culture. It is a building, but there are no blueprints that turn I-beams and cinder blocks into solemn sanctuaries for the human spirit. It is a recipe, but most of the ingredients are based on understanding, empathy, and advocacy and cannot be harvested from a field or orchard. It is a sudden clarity of vision achieved by the removal of the many misconceptions that have formed cataracts so severe that they have blocked light and distorted purpose for decades. It is a shared mindset formed by a unified awakening and call to arms determined to change the curses long embedded into the constellations of children's stars.

Educators must realize that they are the last resort for children who need adult guidance and supervision in their lives. Children need to know that they belong to a place where everyone appreciates their abilities, if only one school year at a time. They need confidence and security, not shaming, ostracizing, and measuring. Adults with the noblest intentions in many cases have failed children by not re-evaluating unquestioned interpretations of scripture that, reflected in our laws, create irrational norms accepted by families as common sense. Adults follow traditions and customs in blind routines that lead to setbacks they accept as inevitable. When in the absence of informed, productive parenting a child fails to grow, when the scales of justice are unbalanced by institutions and the adults who run them, and when the service of churches allows the ancient commands of religious dogma to drown out the softer songs of hope and love, the child becomes a free-falling victim of things beyond his or her control. The school stands as the last bastion of hope for the unassuming child. While the intention is to include all stakeholders in the mission proposed in Part II of this book, they must first be willing to reconsider the rationale behind some calcified assumptions and habits. Times are changing, and these stakeholders have the power to influence positive, powerful growth.

Schools tend to struggle with negative energies so much because they are not consistently effective in using strategies that develop the whole child. Generally speaking, teachers are more heavily trained in cognitive "drill, practice, measure" exercises than they are in social-emotional learning, especially in the higher grade levels. Many teachers were trained to be strict, content-focused ambassadors of their majors' content, as framed by the written curriculum. Others become strict disciplinarians because they seek order and obedience in their classrooms. Undesirable behavior, in these content-centered climates, is rarely avoided through the sort of planning designed around motivation and engagement; it is instead quashed by threat of punishment or negative consequence. There are nevertheless some classrooms void of structure and expectations that can be equally destructive. Additionally, some teachers are under-trained by colleges and universities in aspects of child development not aligned with cognition and content mastery, especially on the secondary levels. While the concept of social-emotional development seems to be developing gradually, it needs a stronger sense of urgency. To educate the twenty-first-century child, the need to first educate twenty-first-century teachers and administrators is the obvious first step. Otherwise the politicians will get all of the data they need to dismantle public education and continue stripping it of funding, as seems to be the case recently. If they only knew that funding the trauma-sensitive, social-emotional learning (TSSEL, pronounced "Tassel") program would save the taxpayer money and improve the quality of life for constituents, they might decide to enhance their investment into children. This is why education needs its leaders to reclaim the reins and advocate for its clientele. Educators do not really need to reinvent the wheel, but they need to re-license the driver behind it.

Part I of this book is intended to make educators aware of this problem that has been hiding in plain sight, obscured by something called "distancing," or the separation between what one could do and what one is willing to do. In many cases, this distancing amounts to a tolerance of the absurd. It is the acceptance of excuses, ignorance, inactivity, substandard ethics, or bias that hinders child development without a plan to improve. It is an assumption that stakeholders' "best intentions" are honorable and selfless, even when those intentions inadvertently hurt children. It is the refusal to see conditions from the perspectives of the children being served, or the unwillingness to understand how those conditions hinder child development. It includes ignoring the problem because it seems massive or else inconsistent with the educator's experiences. It is the mindset that an identified problem is someone else's responsibility. In a trauma-sensitive environment, distance is closed through observation, listening, caring, and knowing how to use the classroom to repair children, and how to foster a culture of belongingness and collaboration for everyone in the building or district. There are no excuses that warrant turning away a child demonstrating an observable need, whether that member of the school drives a bus, sweeps the hallways, or sits behind the largest desk. Part II will detail how everyone in the building can develop TSSEL strategies that positively influence every person in a child's spheres of support.

Everyone in the school culture and its stakeholders must understand their importance to the TSSEL culture and be trained to develop strategies related to their interactions with children. All adults, as mentioned, including bus drivers, custodians, teacher assistants, counselors, nutritionists, nurses, social workers, resource officers, volunteers, and of course, teachers and administrators have critically important roles. Training must be ongoing to refine competence; new employees must be indoctrinated as soon as possible. Everyone who comes into contact with children in a school needs to understand his or her role in the culture. Dedicated individuals sharing the responsibility, mission, goals, and objectives of the school evidenced by service to whole-child development will not fail. Members of the TSSEL school culture are skilled ambassadors, eager to promote the school in the community and home when the opportunity arises. They are part of the marketing and branding of the school, which should accurately reflect pride, purpose, and performance. They understand that even the smallest gesture can have profound effects on a life.

The trauma-sensitive school is more than friendly, dedicated personnel; it is an army of trained staffers who take informed, deliberate action based on best practices strategically aligned with positive, long-term results. These beliefs and practices pulse through every vein in the observable and unseen performance of the school, from greetings at the door to the instructional strategies that blend curriculum with a prescriptive, needs-based process. It involves a code that, reinforced by trust, demonstrates an empathetic awareness of the forms of diversity and addresses the blind spots schools have tolerated much too long. It attacks the practices that threaten children by including parents, politicians, pastors, and people in educational seminars, video conferences, and roundtable discussions. These schools advocate by strengthening weaknesses and decreasing the severity and regularity of threats to children. Finally, in a TSSEL school it is understood that many adults entrusted to care for and protect children are also victims of trauma and need non-judgmental support as well. The trauma-sensitive school culture assists teachers by extending support and understanding to those most directly aligned with the mission. Essentially, before a school can reach its full potential, it must become a place for healing as much as it is a place for learning.

As an adult serving children in a school, it is so easy to fall victim to the negativity that surrounds traumatized people, especially children. Without understanding the nature of the problem, the behaviors of the traumatized child can be taken personally, as if the child is being disrespectful or confrontational. Often the traumatized child's behavior becomes more rebellious when the adult assumes an authoritarian role; a brief outburst or comment steeped in frustrations can often escalate to rage when the adult inadvertently triggers the oppression central to the source of the child's trauma. These children lack the capacity to handle themselves like an adult might, and frankly, if the home is characterized by aggression, perhaps they are mimicking other adults in their lives. Children who are traumatized by adults will resist another authoritarian adult seeking to control them. So much undesired behavior is the result of the traditional school culture, often rising out of low student and teacher morale; in the trauma-sensitive school, the focus is on converting setbacks into positive momentum. Adults exhibiting patience, understanding and listening skills are more likely to forge productive relationships with children and become more successful educators in the process.

All of the adults in the school need to begin the transformation to a TSSEL school culture by understanding one simple concept that will serve as the foundation for all other professional development: "Schools were not constructed so that adults could have jobs." The taxpayers did not spend millions of dollars to construct an edifice so that grown-ups could get paychecks and pensions. Children are not unwanted little people serving as obstacles between the teacher and his or her retirement; they are the clients. Of course, this intentionally humorous phrasing has an element of truth to it, in that there are some teachers who will have bigger attitudinal challenges than others during the transition; in dealing with those teachers, patience and an open mind are your biggest assets. Some will attack the premise and refuse to change. This is not a quick fix but a long-term project. To use a hyperbolic metaphor, children are not to be treated like inmates; they are to be treated like patients. It is not beneficial to have traumatized children tiptoeing around rules that change from room to room, hall to hall, teacher to teacher. Some students are reprimanded, punished, and flunked throughout the day, bullied in the restrooms, yelled at by bus drivers, and spanked when they get home because a teacher called a parent who just had a bad day at work. They are barked at by teachers to "Be quiet!" and "Line up!" as if these adults spent their planning time the night before watching prison films. Many students never hear their names uttered in a positive, supportive way. Talking *at* someone has a different effect than talking *to* someone. Children can be treated like unwelcomed house guests, often made to feel unwanted or merely tolerated. This is why the TSSEL attitude is so important: It is a cost-free choice that reflects character and an understanding of the employee's ideal role in the life of a child. Teachers need to learn how this will help them earn the respect of students, parents, and colleagues. Once stakeholders and children begin to notice the differences, resistance will yield to acceptance.

The adults in the TSSEL school culture are actually the guests, even though the school staffers have *in loco parentis* responsibilities. That does not mean dominance over children, however. The adults form a system of support, and that starts with an awareness of children's deficiency needs and the skills to help that child meet them. Words can uplift or destroy; adults facilitate the language and tone of the school. Support does not come from the top down but cradles the child from all sides. Any adult who fails to understand this concept and is unwilling to learn is not a good fit in a trauma-sensitive school. It is imperative that staffers understand all aspects of the mission. Obedience is not one of Maslow's deficiency needs, and subservience is not going to benefit child development.

Trauma-informed teaching understands that relationships are more important than content. Please re-read the previous sentence, for emphasis. Trauma-informed instruction is not another new thing for teachers to do; it is a new mindset that requires that the teacher understand new priorities based on a new vision of the school's purpose. The focus is shifting away from information acquisition that has teachers providing content for a week and testing on Friday. Education is becoming a process of supportive, integrated collaboration using social-emotional, experiential learning in a connected village to facilitate whole-child development. Content is simply the recipe used to prepare the main course; it is not the main course itself. If content is tied to relationship building and the establishment of belongingness and self-esteem, it becomes valued. Think of it like a song that triggers nostalgia. It may have been decades since it was last heard, but a few familiar notes revives every word of the lyrics and transports the listener back in time, where they become reacquainted with the faces and places of a lost era. The meter, the voice, the instruments, and the magic of some significant moment combine to create something the brain cannot discard.

7

The Trauma-Informed Teacher

The miserable have no other medicine
But only hope.
—*Measure for Measure*, 3.1.2–3

Once a child enters kindergarten, no adult spends more time with them than the teacher. Teachers spend approximately 1,200 hours each year supervising students, and many have the same group of children for the entire school day. To put the amount of time in a perspective adults might grasp more easily, consider that if students were workers, they would spend 27 weeks per year as a full-time employee in the presence of their bosses. On average, according to the U.S. Bureau of Labor Statistics, the elementary school teacher spends nearly three (2.96) hours per day with the elementary school–aged child if averaged over all 365 days in a calendar year. Parents, in comparison, spend a total of one hour per day with their elementary school–aged children. It should be noted that the educationally or developmentally productive interactions between the parent and child are rather minimal, totaling less than 20 minutes per day, on average.[1] In essence, the teacher is constructively engaged with the child about nine times as long as the parent.

Primarily during the pre-kindergarten through elementary school years, then, the teacher may be the only adult engaging a student in meaningful activities that stimulate positive interactions between child and adult. That puts the teacher on the front lines of the battlefield, in the trenches and foxholes with the traumatized children they serve. This is where the awareness, the commitment, and the training must be realized and applied, because the teachers are the most important adults in any school. They have the most access to the child and the skill and opportunity to have a profound impact on development. While this is not to suggest that middle and high school teachers are excused from this responsibility, social-emotional development is most effective when the students have a strong foundation in the TSSEL process. While the form of support may change as the child grows older, it is needed on all grade levels.

Since parents are at the center of the domestic adversities detailed in the adverse childhood experiences study, it is reasonable to assume that the students with multiple ACEs are not characterized by healthy, productive relationships with an adult beyond their time at school. Teachers need to understand that nearly as toxic as the actual emotional, sexual, and physical abuses (including corporal punishment) that create a large percentage of traumatized learners, there is the constant fear of being traumatized at any given time. This is also applicable to some soldiers who were never engaged in combat but were constantly under the threat of it. In the brain, the amygdala fires and decelerates natural brain functioning when there is the threat of being victimized. These children suffer from stressors or triggers most people do not anticipate, such as seeing a parent's car roaring up the driveway and praying that the driver emerges in a good mood. Or hearing the profanity-laced arguments at the other end of the house, wondering if the escalating anger will spread. Or watching a disgruntled parent pull another beer out of the refrigerator before sitting down at the table to go over report cards. It is the threat of such things that keeps children's brains in defense (or survival) mode. This erodes the child's feelings of safety, belongingness, and self-esteem just as much as an actual ACE at times. It is up to the teacher as the last and only hope to help the child learn to cope and become resilient even when no bruises or cuts signal the need for an intervention. The teacher understands that misbehaviors are often the telltale signs of emotional abuse and should assist the child whose actions are nothing more that undisciplined cries for help.

The trauma-informed teacher understands that reactionary outbursts can be signs of overwhelming emotion and are often caused by things that occur before the child enters the classroom. Armed with strategies to help children cope and become resilient, these teachers can approach uncomfortable situations more effectively. Knowing that it is not imperative or even significant to identify the circumstances behind an emotional disruption, teachers rely on an awareness of the severity of the cultural problem as a basis for understanding. Teachers must not be defensive; they need instead to see the behavior as a form of outreach. The TSSEL is a healing culture that is actually designed to gradually eliminate the number of behavioral issues by decreasing stress levels. While Part I of this book spent extensive efforts to demonstrate how environmental forces trigger traumatic reactions, it is not the teacher's job to identify the reason each child acts out. They simply remain consistent with their roles in an environment designed to support without judgment. The "rising tides lift all boats" theory in action, in other words. Teachers must remain vigilant, compassionate, supportive, and trusting. They may be the most important person in many children's lives.

The Dogs of Leadership

Before the trauma-sensitive culture becomes a shared vision, it must become a shared passion. Everyone must see the problem and understand why every detail is important. That passion must then evolve into shared ownership. Teachers are an educated resource with first-hand knowledge of the uniqueness of the school population. While the underlying premise does not require that teachers know which children are traumatized or how severely, they have the connections and background knowledge of the student body to advocate effectively for all children. They must be empowered to make the critical decisions that are applicable to a population. In addition, everyone must lead and, at times, follow. It requires motivated, empowered, autonomous internal stakeholders with high morale and collaborative skills. It also requires reflective practitioners, a team that collects and analyzes data and facilitates the process of growth even when goals are being reached.

It might be an understatement to point out that the first few steps, the things done before a school-wide action plan is ever developed, are critically important. Not only do the staff and faculty need to understand trauma's sources and the extent of the negative impact it has always had on learning and human development, but they need to understand how it has impacted them. Teachers, counselors, and social workers, to name a few, carry their own traumas, and when they come face to face with the stressors that students face, they expose themselves to something called "vicarious trauma." All staffers will need to examine themselves and understand how their own traumatic experiences might affect their temperaments, attitudes, and biases. The school leader will need to understand that maintaining motivation, once the shared vision is created and the mission developed, will involve persistence and trust, especially before results become evident. While many educators are themselves the products of authoritarian leadership and may believe that it was great for them, the focus should never be on an individual case or the experiences of the self; leaders must do what it takes to serve every child effectively. Educators must not promote success in terms of rates but determine why some students are not successful. It calls for a shift in the way schools and classrooms are led. This new form of leadership, whether it be in the office or the classroom, is modeled every day because it is grounded in informed and ethical practice. It is about empowerment and belief in teachers' expertise, which should be developed through constant training and reflection. If teachers do not trust the leader, they will not follow the leader. Therefore, the school leader needs to demonstrate willingness to care for teachers' needs (just as the teacher must demonstrate a willingness to care for students' needs). If they are to feel safe in taking chances in the best interests of students, teachers (and other staff) need to have their needs met as well. They should be shown support during interactions with parents or skeptics and provided emotional support to overcome frustrations certain to arise along the way. A school is only as good as its teachers and the culture is reflected through them above all others. If change is to occur, the leaders earn trust by supporting teachers in much the same manner that teachers do when supporting students in the TSSEL school.

Next, the leader must establish a strong sense of belonging, one in which each staff member becomes an important part of a cause that is much larger than any one individual. This is the key ingredient to the culture, and it starts with these soldiers on the front lines, as it were. Here, morale-boosting social celebrations and constructive criticism help establish strong relationships across the school and into the community. Efforts need to be recognized and all ideas need to be considered equally. School leaders can gauge this by noticing staff members who contribute to the cause even when they think no one is watching; those individuals have assumed leadership roles and have personal investments in the school culture. To facilitate this process, the school leader must pay attention to the micropolitics of the school, understanding where collaborative networks are strong and where they are potentially destructive. Perhaps the best way to determine belongingness is to gauge the degree to which the school staff demonstrates ownership of the concept through a willingness to collaborate, share, and sacrifice for one another and the greater good. That is not to suggest that the leader needs to observe this in all teachers and members of the staff before launching the TSSEL culture; if he or she observes it in the influential leaders in the school (especially the leaders who deal effectively with negativity), buy-in has a better chance of happening at the highest levels. Later, in chapter 9, a simple, observable process will be introduced to help measure attitudinal growth by marking ideological levels along the way.

Only when trust has been established, ownership taken, and a sense of belongingness felt should the leader establish specific expectations. The team members need to know what their roles look like within the new culture, and they need a voice. In an environment built on genuine trust and belongingness, the leader will provide structure and direction that direct the flow of positive energy without robbing team members of opportunities to contribute to its creation. If the leader is like the lead dog pulling a sled, moving determinedly forward and expecting everyone else to follow, without a say about the direction or pace, he or she does not develop leadership skills in others. The rest of the team, which does most of the pulling, rarely see the leader's face unless there is a problem.

Other leaders are watchdogs, observing and waiting for an eventual crisis or error before springing into action. The watchdog has no real direction and is focused on negative threats to the norm. Unlike the lead dog, he or she has the ability to see when a follower falls out of line, but the watchdog does little more than bark furiously and attack problems. If the watchdog were proactive or motivating, it might eliminate most problems before they become serious.

Then there is the lapdog, the school leader who has forgotten who is served and tends to please the superintendent. It could be due to the fact that the superintendent wants to micromanage the school, robbing the school leader of creative autonomy. The lapdog is paralyzed by second-guessing and approval-seeking; they measure self-worth by how many pats on the head or "good dog" comments they hear. While it may not be their fault, lapdogs lose the ability to lead, bound by leashes and doubt. They may see ways to improve beyond the purview of the boss, but lapdogs are usually unmotivated because they serve not a greater good but a person who does not trust their leadership decisions. Because they are more focused on pleasing the boss than supporting the staff and students, they lose trust and respect in those groups as well. They tend to become managers that have long careers "holding down the fort."

Then there is the companion dog, a leader who wants primarily to be liked and fails to address problems or make unbiased decisions when the need arises. The companion dog wants to make people feel better and develop friendships and relationships, but that is only part of the job. They base decisions on pure interpersonal emotion, so they are often manipulated. Eventually, the staff loses respect for companion dogs because there are times when a leader needs to take charge and make tough decisions for the greater good. Anyone can lead 95 percent of the time; companion dogs disappear during that critical 5 percent when they are most needed, when the leader earns respect and demonstrates mettle. While there are times when the leader may have to temporarily assume all roles, the transformational leader needed most is more akin to the sheepdog.

The sheepdog watches from the back, allowing and encouraging members of the flock to step forward and lead who share the vision and are empowered to lead from within. The sheepdog knows the job and does not need to be managed. This person is aware of the natural hazards and where the terrain is challenging, navigating the flock around these pitfalls. When a member of the flock falls out of line or becomes vulnerable, the sheepdog is there to help guide the wandering lamb back into the fold in a nurturing, positive manner. The sheepdog never loses sight of the flock or the path to the corral, but remains out of sight when the flock is marching in the right direction. He or she trusts the sheep who stepped forward to lead and lets them do their jobs, knowing that trust is important. In many cases, these sheep have seen the sheepdog fight off wolves and pull lambs from rapid streams, so they trust and respect the sheepdog, who has demonstrated dedication to their best interests. And while the sheepdog remains in the shadows for most of the journey, the flock arrives at its destination as a team, safely and successfully. Trust, belongingness, and expectations are all demonstrated as the sheepdog follows the flock from where it started to where it wants to be.

"The Readiness Is All"

Later in this process, the leader will encourage divergent approaches and perspectives as the team of instructors brainstorm and design data collection strategies to guide practice, but at this stage, it is important that all feet are toeing the starting line, waiting for the signal to begin. Much of the information contained in the next two chapters comes directly from or is indirectly influenced by the Trauma and Learning Policy Initiative (TLPI) developed through collaboration between the Massachusetts Advocates for Children and Harvard Law School. Since the purpose of this book is to synthesize information from several areas of expertise to arm leaders after an emotional call to action, training should be empowering, cost efficient, and simple. The information about trauma sensitivity is largely based on material made available through the TLPI, especially its website Helping Traumatized Children Learn (https://traumasensitiveschools.org/), and the document "Unlocking the Door to Learning: Trauma-Informed Classrooms and Transformational Schools," by Maura McInerney and Amy McKlindon. It is strongly suggested that anyone serious about developing a trauma-sensitive, transformational school culture become familiar with these resources that provide the context for much of the content to follow.

Satisfactory answers to the following questions are an indication that the team is ready to begin the TSSEL process:

Once the faculty is aware of the severity of trauma, what are the expected outcomes?

This question should be based on an awareness of the problem in relation to perceived needs. If the teachers cannot uniformly answer this question, there is a problem with the vision or their understanding of what the trauma-sensitive approach is or can do. Keep in mind that up to this point, most teachers will agree on the problem and commit to the proposal, but many may have very different views on how the plan is to become a reality and what the outcomes should be. The differing opinions are expected and can lead to more diverse thinking about best practices when the process goes to committee. It should also help shape the program, its vision, and its leadership opportunities.

Is the faculty informed, motivated, and on board, sharing the vision? What percentage of staff sees student trauma as something that does not exist? What percentage of the staff sees student trauma as something that is someone else's problem? What percentage of the staff feel empowered to build resiliency in traumatized students?

After painstakingly demonstrating the ways in which trauma impacts children's abilities to learn, the school leader needs to make sure that there is general consensus that the faculty is mentally ready to proceed. There may be a small number of skeptics, who can be teamed with positive leaders. In addition, the school leader now has a type to seek during the hiring process. Here the leader is going to make sure that the personal biases of the teachers that run contrary to the effort to address the problem are not left unattended. Frankly, there will probably be some teachers who think the Bible belt is a strap of leather with a Proverb burned into the inside, and they will defend the rights of parents to use physical force to beat their children. They may dismiss the data and oppose the softness of a TSSEL school culture, especially if they feel supported by punitive actions taken against "misbehaving" students. They may not buy into the therapeutic, restorative justice approach to behavior issues. They may be unable to effectively embed social-emotional competencies into lesson development. They will feel that this nurturing, "feel good" approach will lead to anarchy. Expect some isolated cases, but if this kind of feedback comes too frequently, the process is destined to fail. A team commitment is what the leader must have at this point. Make sure that the process of determining actual perspectives is one that permits objective, honest responses. People will tell the leader what they think the leader wants to hear at the time, especially if they feel pressured or believe that an honest response will bring repercussions. Trust, remember? Part of establishing that trust is a willingness to provide lanes for communications that are untraceable until that teacher feels comfortable communicating in more direct venues. Regardless, do not launch the ship during low tide. If some teachers blame the students for all behavior issues without considering the child's deficiencies or their roles in helping the child develop these needs, assign a mentor. Revisit the awareness stage if needed, but the leader cannot attain buy-in or commitment if the staffers are not in agreement about the problem and motivated to collaboratively move forward.

What do we need to purchase or modify to facilitate this process effectively?

One of the biggest reasons that poverty is the primary variable when considering a child's likelihood for success in academics is that it is a symptom of things such as parental education and marital status. In the United States, 80 percent of school construction and building maintenance is funded locally.[2] In lower income areas, ACEs are more prevalent and conditions are often more challenging than in more affluent areas. So it is likely that the schools that need trauma sensitive schools the most are more prone to be limited in terms of support and resources. For this reason, this transformational approach using a trauma-informed instruction and social-emotional learning model will assume the school is not a massive architectural marvel with unlimited resources supported by an endless river of gold flowing directly from the community into its budget. The intention is to keep this book as authentic as possible, catering to actual circumstances of the schools that need it most. Therefore, this program described is built with a realistic budget in mind. There will be no additional staffers needed; training and a (recommended) social-emotional learning (SEL) assessment program is enough to get started with decreasing costs as the program matures. While it is difficult to craft a text that understands all of the threats and nuances in every needy school, this is a promise to try. However, it should be noted that trauma-informed teaching strategies are most effective when structured and guided by SEL guidelines. Social-emotional learning has been proven to be effective in all types of schools, so it will be most effective when implemented where it is most needed. Research suggests that SEL program benefits can be similar for students regardless of socioeconomic background, race, ethnicity, or school location.[3] In an article for *Educational Psychology*, Pamela Garner wrote, "Minority students may benefit from having early access to SEL instruction and SEL interventions may mitigate factors that put students at risk for poor social, emotional, and behavioral development"[4] One of the suggestions is to develop spaces for students to meet privately with counselors, social workers, and mentors, depending on the specifics of the program. Later in this book, the hospital model, a therapeutic intervention program, will be described and recommended. If adopted, the in-school suspension room will need to be converted and technology and software may need to be purchased, in addition to workstations. Again, this is an example, one that is recommended for advanced programs.

What skills, dispositions, organization, community relations, and so forth, must be in place to begin?

The answer to this question is important because it requires a self-assessment of dispositions and an analysis of critical competencies. Essentially, the car is taken to a mechanic before a long trip to assess its ability to complete the journey. In *Hamlet*, the young prince contemplates his death before a duel normally considered sport, sensing treachery afoot. He confides in his friend Horatio, "If it be not to come, it will be / Now. If it be not now, yet it will come. / The readiness is all." (5.2.235–237). The play is a bit frustrating because the ever-pensive young prince's tragic flaw is his inability to act when the best opportunities arise. He is plagued by conflict between his values, interpretation of facts, and social stigma. He acts only when the window to do so closes on him, making his fight a desperate battle against all odds. "The readiness is all" might mark Hamlet's failure, suggesting that he still lacks the readiness to act moments before his death. It is perhaps a dramatic analogy, but there is a real need to determine the readiness of the troops before heading off to fight for the cause. A favorable response is imperative before beginning, and the leader should understand that since motivation and commitment are as ephemeral as they are essential when not tied to action, readiness is a window that opens and closes rapidly.

The Trauma-Informed Classroom

Teachers will be involved in every phase of the TSSEL school culture. They are too important not to lead this process, especially in classrooms. For that reason, it makes sense to prioritize teachers with substantial training and resources. It is also recommended that the training be conducted by the instructional coach with the assistance of any combination of counselors, social workers, and school psychologists. It is important that teachers comprehend the depth of support offered by the staff that will directly help design and oversee the curricular and management needs of the teacher. Teachers should not be asked to do more; they should be supported to do things differently. Videos can be developed so that teachers can view segments and respond with attitudinal surveys, providing valuable feedback for leadership, who need to know what changes are being made in the classroom to defuse the impact of trauma brought into it. It is also suggested that staff members become trained in improvement science so that they can help individual teachers gauge progress more efficiently and monitor the school-wide effort. More information about improvement science can be found on the website of the Carnegie Foundation for the Advancement of Teaching.

As mentioned in Part I, the basic framework for reaching maximal academic and social-emotional learning is directly related to Maslow's motivational model, also known as the Maslow hierarchy of needs. The so-called deficiency needs are the most basic for survival, and they must be met before the growth needs are met. These deficiency needs range from the most basic needs to sustain life, such as food and water, to the need for love, belonging, and esteem. It is only once these needs are met that teachers can successfully develop the cognitive and aesthetic needs that form basic human intelligences and lead to more advanced growth toward self-actualization and transcendence. While some schools erroneously assume the basic needs are met—if they consider them at all—many endure frustrations and failures because they have not factored in the effects of the broken, fragmented, or absent deficiency needs.

Strategies for Natural Disaster Trauma

While trauma-informed teachers are very good at minimizing the effects of trauma, they have thus far been unable to divert tornadoes, thwart hurricanes, funnel flood waters away, or extinguish wildfires. Trauma-sensitive school cultures, however, understand that proactive strategies empower children and families by meeting their physiological, safety, belongingness, and especially esteem needs before, during, and after the foreseeable disaster. Natural disaster trauma is unique in that school staffers may in certain instances have some idea the natural disaster is coming. That provides a unique opportunity to help minimize the severity of the trauma before it happens. Knowledge of Bronfenbrenner's nested systems of support is extremely helpful in such scenarios, in that awareness of the exosystem helps orchestrate support for students and their families. There are probably no better reasons for the school, parents, and community to be actively engaged in supportive, communicative networks. For teachers, their primary responsibility is for the safety of their students, so anything that can be done proactively to minimize the threat and maximize the students' resiliency levels is strongly recommended. As suggested by the National Child Traumatic Stress Network, there are many details to consider that relieve stressors and empower victims. Some general guidelines are as follows:

- **Empowering the Children:** Children need to be empowered to contribute to their own safety; it helps minimize the damage to their deficiency needs and creates autonomy that enhances self-esteem. While the preparation windows vary depending on the type of disaster, there are specific strategies that children can do in school to help cope during and after the disaster. For example, children can create a checklist in class that helps them prepare for the storm. The list should include things that will help calm the child during the event, such as packing a backpack with favorite toys, batteries, a music player with headsets, paper and pencils, flashlights, snacks, medications, and important phone numbers. Children benefit from having some control, so helping secure, for instance, safe locations with food and water for pets is something helpful that they can do. (Losing pets is a traumatic event for most children.) In addition, teachers can send home information packets, to be shared with parents, that include evacuation routes, elevation maps, and community centers with vital resources. The National Child Traumatic Stress Network should serve teachers as a valuable resource to help inform not only the students but the network of support around them. For example, it includes a list of activities for children that require no electricity or materials. Giving children strategies to stay occupied not only calms them but decreases the degree to which they might irritate their parents, who might already be tremendously stressed.

- **Empowering the Parents:** Children notice when adults become stressed or afraid. They may not realize what it means when they watch news alerts featuring disturbing images and grocery stores full of panicked shoppers competing for bottled water, batteries, and other staples. By giving the parents assistance in developing a plan and providing options, the child's exposure to panic and chaos decreases. Teachers and the school can serve as the agent for helping parents overcome the overwhelming amounts of pre-catastrophe preparation. Consider that a hurricane is tracked at least one week before it hits land. During that time, teachers can reach out to the community to collect key information, such as the location of temporary shelters, tips from first responders, or evacuation routes for families living in lower elevation levels. This information can be linked through the school website, emailed to parents, or sent home in information packets. In fact, there are other resources, such as a computer application called *Help Kids Cope*, for example, that can be downloaded to help parents before, during, and after a hurricane. It should be noted that decreasing levels of anxiety in parents decreases their levels of frustration. By making them aware that there are resources available and that there is a network of support to help, parents feel more in control.

- **Empowering the Community:** Emergency services and agencies are available in most communities, but because of the inaccessibility of reliable communication networks, the community may need help getting word out to the citizens. Some elderly residents do not use cell phones or the internet, so they may be uninformed about the storm. Through collaborative planning with the relevant agencies, the school can help create and distribute information. There are many ways this can be done, such as having each student give out three information packets to the elderly in their neighborhoods. In addition, school leaders may offer their facility (or part of it) as a shelter if needed. Often, trucks and power workers need a place to park or could use a distribution center for bottled water and food. The school gymnasium is often used by the Red Cross to accept blood donations or provide bedding for the suddenly homeless. Teachers can help in many ways as volunteers that lead community efforts. Again, the best resource available at the time of publication is the National Child Traumatic Stress Network website, which offers volumes of information to assist in all forms of trauma-related childhood experiences.[5]

Helping children and parents cope in advance with the violence of a storm and its aftermath may obviate the need to deal with the negative energies that the unsupported child might bring back when the doors of the school reopen. A school culture cannot reverse the path of a storm, but it can help reduce its levels of anxiety for those it serves. While a disaster is tragic, it provides an opportunity for the staff and leadership to demonstrate character by offering its building, personnel, and resources to lead the community through a time of crisis. It is an opportunity to put aside petty differences and empathetically work with all people who serve children. There is something about a catastrophe that brings the best of people to the forefront, and the school should seize the opportunity to meet as many needs as possible during times of great demand.

Strategies for Coping with Vicarious Trauma

Any school leader attempting to train educators to employ a trauma-sensitive approach must be aware of the repercussions. Teachers, administrators, counselors, and others in the school setting who work with students on a whole-child developmental model are exposed to a tremendous number of stressors related to multiple possible forms of trauma. There is no degree of preparation that readies someone for the sometimes painfully difficult transition from a one-dimensional authority figure to a three-dimensional nurturer. The gut-wrenching shock, the heart-dropping sorrow, and the mind-bending frustration create high levels of secondary traumatic stress (STS), also called "vicarious trauma." While this form of trauma has been well studied in law enforcement officers, fire fighters, social workers, doctors and nurses, therapists, and child welfare workers, there is little research to gauge its impact on school personnel. In the few studies that have been conducted, however, high levels of STS have been diagnosed in professional educators.[6] No program that requires the courage and compassion to undertake such a noble endeavor should disregard the impact such interactions might have on school personnel.

Educators are products of the familial and societal problems detailed in this book, which is to say that many are burdened by the effects of long-term trauma. They have other stressors associated with adult relationships, finances, parenting, and professional pressures. Trauma-sensitivity and social-emotional learning requires patience and positive dispositions. Training and support structures for teachers are essential and must not become a corner cut when constraints such as time and budget become issues. This concept requires a positive, supported, and informed workforce. A multi-tiered system of support (MTSS) model for teachers is something that may help teachers cope, with more support offered for different degrees of trauma. School psychologists and counselors can become support options for staff.

In summary, the psychological well-being of all staff members is critical to the trauma-sensitive school culture, and support for all stakeholders must be effectively addressed.

8

Trauma-Informed Instruction, Social-Emotional Learning and Maslow

O, she doth teach the torches to burn bright
—*Romeo and Juliet*, 1.5.51

There is strong evidence that school-based social and emotional instruction increases academic achievement for all students, including those living in poverty. Furthermore, it develops the skills traumatized children crave because they are deficient in the developmental areas like self-confidence, social and emotional skills, and prosocial behavior. In addition, social-emotional learning (SEL) has routinely been shown to reduce depression, anxiety, and social withdrawal.[1] Furthermore, studies have shown SEL reduces delinquent behaviors such as bullying, which suggests that levels of frustration and anger are being replaced with a sense of belonging and higher levels of self-esteem.[2]

According to Maslow, belongingness and self-esteem are fundamental to cognition. Social-emotional learning interventions for pre–Kindergarten through high school graduation have been shown to improve achievement in mathematics, reading comprehension, and (to a slightly lesser degree) science.[3] By triangulating what we know about needs, trauma's many causes, and the overwhelmingly positive research associated with social-emotional learning, it seems that all schools should be built on trauma-sensitive approaches that feature informed teachers and TSSEL school cultures. Quite simply, trauma is the *why* and social-emotional development is the *how*, the recipe for positive whole-child development that increases academic performance through positive, therapeutic, relationships. If done correctly, it works.

Meeting Physiological Needs

The most basic needs are physiological, and any weaknesses or failures to fulfill them have a profound impact on the brain. Since teachers are blind to what the child experiences beyond the school setting in most cases, it is reasonable to assume that the student has water, food, warmth, and shelter at school but may not have the same necessities elsewhere. Teachers in communities with large populations of students classified as economically disadvantaged should be on high alert and develop a plan to offset the impact of these deficiencies should students display possible reactions to having their physiological needs go unmet. Regardless of whether or not the teacher or school leaders feel it is the school's responsibility to meet these needs, doing so is a way to improve learning, and that is the responsibility of the school, an urgent one in the case of the transformational or "turnaround" TSSEL school.

So how does the teacher address deficiency needs that are physiological? These things are provided for the most part by the taxpayer, not the teacher; however, if the teacher and school administrator are aware of a few basic details, they can improve learning using creative approaches to meeting this basic need. Glutamate, according to a recent study published in the *Journal of Physiology*, is a neurotransmitter that is usually elevated in children who have been victims of violence, such as physical or sexual abuse, spanking, or bullying. Higher levels of glutamate increase the likelihood of aggressive or violent behaviors. In some children, seizures are a serious risk. What decreases glutamate levels? Water. Teachers can control behavior issues and decrease the probability that a child might have a seizure by making sure students are hydrated.[4] Insulin receptors are also altered by chronic stress or prenatal exposure to alcohol. As a result, the child experiences fluctuating blood sugar levels that trigger learning difficulties and behavior problems. Allowing these children access to a glucose-containing drink when that child demonstrates the symptoms is also suggested. Of course, there should be pre-arranged protocols established before any beverage is provided to a child suffering from altered insulin receptors.[5]

These examples demonstrate opportunities to use an awareness of Maslow's hierarchy of needs and how research in these areas can reveal some of the reasons students underperform. With this information, schools can develop a strategy to address these issues, once believed to be beyond the control of the teacher. The solution could be very simple, something like snacks. Some scheduling can cause students to go long periods of time without eating. If data shows that behavior incidents increase and learning decreases at certain times of the day, it could be solved rather easily with a snack period with water. In addition, education about sodas and how caffeine and certain foods can dehydrate children should be shared with the children and their parents.

Another example has to do with body temperature, in this case warmth. Labeling children's jackets with athletic tape that identifies the child's teacher, room number, and bus number can help prevent the loss of these items, for instance. Waiting for buses in temperatures below freezing is counterproductive and leads to sickness, which leads to absenteeism. Many of these jackets are tossed into the school's Lost and Found, never to be claimed. The method of labeling, if adopted school-wide, gets the jacket back into the hands of its owner as quickly as possible. It also helps the child avoid spankings and verbal abuse at home. While water and snack breaks and jacket labeling may make only a small differences, small differences add up.

Meeting Safety Needs

Perhaps no other emotion disrupts cognition more than fear. While the school's primary responsibility to a student is safety, the teacher needs to understand that safety to a traumatized child is a state of mind, not a practiced drill or laminated evacuation floor plan beside the door. Without a sense of security, some students feel vulnerable, sending them into defense mode, essentially locking down the brain from higher functioning and social development. Few teachers have never had the experience of seeing a child suddenly become overwhelmed with terror when there seemed to be no reason for the reaction. In fact, lockdown, tornado, and fire drills have triggered traumatic episodes in students who have had homes burn down or had to hide from an intruder until police arrived. As explained in Part I, the amygdala sends the brain into lock-down mode, essentially prohibiting the hippocampus from converting short-term memories into messages it distributes to the various regions of the brain where they can become building blocks in the process we call learning. There are things that happen in the classroom that can be changed to minimize the fear factor.

For example, the authoritarian teacher often abuses authority and resorts to bullying in the name of order and discipline. This teacher frankly has no place in the trauma-sensitive school if he or she is unwilling to understand the needs of the students. The TSSEL teacher, on the other hand, surveys the environment and minimizes potential stressors that can threaten students' sense of security. These teachers plan cooperative activities, emphasize positive reinforcements, use a calm tone, and allow for the child to have input. Children feel empowered by "voice and choice," a process that gives them control and establishes autonomy. The room should be clutter-free and students should be trained to operate within a framework of mutual respect. Children, in other words, need to feel safe to take the risks that lead to their learning. In addition, TSSEL teachers watch for signs to inform decisions and proactive planning. Are children subdued or aggressive after earning a low grade for the quarter? It seems odd that safety and assessment should be linked, but if the assessment triggers violence in the home, how grades are delivered might need to be revisited.

Fear is a state of vulnerability and helplessness, and the classroom teacher cannot control things beyond the classroom, such as the weather. Between 2016 and 2018, the areas surrounding the University of North Carolina at Pembroke were twice hammered by hurricanes and flooding. The community suffered loss of life, home, pets, electricity, and resources. Many families in Robeson County, the state's poorest, had no insurance; they lost nearly everything they owned. Some schools were closed for over a month as they repaired damages and removed the toxic mold. According to a CNN report, 14 percent of all children in the United States will experience trauma in some form or another following a fire, tornado, flood, hurricane, or other natural disaster. A study of post-traumatic stress disorder in children identified in the CNN article states that 29 percent of children following Katrina were still traumatized within one to two years following the event.[6] That is to suggest that nearly one third of the children in the areas surrounding Pembroke will experience disrupted levels of functioning for a period of up to four years. It is devastating to consider that when Hurricane Florence blew into their lives, some children were still experiencing disrupted cognitive functioning as a result of Hurricane Matthew.

Of course, teachers are amazing people, and they are usually vigilant. Knowing things such as which students have food allergies or issues related to pre-planning evacuation routes (for students with hearing, visual, or disabilities that limit locomotion, for instance) helps meet safety needs and gives parents peace of mind. Other staff members that are not accustomed to supervising children could be trained to help monitor the building for potential hazards. Anyone without a visitor's pass in the building is everyone's concern and must be addressed. The TSSEL-trained staffers need to be aware of bully hot spots and monitor them when possible. If there are children with diabetes, allergies, or epilepsy, the staff needs to know how to administer epinephrine, insulin, or seizure protocols. Children involved in custody battles should be watched in parking lots and bus loading zones. Preparation, empowerment, and information are tools that the teacher can use not only to protect students in the present but to help them deal with the anxieties that can threaten children's resilience in the future. There are literally dozens of ways to improve safety in the school if the word *threat* is defined broadly, as it should be. None of this involves burdening teachers with more responsibilities than they already have, and it is not asking them to do more than to stay alert and prepared.

Meeting Love and Belonging Needs

According to *Psychology Today* contributor Dr. Karyn Hall, "A sense of belonging to a greater community improves your motivation, health, and happiness. When you see your connection to others, you know that all people struggle and have difficult times. You are not alone. There is comfort in that knowledge."[7] In many schools, belongingness is left to chance. It is the hope that the learned and hidden curricula will produce a well-balanced, appreciative student who sees his or her role in the school community and flourishes. In some cases, there is a program or plan to blend belongingness into the school culture, but many are little more than paper policies that are difficult to measure, monitor, or oversee. For traumatized children, it can be a profound experience, perhaps providing a family where they are validated as human beings. If children do not find this sense of belonging at home, they crave it at school. If not at school, they will find it somewhere, often among similar people seeking some form of communal acceptance. Friends are frequently determined by similar coping choices, as among drug cliques or gangs. A positive school culture based on establishing a sense of belonging for everyone can literally save lives.

Take Norm, the character from the 1980s sitcom *Cheers*, for example. Norm is a middle-aged, obese, unhappily married, unemployed accountant. While the world has been unkind to Norm, he arrives at the bar daily, entering to the welcoming shout of "Norm!" On one hand, he is there for the alcohol and its power to temporarily remove him from the pressures of a competitive, belittling society. On the other hand, he needs to hear his name chanted in a loving and accepting greeting as he walks through the door. As the theme song has it, Norm needs to go where everybody knows his name and they're always glad he came.[8] Norm finds his family in a bar beneath the busy streets of Boston where he buys his sense of belonging along with his beer and where his only extended family members are misfits who likewise seek refuge in the bar. A middle-aged mailman, Cliff, who lives with his mother is a part of this unit, as is a retired major league baseball player, Sam, who yearns for the adoration and faded glory of his youth, ironically cut short by alcoholism. Finally, a psychotherapist, Frazier, joins the group and doles out obvious Freudian analyses of his friends while his own life is in shambles. Ironically, beer is served by a verbally abusive waitress, a single mom with several children to support. *Cheers* was the nation's favorite show for nearly a decade, perhaps vicariously luring millions of viewers into a depressing, underachieving family tucked away in the bowels of a large New England city. Looking beyond the comedy, the show's fans might have thought it sad that the characters' alcohol-induced happiness comes from a place established to profit from their self-medicating. How many viewers wondered, as they laughed, what happened in the characters' lives that drove them to the bar?

Perhaps it is not entirely appropriate to compare characters on a television sitcom to children escaping tragic home lives at school, but it is a fair reminder of the human condition, and of what happens to people who do not have their needs met when they are young. Norm, for the most part, is a comical character who earns our laughs through his biting sarcasm; we embrace him lightly while admiring his wit, which is of limited use to an unemployed accountant. He missed his calling, perhaps, and now wallows in the ditch beside the path he did not take. It is not hard to imagine Norm as an ACE casualty, approaching a premature death as a victim of adversity.

Teachers can learn from Norm. First, he is greeted as he enters the door, immediately establishing his value, if only momentary, to the inhabitants of the room. It is the highlight of Norm's day and makes him feel appreciated. This practice of welcoming students is a good one for teachers to adopt. In a recent study, it was found that "when teachers started class by welcoming students at the door, academic engagement increased by 20 percentage points and disruptive behavior decreased by 9 percentage points."[9] There are several reasons this simple practice is so fruitful. In some cases, the simplistic greeting of the teacher may be the only kind words that student hears, as is the case with Norm. Children who are traumatized by adults who supervise them often seek approval from those same adults, even the abusive ones, and their moods may be altered by misinterpretations of facial expressions or comments. A welcoming smile can help establish trust and lighten the emotional burden a student might be struggling with on a given day. As mentioned, students need to feel invited and wanted, not afraid of the teacher or of failure. By increasing engagement by 20 percent, it is as if the teacher creates an extra day per week to work with the student. Increased engagement also results in a decrease in disciplinary incidents, converting the potential for negative energy into positive energy.

The greeting is where it begins, a smile and kind word that filter away problems and make students feel safe and welcome. When the teacher trusts and demonstrates confidence in the ability of the student, the greeting has the power to wash away a lot of the negativity each child routinely carries. It is imperative that the teacher prepare the student to adopt the most beneficial mindset, which is directly tied to feelings and behaviors. In other words, learning is social for these students, and their mannerisms and emotions play a key role in the learning process. The greeting at the door is a positive mood setter. A friendly gesture from a teacher who has taken time to learn about a student beyond the limitations of the classroom is powerful, and might lead to less time spent on damage control during the class. Teachers who understand their students know their favorite pet's name, for instance, or the college team they support during basketball season. They understand their favorite music and latest styles. They notice when one child gets a new pair shoes or a young girl fixes her hair a different way. It makes a huge difference for a child seeking an identity and place in a world where he or she feels unwanted everywhere else they go. In short, when a teacher understands the importance of a series of small gestures, it can make a huge difference.

Of course, once students enter the classroom, the challenge becomes more difficult because there is a higher degree of difficulty for the teacher; the individual, cute, smiling faces become a large mob of noisy faces. All of the individual problems coagulate into a web of complex volatility, it would seem. The teacher has an obligation to teach the content and develop the skills detailed in the written curriculum; however, the manner in which it is taught is what defines trauma-informed instruction, which is dedicated to holistically developing children through social-emotional learning. That sounds complicated, but once the teacher and school staff understand how trauma affects learning and how to overcome the damage, it becomes common sense. The light comes on and the teacher knows which strategies and activities best achieve the desired cognitive, emotional, and psychological results. The social setting of the classroom and how students collaboratively work on tasks are not specified in the curriculum, but they present an opportunity for the teacher to change lives and lead students down the path that leads to self-actualization. They are, in other words, how the teacher can forge relationships and provide opportunities for self-exploration. It is not necessary that the teacher identify trauma or the source of suspected trauma in each student; it is enough to understand that trauma exists on a large scale and that every class presents a challenge to protect and empower children from the external threats, whatever they may be. Failing to see this is blindness that leads to much misunderstanding. It should be noted once more that there are no cookie-cutter recipes for success; teachers must develop their own strategies, which should be consistent with recommended practices, based on the personal strengths, and incorporating knowledge of students and their external support systems. Remember, the TSSEL school culture is about trust and relationships, so the proper courses of action are not easy to define without first understanding the dynamics that surround the development of these two critical necessities. While the possibilities to cultivate a sense of belonging are too numerous to list, some basic strategies largely inspired by *Teaching Children from Poverty and Trauma,* a report written by Ernest Izard, may help guide the process. (It should be noted that much of what Izard suggests is based on the competencies described by the Collaborative for Academic, Social, and Emotional Learning [CASEL], an organization dedicated to enriching lives with social-emotional skill awareness and development. The CASEL competencies are the best resource for any teacher or school seeking guidance in this area.) The strategies:

- **Build positive, enriching, relationships.** As already suggested, you should get to know your students, but take it a step further and give them the opportunity to know one another. Develop peer projects, make group assignments, and have Socratic discussions. Develop "circles of trust" where students collaboratively build social-emotional skills such as empathy. Avoid activities that could be embarrassing or humiliating, such as reading aloud to or competing with the class. The classroom should be dedicated to positive, enriching relationships, so do not plan activities without considering the risks each student must take to succeed. "The first thing an educator should do in his or her interaction with a student from poverty or one who has been traumatized," writes Izard, "is to acknowledge the student's resiliency."[10] Many high school students could drop out, but they do not. Many smaller children emerge each day from homes where poverty, drug and alcohol abuse, and domestic violence have become familiar, but the child smiles back when greeted. The teacher may not know the details of students' lives outside of school but understands how difficult they may be; this gives the teacher perspective and empathy. Acknowledge the simple task of coming to school and establish it as the place where students are appreciated.
- **Develop a calm voice.** Teachers model desired behaviors, and that should extend to maintaining the right tone of voice. The teacher should not only refrain from negative, authoritative, or condescending comments but should speak in a voice that neither triggers reminders of trauma nor elicits other negative reactions. Teachers need to come up with methods, such as holding up a hand or flicking the light on and off once, of silently requesting the students' attention. Once that goal is achieved, the teacher's volume should remain low and the tone should be calm. Always remember that students should be spoken *to* not *at.* There is a difference.
- Since trauma-informed teachers give students a voice as well, the teacher must also understand just how important and powerful

that voice can be. An article at the website Yoga Calm echoes this idea: "One thing we often hear in one of the trauma groups … is how often they perceive that their feelings, concerns, desires, and so on weren't truly grasped by the adults who want to help them. They express a sense of being denied a voice in their own lives."[11] Often children who have no voice anywhere else will speak in frustrated bursts that can be misconstrued as disrespectful or confrontational. Help children find a calm voice and listen when they speak. It is therapeutic to find the composure to communicate to an adult calmly and be heard. It builds confidence and strengthens the relationship, and prevents misunderstanding.

- **Teach emotional skills.** Emotions are basically how humans react to the environment and how others interpret people as individuals. Students should be aware of their emotions and demonstrate the ability to understand them. Emotions are the senses used to establish relationships, communicate, appreciate, and they are the foundation for many more quality-of-life skills. Brain-based learning expert Eric Jensen uses "gratitude" as an example to illustrate this concept, noting that it is often unrefined in children living in economically disadvantaged homes and neighborhoods. He adds, "Students from poverty and those who have been traumatized are no different from other students in that all children are born with only six emotions hard-wired in the brain."[12] A failure to develop one of these emotions is like losing one of the senses. Children who live in poverty often have an underdeveloped concept of gratitude. Trauma-sensitive teachers with a large population of economically disadvantaged students must model gratitude daily, but there may be times when that is not enough. If students demonstrate the inability to respond to a situation, the teacher needs not to correct the student but to embed that situation into the lessons. To extend Jensen's example, gratitude can be taught in history lessons, reading or literature discussions, science projects, or during role-playing activities. For example, the teacher can ask older students to explain the range of emotions they think freed slaves might have experienced after the Civil War. Gratitude would not be the only emotion in that case, but it might be one complicated by a range of other emotions. With younger students, a teacher could have a roundtable seminar to discuss Aesop's fable "The Lion and the Mouse" and ask the children, "Why was the lion nice to the mouse after the mouse chewed through the net that trapped the lion?" In a science project, the class might discuss what a polio patient would have said to Jonas

Salk after he invented the cure for the disease. While there will be a section on social-emotional teaching strategies later in this book, these are prime examples of how a teacher develops lessons that incorporate social-emotional development into the curriculum.

• **Teach self-regulation.** Traumatized students often have difficulties regulating themselves in some situations. They do not always enter the classroom calm and collected; they bring frustrations and anger as well, which is why a whole school, holistic approach to child development through trauma sensitivity and a curriculum based on social-emotional learning is so critical. Many students have not been taught empathy, emotional skills, or self-control; they are essentially reactive time bombs who do not have a sense of control, so they are often controlled by others or by circumstances. As a tool for helping students gain the self-discipline to handle situations appropriately and without personal risk, there are some strategies teachers can adopt that help students learn patience and poise while minimizing disruptive behaviors. Disciplinary action does little to correct undesired behaviors; it actually increases the levels of frustration and diminishes the sense of belonging. So how can teachers develop self-regulation in traumatized children? Here are some examples.

Once students enter the classroom after being greeted, the next step is sometimes called the "warm-up activity." In the study previously mentioned, about the impact of greetings at the door, engagement increased by 20 percent. That increased engagement most likely occurs during the warm-up activity, according to a case study involving three students identified as "at risk" whose engagement was an average of 24 percent higher during the first ten minutes of class.[13] It has been suggested that the teacher play classical music or soft jazz during this time because it has soothing effects that can calm students following the transition from class to class. But for traumatized students, it has increased value, according to an article in *Psychology Today* that quotes English inventor John Armstrong, who said, "Music exalts each joy, allays each grief. Expels diseases, softens every pain, subdues the rage of poison, and the plague."[14] Of course there is a bit of hyperbole in Armstrong's statement, but the essence is not lost. Music changes moods, soothing stress at times like pouring cold water over a burn. Once the teacher greets, calms, and preps the students for the lesson, the likelihood for success is much greater. It should also be noted that the music can also be used to call a "time out." If student engagement decreases or the activity leads to behavior that is too animated, the teacher simply turns on the music again. Students are trained to know that is the signal for silence and calm introspection, or even meditation at times. According to the NEA handbook and the National Institute for Trauma and Loss in Children (TLC), some self-regulation strategies are taken from yoga exercises.[15] Once the music is turned on and the students halt activities to sit silently, for instance, the teacher can lead the class in a deep breathing activity. The students might be told to imagine themselves sitting under a tree in a field, surrounded by fragrant daisies and feeling the sun or a breeze on their cheeks. Then, once the mood is more subdued, instruction can resume. The self-regulation strategies might vary according to the grade level, so it is a good idea for the teacher to maintain a menu of these interventions if this technique is to be exercised.

Finally, many students panic if they find themselves in a situation where they anticipate there will be no due process. If a teacher intervenes in a conflict, or the administrator is called to assist, remind the student that he or she will be given an opportunity to explain their position in private. Afterwards, ask students questions that are not judgmental or cross-examining, but open-ended, geared toward an opportunity to reflect and retrospectively self-regulate. When students understand that they will be given an opportunity to explain themselves, they calm down and are less likely to become as reactive in the future. When students are being taught the SEL core competencies throughout the school, they are more self-aware. Remember, the object is to get the child to become aware of themselves and develop self-regulation strategies, so even if the behavior exhibited is not ideal, a conversation in which the student is able to discuss how social-emotional breakdowns led to the issue is progress. This reflective self-assessment is what many educators think punitive consequences (parent contact, in-school suspension, out-of-school suspension, and so forth) are supposed to accomplish. Many think being grounded, isolated, exiled, or beaten "teaches kids a lesson"; the problem is, the adults usually have no idea what lesson was taught. Even afterwards, when adults ask the child, "Tell me what you learned," the honest answer might be that the child learned to say what the adult wants to hear and, in the future, not to get caught. A voice to reflect, acknowledge, apologize (if they feel it is needed) is empowerment that leads to growth, not merely a fear of consequences. Students have a keen sense of fairness and they understand that they are powerless in most situations. "Voice" is definitely a factor in self-regulation during stressful situations and it can be a very effective skill for both teacher and student.

- **Teach empathy.** Teaching empathy also builds self-regulation skills because it teaches students to see the world from alternative perspectives. It is very important that children learn empathy because there are so many situations in life that require one to interpret the pain or struggles of others. Relationships are very difficult without it. Students developing a relationship with a teacher who models empathy are more likely to incorporate the skills into their own emotional resilience. But since trauma impedes normal brain development, post-traumatic stress disorders (PTSD) in children are often characterized by both stunted growth in areas of the brain that develop empathy and an inability to adequately interpret facial expressions or body language. This problem, if not addressed in childhood, creates social-emotional difficulties into adulthood. In their book *Neuroscience for Social Work*, Holly Matto, Jessica Strolin-Goltzman, and Michelle Ballon note that "survivors of complex childhood trauma often struggle with their ability to experience compassion and empathy toward themselves and toward other people."[16] Meditation, a self-regulation strategy as well, has been proven to be an effective exercise to mediate the harms attributed to the deficiency of this function.

True virtue in the field of education leadership is found in one's ability to see every challenge from the perspective of the various stakeholders while applying all that one learns from that experience to serve the best interests of the child. Reasonable questions to ask include the following: How will my decision impact this person or that group? How can I create a solution that best serves everyone impacted so that everyone can better serve the student? The trauma-sensitive teacher is constantly aware of this dynamic in his or her leadership behaviors and strategies. The stronger the elements of trust and belonging in a classroom or school, the more powerful the lessons derived through modeling will be. Embed these lessons, such as "The Lion and the Mouse" activity, into lesson design. While the mouse, for example, demonstrated empathy when he freed the lion, he was also demonstrating gratitude for having his own life spared by the lion before, when the lion showed him empathy. On a secondary level, there are works of literature that present an unexpected point of view, one that may even be less than popular. After reading the epic poem *Beowulf,* for instance, in which the hero kills the monster Grendel for invading a dining hall and eating drunken soldiers while they slept, a teacher might assign John Gardner's *Grendel*. Gardner tells the story from the monster's point of view, explaining his position in an attempt to elicit an empathetic response from the reader while vilifying Beowulf, the epic hero. Alternatively, a teacher might allow students to think of movies in which the protagonists are outlaws or even villains (e.g., *Joker*, *Bonnie and Clyde*, *Robin Hood*) and examine how the directors compelled the audience to develop empathy for these characters. Once accomplished, an activity or discussion might help students personalize the power of empathy.

Meet Self-Esteem Needs

The fourth and final level of Maslow's deficiency-needs model is esteem, which should be regarded as self-love, and not specifically confidence, which is indeed a desired outcome. Esteem is one of the first things destroyed in children who are traumatized and the most difficult to restore. Trauma robs children of a belief in who they are or how they fit into the mosaic of their worlds, which obviously destroys self-confidence, or the belief in what they can do. Low self-esteem causes students to devalue themselves, creating a feeling of unworthiness. It is the most challenging need for a teacher to meet, but the rewards are tremendous.

There are many things a teacher can do to help a child overcome the damage. It is important for a child to know there is at least one place or one family in which he or she is valued. A place where, to quote the *Cheers* theme song, "everybody knows your name, and they're always glad you came." Esteem is the product of having all other deficiency needs met, both the basic (physiological and safety) needs and the social-emotional needs. There are certain skills aligned with the development of self-esteem that are beneficial to students, and a teacher's failure to master them can have an adverse effect. However, when teachers consider why they teach, the calling they answered and answer every day, it generally has to do with how educators change lives for the better. That is the motivation that drives an educator, one that is often buried beneath a mountain of standardized testing, low wages, negative publicity, long hours, and overcrowded classrooms. The success stories and career highlights educators share with one another are rarely based on content retention. You never hear a tissue-dabbing, moist-faced educator sharing a story about curriculum alignment, for example. You hardly ever hear a math teacher bragging about how the Pythagorean theorem helped a child assist Mom and Dad in saving the farm or how showing growth on a standardized test opened doors at Harvard for a quiet, shy, poverty-stricken adolescent.

You hear stories about resilience, relationships, and courage. Teachers' fondest memories are of students experiencing epiphanies or overcoming obstacles. They are stories that feature a child developing as a social human being, where the student overcomes some major crisis or accomplishes some remarkable, unexpected feat. These moments are often related to Maslow's esteem category, in which the student's anxiety and feelings of unworthiness are converted into a love for the self. When that happens, it is indeed magical. It may not be the reason one might enter the field of teaching, but it is the reason one remains. It should be noted that many of these tales are memorable because the child somehow defied the odds, unlike others in similar predicaments who failed, vanished, and go unmentioned in the teacher's lounge. Those who do not overcome the odds are the children for whom and about whom this book is written. We need to save them all.

Shakespeare writes, "This above all: To thine own self be true" (*Hamlet*, 1.3.84). Being "true" is often interpreted as being honest, but Shakespeare's ambiguities often allow for multiple meanings, giving flexibility to the script. If it means devoted, as in being true in a relationship, then it is very applicable to Maslow's fourth level. Esteem is a love of the self (not in a conceited way, obviously) and this quote treats the character and the self as separate entities. To extend this, the self then is something to which one must show devotion, and that means it becomes something that is respected. In other words, self-love is not confidence or conceit; it is an obligation to the self to reach one's full potential, or as Maslow says, to self-actualization. Often the introduction to this rather famous quote from *Hamlet* is omitted, but it should not be. "This above all" is extremely significant because it concludes (in the play) a long list of idiomatic bits of advice given by Polonius to his son, Laertes. The most significant advice the father can give his son before he ventures out into the world amounts to "be devoted to yourself so that you may reach your full potential." To find that passion within that motivates you to defy their stars and venture beyond them.

The great thing about teaching is more than making children smarter; it is making them whole. Like Shakespeare, Maslow does not use the word *self* lightly. Self-esteem, which leads to self-actualization, develops when the conditions are right and the student decides to grow. Relating this to CASEL SEL core competencies, it starts with social-emotional competencies dedicated to the self: self-awareness and self-regulation. The journey to understand the full potential of the self includes the other SEL competencies (social awareness, relationship skills, and responsible decision-making). So to reach Maslow's pinnacle, self-actualization, the student must first develop the SEL competencies along the journey toward that goal.

That is the focus and primary objective of the trauma-sensitive school, but a vast majority of students never reach self-actualization, which is the realization and application of one's full potential. This is why SEL competencies and development are so desperately needed—to help the student become devoted to the self so that they can become resilient in their journeys toward self-actualization. The following are key strategies that help facilitate the development of self-esteem.

Teach Hope. As indicated in Part I, the adverse childhood experiences (ACE) study strongly suggests that about two-thirds of students suffer from at least one adverse childhood experience. Another study concludes that 62 percent of children in the South (as opposed to 41 percent everywhere else) suffer cognitive impairment as a side effect from spanking.[17] In addition, bullying and things like natural disasters are other stressors that impact cognition and, through fear, interfere with the meeting of deficiency needs. Poverty intensifies levels of frustration and increases the percentage of students who fall victim to the traumatic adversity explained in Part I. Their lives are violent, horrifying places, and many children believe it is entirely or primarily their fault. In Martin Seligman's theory of depression, this is called "learned helplessness."[18]

For every teacher that is patient with this process of teaching hope, hundreds of lives can change for the better. Teachers need to be aware that the quiet, at-risk children are more likely to have given up than the boisterous children with behavior problems. They are often hiding guilt and shame, and they fear being exposed. They do not seek attention; they deflect it. Their behaviors are more aligned with a feeling of helplessness, not with anger or rebellion. They need encouragement and hope to build self-esteem. If the teacher is a disciplinarian, then he or she becomes the police force in the classroom, focused on the rowdy behavior issues and ignoring the hopeless. It is the hopeless children who become the tragic casualties in many cases. They live in a world where the adults' rights and conveniences are considered more sacred than children's needs. The laws protect the parents' right to hit or shame children; some churches either endorse corporal punishment or do not address the matter; schools punish students using methods that force obedience over inclusion. Adults responsible for the care and well-being of children see the roles from their own perspectives, as if children are supposed to be better at their jobs than the adults who supervise them. So the children who do not buy in to the school programming because the school is not meeting their needs are voiceless and ostracized. They are hopeless.

The teaching of hope extends to the ways children are measured, which will be discussed later. Figuratively, the red ink of error needs to transform into green branches of growth. It does not matter how things have always been. Change is needed because so much more is known about how kids learn today and, more importantly, why they fail. There should be no student in any school void of hope, no student mathematically or systematically eliminated from reaching his or her full potential through a process of labeling and one-dimensional assessment. With hope, students find the way out and the way up. When the focus is on labeling, disciplining, and evaluating, we are running a system of selective filtration. It is a system that features teachers who fail students while totally detached from the fact that they are unable to teach them. How can a teacher remove himself or herself from a shared responsibility for academic underperformance? If academic performance is what the teacher is hired to facilitate, then how can anyone blame the students for failure? Some teachers boast about their high standards and rigor, implying that the students are to meet the teacher's goals and if they do not, they are judged accordingly. Have high standards and be rigorous, but make sure the standards and rigor are reachable and assure that every student in the classroom is given the support needed. The best teachers take in students who are broken and fragmented and send them away whole. The TSSEL teacher has lofty expectations and shares the responsibility in meeting them. There is no process of elimination in the TSSEL school. If a student fails, the TSSEL school needs to make sure that it in no way provided a disservice to the child who needed it most. The faculty should adjust to prevent losing any child. There should be no gap between what the school was capable of doing for the student and what it did to help the student succeed. It is important for all of the adults in the student's macrosystem to acknowledge that the student did not fail but was failed. We do not improve performance by raising standards unless we fortify and elevate the foundation first. It is critically important. The sheepdog facilitates a collaborative journey where all under his or her watch reach their destination. All stakeholders are confident that this is the case, even when confronting challenges along the way.

This is not to suggest that academic rigor is a bad thing, but it is not the only or the largest thing. Ignoring the stressors and influences that occur at home and in the community, on the buses and in the bathrooms, is not meeting the needs of the child, regardless of how rigorous a teacher makes the lessons. Every success in education trickles back to Maslow's simple model. Since trauma-sensitive, social-emotional approaches provide positivity and hope, the teacher helps meet the deficiency needs of the student.

Use meaningful touch. There are obviously legal concerns that touching a child might be misinterpreted. Understanding the risks is important, but the benefits must also be understood so a teacher can exercise professional discretion; trust and reputation can help minimize or eliminate any gray areas between reaching out and inappropriate touching. Touching can be very instrumental in developing rapport with students, and there is brain science to support it. According to Ernest Izard, author of *Teaching Children from Poverty and Trauma*, appropriate touching with direct eye contact has been proven to increase levels of oxytocin, a hormone that not only elevates good moods but also strengthens the immune system.[19]

For those who are uncomfortable with physical touch of any kind, the recommendation is to communicate with the students in a pleasant, positive, complimentary manner while making direct eye contact. Speak to students personally and not "at them." The eye contact becomes the embrace or the substitute for the pat on the back in that situation. The decision to touch or not is usually left to the child. It would be an oversight to present this strategy without mentioning that to some children, being innocently touched by an adult could trigger a defensive reaction. While that would be a strong indication that there is a serious problem at home, respect the child's wishes and report the unusual reaction to the counselor for feedback.

Give students a sense of control. The most important form of the curriculum is the hidden curriculum, which exists alongside the learned curriculum. Basically, the learned curriculum is, despite the intentions of the taught curriculum or the tested curriculum, the outcome of what happens in the classroom. The teacher's intention really is of no significance unless it is aligned with what is actually learned. For example, a teacher can lecture for an hour on the three kinds of rocks—metamorphic, sedimentary, and igneous—but the students might learn only that they hate lectures about rocks, perhaps because they doubt that understanding a boulder's genealogy and composition will ever come in handy. The teacher must design an activity that supports the content in some way to make the content meaningful. Hands-on, collaborative experimentation, which is why labs are so important, in this case would be a start. A trauma-informed teacher develops lessons that include social-emotional objectives, so the likelihood for skill development beyond content objectives found in the written curriculum is much higher. It becomes personal and significant because it is woven into the life-saving mesh of self-discovery within a process of self-recovery. Lesson design should incorporate student suggestions and offer interactive opportunities not only to develop strategies but to customize the organizational structure and procedures that have traditionally been focused on cognition. They select the method of assessment and provide and receive peer feedback. In the example of teacher lecturing on rocks, had the teacher given students samples of each kind of rock and allowed them to discuss how each might be important in various ecological settings, it may have been more productive.

There are basically three areas of support that facilitate student choice that are identified in a recent study by Hanover Research. They are as follows:

- **Organizational autonomy support**. Under this kind of support, students are involved in activities such as selecting class rules or activity protocols, assessment processes, group members, or seating arrangements. Students might be allowed to collectively establish deadlines and schedules, and to suggest assessment strategies.
- **Procedural autonomy support.** Here students develop their own roles and procedures within the context of the rules and protocols they have developed. Students in this phase of autonomy choose materials, how their work will be displayed or submitted, and how competence will be demonstrated. They may develop group goals, assign responsibilities, and create a timeline to achieve the goals.
- **Cognitive autonomy support.** Once students have been given choices, the teacher creates an activity and rubric, an open-ended task that facilitates collaboration and divergent thinking. Students might be allowed to decide on a concept and a strategy. They share expertise, solve problems, analyze multiple options before deciding on a method to fulfill the requirements of the rubric. The students understand that the teacher is detached from the activity, except as a monitor or periodic consultant, so they are less inclined to approach the challenge as if teacher approval is required or that there is only one acceptable product.[20]

While the process of giving students control is much more complex and extensive than is illustrated here, it will enrich learning and involve many 21st-century skills that are vital to successful connections between classrooms and the professional world. Teachers monitor student engagement in activities instead of spending time dealing with off-task behaviors. While it takes some faith and must be done correctly to be successful, in most cases, the students will rise to the occasion. Upon reflection, rarely do students need to be disciplined when they are having fun in a structured, collaborative activity. Why is that?

Work with students who lack self-regulation. As mentioned already, the trauma-sensitive culture requires patience. It should be noted that most of the focus on correcting behaviors is handled proactively, before there are disruptions, victims, and consequences. Trauma-sensitive cultures are not built in a day, a week, or even a year. They evolve, helped along by the dedication and attention to detail exercised by the stakeholders. Teachers need to understand the reasons traumatized students are usually more withdrawn or behaviorally aggressive. As Izard writes, "All behavior has a reason that drives it.... Students from poverty and those who have been traumatized act out because they have experienced a lack of control in their lives due to a lack of resources, emotional support, and understanding."[21]

Teachers also have to maintain order and safety, so there will always be a need, unfortunately, to refer to the disciplinary codes to determine which sentence appropriately matches the crime. This disciplinary action does not represent justice or reform when it involves a child; it is a failure every time it occurs, and a strong trauma-sensitive culture will gradually and dramatically reduce the frequency of these occurrences. The school needs to see it that way and do all it can to minimize that failure instead of blaming the students or the families behind them. Schools know their demographics and need to develop strategies to meet the needs of the population they serve. This is not to suggest that students can do no wrong and that all undesired behaviors are preventable, but the trauma-sensitive school that focuses on social-emotional learning is designed to address a lot of the unseen causes of inappropriate behavior, and within an environment that minimizes the likelihood that it will be triggered. In chapter 11, a hospital suspension model will be introduced that is an alternative to the punitive processes aligned with undesired behaviors. Essentially, strategies that utilize the expertise of the support staff are recommended, bypassing the current prison-style system of punitive consequences. Fortunately, the positive behavioral interventions and supports (PBIS) process is designed to meet the needs of the trauma-sensitive school. Most of what has been discussed in each of these subsections is part of the process. These are some of the expectations if administered with fidelity:

- reductions in major disciplinary infractions, antisocial behavior, and substance abuse.
- reductions in aggressive behavior and improvements in emotional regulation
- improvements in academic engagement and achievement
- improvements in perceptions of organizational health and school safety
- reductions in teacher and student reported bullying behavior and victimization
- improvements in perceptions of school climate
- reductions in teacher turnover[22]

Use expressive writing or drawings. Expressive writing is a low-risk opportunity for children to apply language to a situation and in the process become less victimized by it. It is not suggested that all expressive writing assignments confront potential psychosomatic disorders, but it is an opportunity for a child to relieve his or her feelings privately to an adult. Following a hurricane, for example, children can write about the storm because all were impacted in some way. An open-ended assignment could be an opportunity for individuals to reflect on personal traumatic experiences, as well as topic choices not associated with trauma. Poverty magnifies and intensifies the impact of trauma, and the way it increases frustration, diminishes life quality, and reduces options is something children accept as normal. Psychiatry patients who participate in expressive writing therapy "have demonstrated improvements in distress, negative affect, depression, and posttraumatic stress disorder (PTSD) symptoms."[23] While the teacher should not play psychiatrist after a perceived traumatic event, he or she can assign a routine expressive writing opportunity, which can improve more than grammar skills. The four benefits for the student who chooses to write about a traumatic event are beneficial because it allows:

- repeat exposure to stressful or traumatic memories, allowing the child to gain distance from them
- creation of a narrative around the stressful event
- labeling of emotions
- self-affirmation and meaning-making related to the negative event[24]

The self-affirmation component is the reason expressive writing is included as a practice that promotes esteem and confidence. Basically, the process provides an opportunity for students to find value in the self in the face of adversity.

If students are too young or for other reasons incapable of expressive writing, the same effect can be demonstrated in drawings or other creative projects. For example, if a child draws a picture of his family, it could open opportunities for that child to discuss his or her reality with the teacher or classmates. The teacher may ask, "Who is this? Why is he frowning?" for example. In 2005, Harvard University psychiatrist Robert Coles, author of *Their Eyes Meeting the World: The Drawings and Paintings of Children,* told me in an interview that children often tell adults what they think the adult wants to hear or they have difficulty articulating complex or emotional situations. To extract a more honest answer, he gives the child a box of crayons and paper, and invites them to draw.[25] Upon completion, the child proudly explains the drawings in a manner that simplistically reveals truths. Coles then asks the child to draw his family. One child drew a brown rectangle around his brother. Coles asked the child why he drew a brown box around his brother. The child responded, "He is dead. That is his coffin." When I asked Coles about the expertise required to analyze children this way, he replied that it does not take a psychiatrist to do it. It is simply a method to help children truthfully explain abstract or complicated concepts in their language.[26] The teacher is never attempting to diagnose, but the student may be trying to communicate with the teacher in the only way he or she can. Paying attention to subtleties can be very supportive.

Teachers need to be aware that with this opportunity comes professional duty. When students have an outlet to communicate in an unrestricted format, teachers must accept the responsibility without judgment. While these assignments can improve the quality of the teacher's understanding of the student and could inform instruction, parent conferences, and social activity design, some information shared with the teacher could also lead to more drastic and immediate action, such as reporting details to the appropriate staff. Fear of this should never be a deterrent; teachers must understand their role and accept the child without hesitation. Nor should a teacher fish for information through open-ended assignments or conversations. Information shared could result in the inclusion of a counselor, psychologist, or even a social worker from Child Protective Services, but trauma-sensitive schools are not places where adults cast about for sources of trauma; instead, the school staff creates an environment so powerfully therapeutic it overcomes unseen or unknown problems. Those problems will emerge when children are given control and voice, so faculty should know that their guidance and assistance may bring about interventions. In those situations, students may feel that the teacher has broken a confidence, but that is a reason trust is so important to establish early in the relationship.

Listen to students. In many classrooms, students (especially those who are deprived of attention elsewhere) compete for the ears of the teachers. They may strive to get the attention of the teacher so fervently that when they get it, they forget what they had to say. At other times it might be revealed that the student simply wanted acknowledgment. This can be frustrating for the teacher, which is why the opportunities for regular and interactive self-expression are important in the trauma-informed classroom. Teachers are also the facilitators, accustomed to being the senders of important information, not the receivers of information that may not seem significant. Listening then, is a filtering process, a skill that requires the teacher to determine the significance, urgency, and meaning of a comment.

The trauma-informed classroom needs a teacher who is a good listener, capable of minimizing distractions such as convoluted phrasing, pacing, bias, and focus to comprehend what the student is attempting to say. A student may reach out at the most inconvenient time and struggle to find the words to articulate what he or she wants to share. An unresponsive reaction or a failure to comprehend the significance of the student's underlying message could cause the student to feel rejected. While traumatized students often cocoon themselves from harmful adults in their lives, they will attempt to communicate with an adult they trust. Established lines of communication and opportunities to hear the students on a regular basis is important and will eliminate missed opportunities. In *Stand Up, Speak Out: The Practice and Ethics of Public Speaking*, the fourth chapter is dedicated to the art of listening, and even though the book is about public speaking, it has a solid message for teachers. Basically, educators should think of listening as a planned process, one that has stages. In the first stage, the teacher establishes an opportunity in which to provide the child or children his or her undivided attention. The teacher needs to signal—by squaring the shoulders to the student, for instance, or removing obstacles between the student and teacher (such as a desk or lamp), and making eye contact—that they can be approached. Occasional facial expressions such as empathetic smiling or nodding demonstrate that the student is being understood, not judged.

In the second stage, the teacher suspends judgment and focuses on what is actually being said and what it means. Children have trouble explaining emotions and may allow them to interfere with what they say. Repeating or rephrasing what is being said can confirm the meaning. Again, teachers should refrain from judgment. Do not interrupt or inject comments that could influence the student to redirect or change the message until the student is finished.

In the third stage, the teacher evaluates the message based on the evidence of what was expressed. It is a good idea to summarize what the student reported in concrete, objective terms that are untangled from the emotions and opinions in the message. For example, if the student says, "She is mean to me because she doesn't like me. That is why she trips me on the bus and calls me names." The teacher summarizes by saying, "She trips you on the bus and calls you names; is that correct?" And the teacher adds, "You feel that she does these things because she does not like you, correct?" The teacher has stated the student's facts and acknowledged the opinion derived from those facts without stating it as agreement.

In the fourth and final stage, the teacher responds to the student. What precisely this mean can vary depending on the reason the student wanted to be heard. The teacher should understand that the student may not want advice or an intervention; it could be that the student only wants to be heard. After listening, the teacher is more likely to respond appropriately than if he or she rushed to judgement.[27]

Listening is important on all levels identified in Maslow's hierarchy of needs, but it is categorized as an esteem builder because that is perhaps where the skill can be most effective. Yes, it is important to belonging, but belongingness can be achieved without the student seeking to express himself or herself to receive feedback, support, or an intervention. The fact that the child is communicating with the adult demonstrates that his or her basic needs (physiological, safety) have been met and that he feels enough trust (belonging, love) to confide to some degree in the teacher. That is an act of reaching out, and an unintentional rejection of that act is reasonably expected to hinder the child's development of self-esteem. It should also be noted that there is no confidentiality between a teacher and student when that student divulges information that requires the teacher file a report. Consider Maslow's pyramid: Safety is a basic need. Any child who reports that he or she is being deprived of these needs in any way requires the teacher to take some form of action.

9

Rethinking Assessment

We know what we are
But know not what we may be
—*Hamlet*, 4.4.48–49

Perhaps it is necessary to remind the reader of something briefly introduced in Part I. After a detailed discussion of the deficiency needs, the foundation of Maslow's hierarchy, it is concluded that the final stage, self-esteem, must be met before the student can maximize success in the area of cognition, something specifically identified as the first component of the self-actualization level. Cognition is the foundation of the growth needs (cognition, aesthetics, and transcendence). Originally, Maslow's pyramid had only self-actualization above esteem, but the need to break the former term down into these component parts (cognition, aesthetics, self-actualization, and transcendence) has since been a clarifying practice. Specifically, these parts provide clarity into what self-actualization looks like in the performance of the learner, perhaps for the sake of analysis and measurement. Since then, there have been other slight modifications, but the basic concept has remained unchallenged for decades.

To simplify this fundamental concept, teachers must not only help students meet the deficiency needs (physiological, safety, love and belonging, and esteem), but they must help preserve them because they are constantly under attack in many cases. If a process common to the development of a growth need damages a deficiency need, that practice needs to be re-examined. It is much like pruning a branch off a tree while sitting on the small of the limb. Most assessment in school is related to cognitive development, the most basic growth need. A 2002 study at the University of Michigan found that 80 percent of students surveyed based their self-worth on academic performance.[1] Note the power of assessment here on the deficiency needs and consider how assessment has evolved in education. For four of every five students, self-worth is determined not by relationships or religion or wealth but by the manner in which the school assesses cognitive development. Undoubtedly, children with fragmented and broken deficiency needs score lower on assessments, as previously demonstrated, so the practice of assessment not only measures one form of student growth, but it actually damages the deficiency needs that are required to maximize that student's growth. It is a critically important side effect that ultimately eliminates students from academia because it pounds them into submission by repeatedly reaffirming the sense of inadequacy that the assessment helped create. This is yet another damaging cycle no longer questioned because educators operate under the assumption that it is necessary and beneficial. In other studies using the self-esteem index (SEI), "self-esteem scores were the only factor significantly correlated with earned grades."[2] In other words, when children are graded, the grades determine their self-images. For students who enter the assessment arena disadvantaged by poverty, ACE issues, or any other element that creates an uneven playing field, they are forced to participate in a process that contributes to their struggles. The current process seems to celebrate the winners while the victims are reduced to insignificance.

Assessment refers to judging a student's rate of academic achievement by analyzing the available evidence. The teacher's role is to create the environment to reach learning objectives and to fairly evaluate the student's (and his or her own) success rate. It is based on the concept that all students are treated fairly and have an equal opportunity to succeed. However, there are many teaching strategies and routines that are designed to expand the student development in areas that are important but difficult to assess fairly. Ironically, these kinds of activities build the skills that are most closely related to the child's ability to develop self-actualization. Competencies and dispositions that are associated with social-emotional and desired professional skills development, traits most associated with successful adults, are often neither graded nor easily assessed. Since students and parents are conditioned to find worth in test scores and academic averages, these non-assessed activities are de-emphasized in the school and not prioritized by students or educators. The national obsession for ranking, labeling, competing, and filtering is part of schooling, and the need to make data-informed decisions to improve efficacy is palpable. Words like *achievement* and *growth* are inferentially related to academic or scholastic ability. How much learning is demonstrated through the teacher's (or state's) assessment? What is the degree of the child's cognitive skill? Functions that measure cognitive development are easily measured and they are important. They are how the teacher provides feedback or communicates progress to parents, and often they determine which programs or colleges will accept students. There are some who say success in life is attributed to grades because students who make better grades tend to earn more money. But there is an argument that lower grades damage self-esteem more than positive scores predict success. In other words, the teacher's instructional strategies and selected measures of success are not measuring skills one needs to succeed but are actually filtering students with different learning styles or fragile self-esteem levels. So if 80 percent of students determine self-worth by their grades, teachers need to understand just how delicate this process is and how to overcome assessment that undermines the over-all purpose of education.

To summarize, the most negative aspects of education are tied to the assessment process. It divides and humiliates on the one hand, promotes and endorses on the other, creating bias despite its intent. It determines what is important and what is not even though it measures only what is eas-ily measurable. There is a difference between an advocate and a judge, and in the attempt to assume a delicate balance between these two roles, edu-cators have repeatedly demonstrated that they are incapable. It should be noted that this is another example of a bad idea that is repeatedly practiced and accepted because it is no longer questioned. To consider the prospect of another form of feedback and progress monitoring is blasphemous to some. Remember, the people who were affirmed and promoted by the sys-tem, their self-esteem fostered by good grades and positive reinforcements, will struggle to see the ugly underbelly of assessment. They will assume that they worked harder and earned it, and in many cases that is true. If effort is being rewarded with positive accolades, then assessment feedback becomes motivation. However, if the a student deprioritizes school in response to red ink and other symbols of failure, then grades are not measuring any-thing more than the student's level of humiliation. Assessment is measure-ment that is used for much more than providing constructive feedback, and that is how it becomes a threat to children. To children of adversity, assess-ment has been weaponized in that it is a threat to expose their vulnerabili-ties. Educators seem chained to this antiquated approach because it is now used to measure teachers, principals, school districts, and state education programs. Pressure from the top trickles down and lands on the shoulders of children. To avoid being labeled because of underperforming students, teachers in assessed content areas become more focused on high test scores than whole-child development because the scores, more than the testimo-nials of the children, will be discussed during their summative evaluations. This is not to suggest that data collected via assessment is a waste of time, but it is time to encourage a wiser approach to child development, one that satisfies the deficiency needs and does not unintentionally weaponize assessment as a form of categorization and accountability.

Self-actualization is not an unrealistic goal. Basically, it occurs when a person becomes that which he or she is capable of becoming. The self, then, represents a holistic developmental process, not merely a cognitive developmental process. Cognition is the most fundamental of the growth needs, which suggests it is needed to fully understand the beauty and value of life (aesthetic development) and the full potential of the self (self-actualization). One might assume that a lengthy, structured educational process throughout the child's formative years would assure that most if not all students reach their full potential. According to Cynthia Vinney, in her article explaining the concept of self-actualization, "Maslow believed that, because of the difficulty of fulfilling the four lower needs (deficiency needs), very few people would successfully become self-actualized, or would only do so in a limited capacity."[3] In 1970, Maslow estimated that the percentage of people becoming self-actualizers is around 2 percent.[4] While assessment practices are not entirely to blame for such a low percentage, they are a part of the problem. It is an indictment of the educational system, which has been mired in mediocrity or worse for decades, its stewards never seeming to realize the importance of Maslow's message. After considering all of the adult influences on a child that inhibit the development of essential needs, from ACEs to corporal punishment to bullying to social injustices and inequities associated with race, gender, and level of poverty, it is difficult to see how a low grade has any productive purpose.

Since stakeholders value what is tested and graded over other important forms of development that are difficult or impossible to accurately measure, flawed or limited instructional delivery and one-dimensional testing practices unfairly label children and condemn them for a perceived weakness that is based on what adults can see. And since it has already been mentioned that greater than half of the public school students in the United States live in poverty, there is evidence to suggest that their most essential deficiency needs are not being met. Some needs, like belonging and self-esteem, are not mandated to be developed by any agency in the child's life. Assessment forces high-pressured cognitive drill-and-practice, culminating in high-stakes testing. When student success affects teachers' careers, the pressure placed on children is unbearable to many of them, especially when they are labeled with a number that reaffirms their biggest fears and demolishes both their sense of belonging and their self-esteem. Many never reach the stage where self-esteem can be established because those who are legally or morally obligated to care for them are ill-equipped to help children reach that stage. Children are demoted or drop out, and teachers and principals are fired, moved, or forced into early retirements. If only Billy and Sue had filled in bubble C instead of D! Perhaps the school should relinquish the power to judge and focus on things too complex to measure.

The school is a last chance for many children to develop skills to repair their lives, so perhaps educators should become more responsible when assessing student growth by understanding the impact that process has on children. Perhaps we should build the very things negative feedback destroys by assessing children using multiple methods and allowing for a student's strengths in areas we do not test to be acknowledged if not celebrated.

To many teachers, grading is a perfunctory task or a necessary evil. Many spend more time developing lesson plans than designing assessment instruments. The child is subject to surprise pop quizzes, tests designed by textbook publishers, or essays with non-existent or poorly designed rubrics. They are voiceless victims of a hectic, assembly-line approach to education that was originally meant to prepare workers for mass production during the Industrial Revolution. Teachers face overcrowded classrooms and the unrealistic expectation of developing meaningful lessons and assessments. Needs have changed, but this basic design remains intact. Parents are usually uninformed or confused outsiders, often frustrated and frantic during the early years and becoming more distant and indifferent as the child ages. They accept the institutional labels that stymie their children. Not knowing what to do, many parents resort to shaming and either threats or acts of violence. In some cases, grades are the only indicator of their child's progress. When grades not only attack the child's sense of self-worth but lead to their being attacked by frustrated parents, there is something tragically wrong with the process. In a March 28, 2019, article in the *New York Times*, it was reported that incidents of child abuse increase by nearly 400 percent when report cards go out on Fridays.[5] Children who face unfavorable odds in school because of variables in their lives beyond their control are being negatively judged, and sometimes beaten, by the adults in their spheres of support. That is not what assessment was designed to accomplish.

The inescapable conclusion is that the way schools assess child development is flawed. Millions are spent on testing and evaluation; schools and school systems are condemned; and, most important, the assessment contributes to the low self-esteem and future struggles of children. And although there are other, perhaps more significant skills than those repeatedly measured, students are not given credit for development in those areas. Much emphasis is placed on improving cognition when unassessed deficiencies are the main reason children succeed or struggle with academics. Students also learn to value what is graded and dismiss or trivialize things that are not. It is this writer's opinion, based on observation and experience, that self-esteem is the most difficult of Maslow's levels to develop, and a very large reason is assessment and the role of the teacher.

Teachers are given a lot of autonomy and power over students in the area of grading. They back their decisions with numbers, stories, and historical data that often assure that all blame falls on the student. But they should not detach themselves from the responsibility surrounding a student's progress. They do not have adequate time to consider all variables in planning; they do not always consider how their differentiation (the modifications a teacher makes in trying to reach students of all learning styles) or lack of it impacts each child. The assembly line is moving and it is crowded. They collect performance and cognitive data, convert it to a number, transfer that number to a letter and brand the students accordingly as the latter drop off that grading period's conveyor belt. It is a necessary evil for the teacher to transition from supporting mentor to an evaluator and judge, one that is not lost on students. What are the odds that any evaluation accurately depicts the degree to which important cognitive development occurred? Do most teachers understand the full spectrum of the responsibility and practice holistic child development with expertise and precision? How many teachers strategically developed lessons that helped meet deficiency needs required for cognition? This is why trauma-informed teaching and social-emotional learning are so desperately needed.

Four out of five students surveyed based their self-worth on academic performance; we owe it to them to get it right. Assessment should not be a destructive process, even when the performance is below the norm-referenced standards we tend to use, as if norms are fair to all students. So what can be done? There are literally hundreds of assessment practices that might be considered alternatives to the one-size-fits-all approach, and it is important to provide educators with information about these alternatives so that, like a doctor, they can diagnose what ails students and provide the appropriate remedies. In terms of assessment, remember that students have been conditioned to value only what is graded. Teachers cannot possibly grade every assignment and activity in a six-hour day, but the students need to be kept on task and engaged. How many teachers have responded to a raised hand to hear the question, "Is this for a grade?" That can easily be translated as follows: "If this is not for a grade, I am not going to put much effort into it" or "If this is not for a grade, it is not important." Remember, four out of every five students have their sense of self-worth riding on the grade they get from the class.

It is not realistic to think that we cannot dramatically change the current system. But more attention and focus can be dedicated to differentiated instruction—that is, instruction tailored to the needs of the student—and feedback. We live in a competitive society that is influenced by processes of elimination and entitlement. (Consider this country's class structure, with its shrinking middle class and burgeoning wealth disparities.) So instead of laboring to budge the antiquated, biased, and unjust systems of assessment, perhaps the most practical and realistic approach is to understand the variables and make decisions that serve the best interest of the student within the current system. If a student's self-value is based on grades, then educators must spend a lot more time considering alternative forms of instructional design and assessment practices.

Nothing drains a student's hope and desire more than a failing mark. Failure is a huge part of the learning process in life, but in school, it can be something that causes shame, guilt, or embarrassment if not embraced as a necessary part of the process. It is often final, and often void of input from the student. Why is failure a negative in school? Students are learning and should be afforded the opportunity to fail. Error is a symptom of risk-taking that often coincides with higher-order functioning. The assembly line may get a little crooked, but the paths of students will straighten out if originality and academic courage are celebrated and not punished. Provide opportunities to revise; if a student wants an "A," give them opportunities to try and try again until they earn the grade they seek. Coach children from failure to success, letting the grade signify accomplishment, not inadequacy. It should suggest that students refuse to quit and are willing to work to convert weakness into strength. Why do we deny so many children that opportunity? Self-esteem becomes confidence, and confidence is, in part, an unwillingness to fear failure and the resilience to rebound from it. In addition, the teacher is given a chance to modify his or her instruction so that he or she does not fail to teach effectively. That grit is what will determine success in life, not some one-dimensional label based on a poorly designed and inadequately assessed cognitive task.

Perhaps the most significant point made in this book is that we need to develop an awareness of the world in which children live beyond school and, more importantly, a strategy to help them overcome the ill effects of that world. Educators often embrace inspirational sayings such as "no child left behind," "raising the bar," and "all children can learn." Yet they create uniform standards of assessment that are based on the assembly line mentality, based on an assumption that all have equal footing. In actuality, assessment is how we determine which children are left behind, how many fall under the bar, and which form of learning is most important. What do those things actually mean?

Yes, all children can learn. That is not a radical concept. Even dogs and cats learn when their deficiency needs are met. Why do we measure learning one way and fail to take into account the critical importance of the non-academic factors that determine success? Maslow opines that the reason so many individuals never become self-actualizers is that schools focus on measurable growth needs, and of those, cognitive development is the easiest to measure. Yet one of the most important applications of social-emotional learning is fair, diverse, and interactive assessment practices. While to do these practices just might well require book-length discussion , the basic concepts will be introduced in this chapter. It should be noted that there are no easy processes for educators, so any similarities to such a recommendation should come with the caveat that individualized applications and modifications are almost always necessary. Textbook-supplied tests that are aligned with worksheets are convenient for the overloaded, overworked teacher but are not always great for the student.

There are some basic questions all teachers and school leaders should be able to quickly answer: What is the purpose of assessment? Why do we give a child a letter or number? Is assessment motivating, informative, or productive for the stakeholders? Does the number or letter a test or teacher might assign a child reflect whole-child development or academic achievement in one basic area of learning? What important components of child development are not measured or graded by schools? Assessment can be fixed if we change our perspectives about it and broaden its purpose. Are we truly assessing learning when most cannot recall content tested two weeks prior? Do educators really understand what learning is and how it is related to whole-child development? And then there is the most important question: How does assessment adversely impact students, especially those who are disadvantaged and traumatized by things beyond their control that are not factored into the equation?

Assessment is the best place to begin when designing a unit of instruction. It requires the teacher to design measures that will evaluate the degree to which outcomes will be mastered. It stands to reason that the teacher would then need to understand which objectives are important to the curriculum. They also need to understand the other standards that are essential to social-emotional learning competencies and those related to 21st-century skills because these pedagogical approaches give learning personal meaning and relevance. The teacher generally selects items that reflect the manner in which students learn (using that word loosely here) the content and can demonstrate some degree of cognitive ability related to it. Aesthetic development, social-emotional skill development, or implementation of experiential or professional competencies (21st-century skills, for example) are difficult to measure effectively or directly. They are therefore deemed unimportant by the student and teacher, who undervalue the non-academic growth that may have been instrumental to lesson designs aligned with the written and tested curricula. This non-academic growth, after all, is not part of the summative evaluation of acquired content. Considering this, educators should be using content to develop perspectives that contribute to whole-child development, and cognitive development is only part (albeit a fundamental part) of that process. Even if cognition reigns supreme over other forms of development, these "secondary" forms enhance and improve cognition.

In sports, athletes are often evaluated by scoreboards, but the greatest athletes understand how things such as weight training and cardiovascular exercises contribute to favorable scores. They learn to recognize conditions and calculate the opponent's probable course of action, split-second thinking made possible by preparation, cognition, and intuition. Those that do not build these skills do not become great athletes. In education, on the other hand, narrow-minded political leaders increase spending on assessment and decrease spending on the arts, or aesthetic development, failing to see how they indirectly contribute to positive test scores. Many educators teach only what is tested, failing to support learning beyond skills obviously linked to increase testing efficiency. In many schools, teachers who do not teach in tested areas are made to feel like non-essential personnel when they actually should play a very critical role. It seems that it is not the quality of instruction that is important but the appearance of quality. If we test English or language arts, biology, and algebra, those teachers and courses become the most important to all stakeholders while others are devalued. It is something we accept without considering the repercussions. How can we have standardized testing in three or four academic subjects and value the others equally? A better question: How can we develop an assessment program that informs growth in all areas of child development?

SEL Assessment

By understanding all of the unintended stigma associated with assessment and how it can be counterproductive if done incorrectly (which is often the case), the teacher should strive to make sure that evaluation is differentiated and covers all formidable areas of whole child development, some of which are not easily measurable using conventional methods. Social-emotional learning includes processes through which teachers, parents, counselors, psychologists, and administrators can monitor SEL development in students. The ability to recognize and communicate feelings, character development, coping, and cooperative decision-making processes are noted throughout a grading period, as are the student's demonstrated inabilities in those areas. Interestingly, the teacher is not the only member of the staff with the ability to record this information, which might be entered into software programs or databases; parents, for example, can team with teachers and counselors to evaluate the development of the child in various settings from various perspectives. Not only does this empower the parent and provide that parent support, it creates a blueprint for success that all parties can conceptualize. Social-emotional learning assessments should accompany report cards or be tools used to frame parent conferences, giving students and parents a fuller range of developments that improve academic performance. This widening of the assessment scope provides feedback in the areas of student performance that build resilience, develop social skills, and improve academics. Since the students will become more cognizant of the monitored behaviors, they will value the practice because, for the first time, it is "graded." This mode of assessment not only improves behavior, academics, self-esteem, and social development but can be a critical resource for professionals and adults who serve students beyond the classroom walls. Parents, for instance, may wish to meet with day care workers, mental health professionals, coaches, and others so that they better understand the dispositions and emotional intelligence of their child. Since this process is designed for schools without rivers of gold flowing into the budget, the author has designed a companion text for ancillaries, including SEL assessments developmentally appropriate for every grade level, that can be entered into most school databases. In addition, it links nicely to the multi-tiered systems of support (MTSS), providing data that measure competencies and skills congruent with each level. It is recommended that these SEL assessments be sent home with report cards so that students and parents see the relationship between the two and begin to value social-emotional development.

Since assessment websites and software are expensive, this book is dedicated to a practical, frugal approach to SEL assessment, one that involves a process that follows the child from kindergarten through high school, with strands featuring items that increase in complexity within the context of a particular CASEL core-competency element as the child matures. Specifically, each item number from each of the 12 surveys is linked to the same SEL competency elements, demonstrating longitudinal growth patterns in each skill area over a 13-year period. Each semester or grading period, for example, all students are evaluated by informed stakeholders, and the system identifies competency strengths and weaknesses not only for each child but for each grade level, school, and district. This aids in the planning process, helping direct teachers and instructional coaches to create curriculum lesson plans that feature activities to strengthen certain skills. For example, item number three on the kindergarten survey is aligned with three descriptors from the first CASEL core competency, self-awareness: (1) identification of emotions; (2) accurate self-perception, and (3) self-confidence. When the student reaches high school, item number three will measure the same skills, prompted by descriptors that have gradually increased in complexity from year to year. A sample of this instrument is pictured in figure 3.

GOAL 1—*Focus on Self-Awareness, Self-Control, and Self-Improvement* THE STUDENT DEMONSTRATES THE ABILITY TO:	*Strongly disagree*	*Disagree*	*Agree*	*Strongly agree*
1. Understand emotions and how they are effectively managed by successful people.				
2. Express hurt without withdrawal, blame, or aggression.				
3. Develop an understanding of the sources of trauma and the long-term effects of trauma.				
4. Practice multiple mental and physical strategies to reduce stress levels.				
5. Identify personal skills related to a career and develop a plan to acquire required certifications.				
6. Identify things about himself/herself that are traits necessary for success.				
7. Select healthy defense mechanisms to protect self-esteem in school and the workforce.				
8. Identify personal competencies still needed to be developed in order to be successful post-graduation.				
9. Reflect on the student's past personal and academic goals and identify learning about the self.				
10. Practice decision-making based on what is right rather than traditional images of success.				
11. Practice emotional self-efficacy by regulating emotional states and eliciting emotional reactions.				

GOAL 2—*Develop Skills to Build Productive Relationships.* THE STUDENT DEMONSTRATES THE ABILITY TO:	*Strongly disagree*	*Disagree*	*Agree*	*Strongly agree*
12. Work well with those who may have different values and beliefs.				
13. Reflect to understand how student collaboratively has helped another overcome the ill-effects of trauma.				
14. Define relationships in the family, school, and community that support personal and career goals.				
15. Evaluate controversial ideas on their merit instead of the individual sharing them.				
16. Explain how the student has grown by developing relationships with members of other cultures.				
17. Evaluate how well one supports the leadership of others and supports those who follow his/her lead.				
18. Identify specific examples in which the student has empathized with others				
19. Evaluate how the majority treats groups in ways that create the appearance of social injustice.				

Opposite and above: **Figure 3. Sample SEL Assessment Instrument**

The MTSS is a framework or school-wide system of behavioral support associated with the response to intervention (RTI) model. It supports the academic and social-emotional curricula, strategically providing immediate, prescriptive interventions that can be intensified as needed. The success of the MTSS model depends on the extent to and diligence with which it is implemented. Kansas has implemented MTSS into all content areas, behavior assessments, and social-emotional learning processes. More than 500 Kansas schools were surveyed about MTSS, and the results are very positive:

- decreasing discipline referrals (77 percent of respondents)
- decreasing special education referrals (63 percent of respondents)
- increasing student proficiency (70 percent of respondents)[6]

Students are assessed on three levels as opposed to one as in the past, and parents, teachers, administrators, psychologists, and counselors have input and voice in the ongoing evaluation of the whole child.

10

Social-Emotional Learning Competencies and Teaching Strategies

Our doubts are traitors
And makes us lose the good we oft might win
By fearing to attempt
—*Measure for Measure*, 1.4.85–87

After a student's basic (physiological, safety) needs are met, the child must develop psychological or emotional needs (belonging, love, self-esteem) in their path toward self-actualization, based on Maslow's hierarchy of needs. Historically, schools have done very little to develop the psychological or emotional needs, probably because they are difficult to assess and educational leaders may not have been convinced that there is a direct correlation between the psychological and the cognitive needs most frequently attributed to intelligence and learning. That leaves many of the toxins of the home and neighborhood in place, creating a resistant undercurrent that pulls children against the momentum of quality academic instruction. The emphasis on social and emotional development has intensified as educators realize that school classrooms and cultures can become microcosms of the world, in which students will need not only intelligence but certain skills, behaviors, and dispositions necessary to reach their full potential. The Collaborative for Academic, Social, and Emotional Learning (CASEL) core SEL competencies have become the gold standard for evidence-based strategies for Pre-Kindergarten–12th grade curricula in the United States. This core of five competencies can be taught in multiple formats and settings, and the implementation of deliberate, escalating strategies has improved behavior, academic achievement, and attendance while diminishing the impact of traumas incurred beyond the walls of the school.

These competencies serve at the center of professional strategies found in lesson planning, assessment, communications, parental involvement, systems of support, and school culture, to name a few. The importance of these SEL competencies cannot be easily exaggerated, and the degree to which an infusion of these skills benefits the students in any classroom or school depends on the degree to which the educators provide social-emotional development for students.

The CASEL Core SEL Competencies

- **Self-awareness.** The ability to recognize and communicate an awareness of one's feelings, interests, and strengths. Self-efficacy and self-confidence, among other skills, are developed in this competency.
- **Self-management.** The self-management skills are critically important for students with ACEs or other forms of trauma. Regulation of emotions, poise and composure in stressful situations, and organizational skills are important in that they help the brain relax so that it can function at maximum capacity. These skills are directly related to academic performance, but they serve a broader purpose.
- **Social awareness.** True intelligence is not what you know; it is how effectively you go about knowing. Problems have many perspectives, and the smart person is one who can open-mindedly examine many points of view before arriving at the best or most appropriate solution. He or she develops opinions based on facts, not other opinions. To see a situation from another's perspective empowers any person with the ability to make friends, understand situations more clearly, and empathize.
- **Relationship management.** No man is an island, and the strength one garners through others is important. Teamwork, relationships, and participating in society are skills we all need, but these are vital for traumatized students. Through an ability to recognize strengths in others and a process of inclusive cooperation, the student supports something of which he or she is a part. Knowing when to trust, when to avoid conflict, and when to seek guidance are important components that help meet the deficiency needs of belongingness and love.
- **Responsible decision-making.** This competency includes students' capacity to make practical, ethical decisions in social or professional situations. Self-esteem development (Maslow's fourth level and the top deficiency need) is evident in this competency.[1]

Social Emotional Teaching Best Practices

Part I of this book focuses on trauma, its prevalence, the reasons it is so readily accepted in the United States, and how it adversely impacts child development. Too often in education reform efforts, we empower teachers with the flavor-of-the-month cure-all without taking the time to fully explain the reasons the effort should work. It is assumed that the theoretical rationale and the research behind the reform effort, the processes designed by scholars and politicians who may only infrequently visit classrooms, are understood. All the teacher needs to do is follow the directions and the results will look like the photo on the box. The *why* is minimally addressed, often without an emotional appeal or logical plea. That is why most such interventions fail so quickly. Teachers need to know why they are being asked to change, and to believe it will work; if they see no reason for it or fail to generate immediate results, they will not adopt the changes for the long term. Change, after all, is based on emotion, not logic, data, or mandate. They need ways to be more effective and efficient without being given more to do. Frankly, giving subordinates more work to do to facilitate growth is lazy leadership and it is not sustainable. The art of any new and improved product is to make things easier, faster, and more productive. Use positive energies to replace negative energies. Too often, the most critical attitudes, those of the teachers on the front lines, are casually glossed over. Compliance is assumed within the framework of mandates and directives, but cultures are not forged that way.

Teachers are also the products of the blindness that was detailed in Part I. They were raised in the same churches, governed by the same laws, and exposed to the same family traditions as those who make school policy. They grew up in similar communities and shared similar values. Educators are products of the system they now must question, which requires strong, objective introspection that could run counter to lifelong beliefs. Most teachers are successful people who may not understand what it is to fail and lose hope; they are unlikely to have ever been a casualty of the system. They are college graduates, many with advanced degrees. They are the survivors, the beneficiaries of the system that allowed them to rise above their childhood classmates, the faces and names of whom many probably struggle to remember. Perhaps people who never played the game are unqualified to advocate for the losers; perhaps the winners of the game are unqualified, too. The purpose of Part I of this book is to show all stakeholders that there is a fog covering the American culture that has normalized the unintentional (and intentional) abuses of its youth to such a degree that most children are physically traumatized in practices that our churches endorse, our laws allow, and our culture embraces. To advocate for those who have lost or are losing in the current system, we must hear from those who know the loser's pain in some form. Part I provides the wakeup call that we all need to understand the severity of the problem and sense the urgency that should motivate any educator to develop a new approach to the profession. It explains the plight of the voiceless and provides the *why* that must be fully understood by the heroes on the front lines—the teachers, administrators, counselors, and so many others affiliated with the school culture.

Trauma-informed teaching is about having empathy for the children teachers serve, a complete understanding of that which was previously assumed or deemed irrelevant. It is about an awareness of the threats to the child that radiate from unsuspecting places, about knowing the child's environment and understanding how to help that child navigate through it. It is empowerment and the advocacy that only educators can provide. Social-emotional learning, on the other hand, is the strategy trauma-informed teachers use to help students overcome that trauma. It is an understanding of the process, its outcomes, and methods to build the child from the inside out. It is an awareness of the things unseen that thwart intentions and how to overcome them. Teachers know how to provide a therapeutically beneficial environment for all children. They heal with one hand and build new support systems and levels of acceptance and confidence with the other. It will be ingrained into the fibers of everything the teacher does because, eventually, that teacher will see the connections; he or she will come to realize how the contribution to the overall school culture is critically important to the team and the students. No longer should a child's social and emotional development be left to fate. Critically important things like belongingness and self-esteem should be built deliberately, not left to the chance that a child will randomly be assigned to a teacher with healthy dispositions. Luck should not be what saves children from the destructive traumas that society so willingly accepts as normal. The social, emotional, and psychological development of the whole child is as simple as understanding Abraham Maslow's hierarchy of needs. Motivation to act begins with understanding the severity of the problem and how to make a difference.

For teaching the whole child, CASEL identifies instructional practices that support social and emotional learning in three teacher evaluation frameworks. In developing this model, they extensively reviewed literature that "focused on the relationship between specific instructional practices, positive learning environments, and student social-emotional competencies."[2] This process was filtered through established findings presented in the CASEL 2013 guide on research-based social-emotional programs. These instructional competencies are:

- **Student-centered discipline.** Teachers need to develop strategies used to manage behavior in the classroom. It should be noted that discipline here does not refer to punitive action; it refers to the developing self-discipline students need to function in the classroom environment. There will be more on this approach on a school-wide model, one that should inspire the trauma-informed teacher.
- **Teacher language.** Teachers must use a method of communicating with students that encourages, reinforces, and motivates. A calm, positive tone that is paired with eye contact and a smile is the recommended method.
- **Responsibility and choice.** This refers to the teacher's ability to give students options relating to classroom operations and learning opportunities, at least to some degree. The idea is to create more of a democracy than an autocracy, in other words. From the teacher's perspective, this may initially seem like a structure-versus-choices dilemma, but it is not. Think of it like a grocery store. There are many choices on each aisle, but the items on the shelves are strategically placed.
- **Warmth and support.** This refers to support each student receives from peers and teachers. The desired climate is one in which students take responsibility for the holistic development of themselves as well as their peers. When students reach out to one another empathetically and supportively in a collaborative effort, they prosper in all aspects of their own development. These environments are part of what is often called responsive classrooms or learning communities. To gauge the degree to which a responsive classroom has been achieved, the teacher needs to watch students interact when they do not realize they are being watched. It is the best indicator of a learned behavior.
- **Cooperative learning.** Cooperative learning can be very effective, but it is one of the most underdeveloped strategies commonly employed. To achieve maximal results, there needs to be a specific academic task that requires a group effort to achieve a collective objective. This is not mere group work; it is a carefully designed, multi-student approach that includes an awareness of developmental social and interactive skills.
- **Classroom discussions.** The classroom discussion is an extremely valuable tool for teachers because it extends concepts, fuses ideas, and enhances understanding by allowing for informed opinions and emotions to be shared. When everyone is engaged, the classroom discussion can be a building process in which students

layer ideas that intensify understanding and the teacher merely facilitates, guiding the group toward a more rigorously considered conclusion.

- **Self-reflection and self-assessment.** Once the teacher and students have developed clearly stated, attainable short and long term goals, it is important that they engage in routine reflection. The writing activities detailed earlier are ideal for this, as are conferences and group discussions. Self-assessment is a valuable tool that creates ownership and accountability for performance-based projects. In a trusting environment where error and failure are acceptable, formative processes, this practice can reinforce positive pathways and eliminate recurring mistakes.

- **Balanced instruction.** This is akin to differentiated instruction, but the term *balanced* suggests that there is measurement between active and direct instruction. The balance lies in the teacher's discretion to use strategies that are directly applicable to the individual and then the opportunity to actively apply learning in various situations. The idea is to use a more direct form of instruction to introduce content or skills before asking students to engage in activities that apply knowledge in a way that personalizes the learning and requires a higher-level of functioning. The premise, however, is not to balance these forms of instruction on a 50-50 scale; it is to understand the importance of each. Ideally, the direct instruction should be minimal but thorough and complete before starting the active instruction.

- **Academic press.** Basically, academic press refers to rigor. The teacher should expect the students who are benefiting from the holistic developmental model established in the CASEL standards to achieve at a maximal rate, but a strict or lackadaisical approach could undermine the effect. Teachers are encouraged to familiarize themselves with Lev Vygotsky's concept of a zone of proximal development, where complexity increases toward unit objectives on an appropriate slope. Rigor is the process of increasing the level of complexity without increasing the level of difficulty. To do this, one understands that adding too much complexity too quickly creates stress and anxiety, and the impact of stress and anxiety on cognition is not productive. The refusal to add complexity, on the other hand, increases the level of apathy or boredom and hinders motivation and growth.

- **Competence building.** Part II of this text has been an exhaustive explanation of how to build social-emotional competencies in students to help them become successful, productive students and, eventually, adults. Strategies have been aligned with Maslow's deficiency needs so that the teacher understands how social-emotional learning fills voids and meets needs. The student needs to understand the self and how that self fits into the greater good.[3]

Remember Shakespeare's advice: "This above all: To thine own self be true." Teachers have the power to help students reach that pinnacle, regardless of how often these children have been bullied, beaten, or neglected. Reaching full potential will no longer be something that only 2 percent accomplish, as Maslow reported. Schools can do much better, and by weaving the SEL competencies into the fabric of planning, instruction, and assessment, they will.

11

Behavior Management

How poor are they that have not patience!
What wound did ever heal but by degrees?
—*Othello* 2.3.391–392

The recommended strategies for creating a positive learning environment in the classroom have been presented and detailed. To simplify the concept, it is essential to understand that the first and most important part of the process is trust. Teachers must demonstrate the capacity to trust students before expecting to be trusted. Broken promises, empty threats, or even inconsistent grading can impede the development of trust. On the other hand, being direct and honest, using rubrics and other measures to create consistency, fairness, social justice, and equity, to name a few, are ways a teacher earns the trust of the class. Once trust has been established, belongingness is the next key aspect of the positive learning environment. There are so many possibilities that could involve mutual respect, collaboration, cooperation, and communication within the walls of the classroom, and they all require that a child feel important. Feeling needed, in other words, is often the result of creating activities and roles in which all students can utilize personal strengths to contribute to a group or whole-class project. Finally, after belongingness and trust are in place, the positive learning environment features challenging, goal-driven expectations. A student who trusts the teacher and classmates and feels a strong sense of belonging will take the learning risks needed to reach goals and exceed expectations. These students find pride and fulfillment in pleasing the teacher and successfully executing their roles as members of a team.

Table 2 includes the three components of the positive learning environment (engagement, safety, and environment), along with the characteristics of each. Note how many of those characteristics are easily aligned with Maslow's deficiency needs, especially those from the social and emotional deficiency need category, strategies that foster belongingness, love, and self-esteem.

Table 2. Positive Learning Environments

Engagement	Safety	Environment
Positive student-teacher relationships	Effectively addressed discipline problems	Cohesive
Teacher academic and emotional support	Emotional and academic safety	Democratic
Peer academic and emotional support		Goal directive
Trust in teachers		Captivating
Personalized relationships		Relevant
Meaningful control		Challenging

Source: Yoder, N. (2014). *Teaching the Whole Child: Instructional Practices That Support Social and Emotional Learning in Three Teacher Evaluation Frameworks.* Washington, D.C.: American Institutes for Research Center on Great Teachers and Leaders, 2014.

While this process reduces or nearly eliminates the need for traditional forms of discipline in schools, since everyone in the building understands his or her importance to every child's development, it takes time and patience. Any effective behavior modification process that does not necessitate patience is probably not child-centered. Professionals realize that a large percentage of behavior issues are manifestations of some form of trauma, that the behavior is a reaction to a deeper issue. Trauma impedes cognitive processing because it triggers so many problems in the limbic system and the prefrontal cortex of the brain, as previously described in chapter 4. Teachers, therefore, must remember not to ask, "What is wrong with you?" and attempt to correct the undesirable behavior. "What can I do for you?" is the better question, one that almost guarantees that the teacher is interested in addressing the trauma, not the reaction to it. This approach may take a little longer than assigning punitive consequences like a basketball referee calling a foul, but it saves time by minimizing the likelihood for recurring disciplinary consequences. The teacher must calmly approach the matter from a new perspective, one that strategically avoids conflict by implementing a therapeutic strategy. This is not to say there are no consequences for undesired behavior—but that there is a different, more informed approach to them. The idea is to resolve and support the student's ability to cope and develop resiliency, not to punish or humiliate. Still, some will argue, "That is what is wrong with education today. Kids nowadays get away with murder. Back in my day..." Ignore them. Any endorsement of a process that has been so tragically disappointing for decades is not worth anyone's attention. When people start seeing positive results, they will develop an understanding that discipline is a process, not a consequence. In the classroom, positive interventions (including consequences) could mean several things, and are not limited to any one strategy. All teachers and administrators need to abandon the "us against them" mentality and listen (once again) to the wisdom of Shakespeare, who wrote, "There is nothing either good or bad, but thinking makes it so" (2.2.250–51). There are no bad children; there are those who react poorly to bad events in their lives.

For example, Billy is having a bad day. It does not matter why; he just is. Teachers rarely know why anyway. He bumps into Chucky, a child not having a bad day until he bumped into Billy. Billy pushes a bewildered Chucky, who pushes Billy back. Billy punches Chucky, who transitions from bewildered to angry rather quickly. He retaliates, and Billy retaliates against Chucky's retaliation. In education, the technical term for this is "a fight." Normally, the two students are sent to the office (separately, preferably) and both are suspended from school. It did not matter that Chucky was the unsuspecting victim who was attacked and went into defense mode and retaliated. According to the handbook, he acted aggressively by committing an act that was not considered self-defense. He could have walked away, but he did not. The consequences for not retaliating might have been worse than being suspended; he would have suffered socially and possibly would have been targeted by other bullies later. Technically, Chucky did not have much time to figure it out; he was reacting in the heat of the moment, a fact given no significance in the school system's code of conduct. That the situation was not monitored and that his anger was justified in that situation are also ignored. According to the simplistic one-size-fits-all policy, his choices were simple: fight back and be suspended or walk away and be mocked and perhaps bullied later. That is how Chucky's day goes south very quickly. He feels violated by the unjust rule in the handbook, approved by the board members that embrace law and order in schools.

Meanwhile, Billy, the aggressor, had never been in trouble before that day. Chucky had a few priors, but was working hard to change his ways. Billy is given three days of out-of-school suspension for a first offense, while Chucky gets six days because this was his third unrelated offense. Furthermore, parents are called, and both children are dragged to their parents' cars to be chauffeured home, where a possible beating awaits.

What exactly did each child just learn? How is the actual source of the inappropriate behavior addressed? Many teachers feel that a principal who does not send a child home for such an egregious violation of Section I, Article 4, subsection 3 of the conduct manual is only asking for more fighting later because students will think there are no consequences (the assumption here is that students fight if they think they can get away with it). While it is understood that the educator's first obligation is to safety (Maslow's second level), punishment has little to do with safety; prevention is about safety. This very common punitive strategy attacks the student's feelings of justice, hope, and self-worth. There is a point where the student hits rock bottom in these areas, and decides he will seek revenge for this social, anarchic injustice and take matters into his own hands. That could mean a rematch, it could mean worse. The actual problem (whatever trauma caused the aggression) goes unaddressed, only the reactions to it are acknowledged in a manner that socially and academically harms the student.

Now imagine that the teacher had greeted Billy at the door with a smile and nice comment. Billy grumbles and looks away. Immediately, she asks him to stand with her until the other classmates enter the room. She looks him in the eye and asks him if everything is going well. He does not respond, so she says, "Billy, we are starting class and I sense something is troubling you. I am going to call Mrs. Jones (the school counselor) to come talk to you." Trauma-informed teachers know how to spot problems before they become bigger problems. However, on this day, the teacher was not at the door for some reason, so Billy slipped by her vacant post and into Chucky.

It seems odd that adults in the children's support systems are the most likely source of the problem or have the best opportunity to circumvent excessive reactions. The parent may have caused the trauma and a vigilant, trauma-informed teacher might have de-escalated the incident, proactively inquiring and seeking appropriate interventions before the fight occurs. However, since it did occur, the same two adults who could have caused or prevented it are the adults administering punishments. That is not to suggest that teachers need to be mind-readers, but scanning body language at the door can eliminate a substantial volume of aberrant behaviors before they become conflicts. In addition, a trauma-sensitive school might have had two or three other adults to spot the problem or de-escalate Billy's ire by simply greeting him before he entered the classroom. It is a reverse butterfly effect, where the student must pass through a gauntlet of kindness and warmth before arriving at his or her destination. It is hard to remain angry in a culture where "everybody knows your name, and they're always glad you came."

Once the matter gets to the principal, the trauma-informed teacher must trust and respect what is decided; it is out of the teacher's hands. The trauma-sensitive administrator should act in the best interest of the child, not cater to teachers' expectations if the two are different, as is the case in many punitive cultures. There are interventions and consequences in the trauma-sensitive school culture, but they are therapeutic instead of puni-tive, and all should approach behavior issues with the intention to support deficiencies, not punish students for weakness in those need areas. Teach-ers and administrators in a trauma-sensitive school culture trust the deci-sions made by others because they are trained practitioners with an eye on long-term benefits. They understand the philosophy behind the actions and all others' attempts to care for the child. Remember that relationships are critically important, so whatever is decided must be handled delicately and at times, creatively.

The punitive systems established to deal with undesired behavior are often adult-centered, authoritative mandates that eventually contribute to the process of elimination. There are no fair or just consequences applicable to misbehaviors if the consequences fail to bring about anything but fear or dread. Current behavior modification models foster recurrences. They damage without repair; the interventions have been determined before violations occur because violations are so cyclical. They ostracize, scorn, and exile the student from the school. It is tragic that educational leaders have not been able to do anything to correct this obviously flawed and inef-fective process. Are they servant leaders? Do any of them have that same dirt under their nails that children of adversity get clawing their way out of poverty and across uneven playing fields, hoping to fulfill an unrealis-tic goal and win accolades meant for someone else? Equity, it seems, is not for everyone.

There is a better way, and it is consistent with the values of the trau-ma-sensitive school. First, one must understand that by removing the child from the school setting, the out-of-school suspension kicks the problem down the road. An out-of-school suspension is the impersonal, legal way of sending the problem out of the school's sphere of influence and back into the jungle where trauma is spawned. It is a bad plan but one accepted as a fact of life, something that was in place before today's educators were born. Educational leaders have accepted a process that requires children to gam-ble with their futures, and the odds they play are dependent upon their zip codes, prayers, ACEs, and face colors. It is normalized institutional screen-ing—systemic, procedural, and largely unintentional elimination. Again, the masses follow doctrine based on flawed logic without questioning why it is widely practiced. Educators do not improve the school by banishing the child with problems; they improve the school by removing the problems from the child. Fortunately, trauma-sensitive schools are obligated to align disciplinary practices to structural ideologies. There is a better way, one that could challenge the blindness or calcified policies that are yet another example of how education is controlled by some rather archaic ideas that seem immune to any form of scrutiny.

Suspending Out-of-School Suspensions

When an undesired behavior occurs, it often begins with the student's failure to self-regulate, which brings a response from the school employee, which in turn elicits a reaction from the student. The situation tends to escalate, in other words. That is understandable, since the code of conduct is based on consequences for disruptive behaviors without considering the fact that these behaviors are not actions, they are reactions. Traditional school employees know that there is a direct correlation between undesired behavior and punitive consequence. The first reaction is often to directly address the violation, as stated above, and that usually triggers a reaction, depending on the tone of the encounter. While this is not to suggest in any way that school leaders should ignore the code of conduct, the school employee does need to be trained to diffuse the situation rather than to ignite it. For example, if a student, Bob, arrives late and throws his books down onto his desk in his classroom in a manner that disrupts class, the teacher's reaction has a lot to do with the seriousness of the action and whether or not consequences will be necessary, or to what degree consequences will be enforced. This is not to blame the teacher for inadvertently triggering or provoking the student even further, but regardless of intent, that is essentially what happens. One of the benefits of the trauma-sensitive school is that teachers have some idea of the family and community beyond their doors and know that many kids carry some pretty heavy baggage. Teachers enforce rules and keep people engaged, and they must maintain control of the classroom to maximize learning and create a safe environment. However, there are strategic techniques that minimize the need for punishment, offering instead means to console, counsel, and coach the student back into a more positive frame of mind. Basically, empowering the teacher with effective, de-escalating strategies decreases levels of frustration in both the student and teacher. The relationship between student and teacher is the most important in the school, so it is reasonable to build around that important dynamic.

In the example, the Bob aggressively demonstrates a high degree of frustration that disrupts the teacher's class. This annoys the teacher, who is also under a high degree of stress (testing, poor formative observations, and a parent that has just been hospitalized, for example). In addition, the teacher is afraid that a public display such as this would be seen as a challenge to her authority, and she has to maintain her status as the alpha figure in that classroom when the climate becomes aggressive and confrontational. Without a plan, that is a lot to process in a few seconds, when reacting to an unforeseeable disruption puts the teacher on the spot. Her reaction to Bob's drama (the trauma and its triggers that result in undesired behavior) determines the fate of the student in many cases. If she thinks, "What is wrong with you?" she is likely to react by blaming the student. She does not consider the likelihood that the anger is a reaction to things that occurred before entering the classroom, whether at home, on the bus, in the bathroom, or between classes. Since the student is not challenging the teacher's authority but is disrespecting the rules, the teacher should assume the "What happened to you?" mindset (as opposed to the "What's wrong with you?" mindset), one more likely to result in de-escalation and a supportive relationship. Paul Gorski of EdChange.org might call this more understanding mindset a "structural ideology," in which the teacher, aware that students contend with a range of stressors from outside and inside the school, helps the student overcome the barriers causing the anger.[1] The teacher realizes that there is something wrong, probably related to the reason Bob is late for class. Although she knows no more than that, the teacher does not allow the behavior to trigger her own frustrations, creating two traumatic reactions on a collision course in one classroom. In the trauma-informed classroom and trauma-sensitive school culture, understanding that Bob's behavior is a reaction to something that occurred beyond the walls of the classroom is all that is needed to make a proper response. The teacher, even with her own problems, has been trained and refuses to take it personally and let it control her emotions. This brand of restorative justice, which replaces punitive measures with efforts to heal, has been proven to be effective in some schools, and it is strongly suggested for TSSEL schools. Much of what is discussed here demonstrates strategies for classroom management that are proven to be effective, but there are times when issues overwhelm a staff member's ability to contain and redirect the behavior, so the office referral is needed.

The first thing a teacher should try to do to condition his or her mind is to abandon the sacred belief that all rule violations require punishment. Schools are no place for street justice. Such a comment sounds outrageous to some, and loosening the grip of control can be hard to do. But with training and school-wide support, it is easy. Bob's teacher had been trained in restorative justice, and applied some of those strategies to refocus him. Sometimes, however, there are constraints such as time, safety concerns, and needed staff expertise that might necessitate a different form of restorative justice.

As mentioned, most suspensions in a school are recurrences, and it should not have taken this long to realize that systemic revenge or some sick cause-and-effect conduct manual is not effective. In many cases, schools are punishing cries for help, failing to see the distress signals to preserve ineffective systems of order. There is a better way, and like so much else, it is simple logic that has been scarcely used because previous attempts with similar strategies were not launched properly. Since the ability to see how habit and routine plague education is, at best, questionable, before this process can be fully effective, the administrator must have overseen staff and teacher training in the following areas:

- **Positive behavioral supports.** School-wide positive behavior intervention support (SWPBIS) and multi-tiered systems of support (MTSS) are examples of frameworks designed to incrementally and methodically improve student behavior and academic performance.
- **Restorative justice.** Restorative justice requires that undesired behavior be corrected, not punished; while this is not discussed in detail, restorative justice is best when addressed immediately and on a smaller scale so that the student or students are refocused and positively engaged quickly.
- **Therapeutic behavior interventions.** The hospital model is suggested when students are not able to return to the classroom immediately after restorative justice has been attempted. While part of the MTSS process and considered (basically) a form of restorative justice, the hospital model is ideal when the student needs to be removed from the academic environment to prevent disruption or his or her own humiliation. It is also a way to see that the students' needs are addressed professionally by experts, assuming the teacher is overwhelmed or the matter exceeds his or her area of expertise. An alternative to behaviors that once necessitated out-of-school suspension, it requires that the student be extracted from the classroom with the idea that his or her behaviors are most effectively addressed by experts (such as counselors or social workers) until all support staff determine the student is ready. This model and process will be detailed later in this chapter.
- **Mindfulness practices.** Trained teachers practice habits of mind that empower students to become aware and knowledgeable about perceptions, thinking skills, focusing exercises, metacognition, visual imaging, and other skills used to enhance mental self-regulation. When mindfulness practices are modeled and facilitated, students develop more control over reactions associated with confusion, panic, and fear.
- **Trauma-informed teaching.** Obviously trauma-informed teaching requires a full understanding of trauma and its influences on cognition and behavior, including instructional strategies that help children develop coping, resiliency, and trust. Understanding

the impact of trauma on the brain, and specifically how it effects learning and behavior, instills understanding and empathy to help educators advocate for the child.

- **Social-emotional learning.** Social-emotional learning involves cultural and pedagogical strategies that shift focus from cognition to a balance of cognitive and psychological development in a climate that prioritizes relationships.

It seems odd that so many would be reluctant to adopt a concept that has been tried and proven to be effective for all age levels and for all demographic subgroups. Remember, it takes a village and that village can create a non-threatening environment that takes students out of survival mode and gives them self-esteem and belongingness instead. Of course the reactions will be different. For example, one school in Washington saw immediate academic results during the first year of trauma-sensitive school reform. Suspensions and expulsions also dropped dramatically, from 798 suspensions in the year prior to implementing this trauma-informed approach to 135 suspensions during the first year of the trauma-sensitive culture.[2] That is a difference of more than 83 percent during the first year of implementation.

In addition to easing Bob's frustration and anger, his teacher is aware that she is contributing to his long-term success by avoiding a potential conflict that could have led to intensified acts of frustration and scarring punishment. While the school culture itself is certain to dramatically impact the number of out-of-school suspensions, there can be other measures in place (e.g., teacher training in restorative justice) that systematically address the policies that schools have practiced for years. Studies routinely demonstrate the connection between out-of-school suspensions and a child's probability for success. Balfanz and colleagues documented that even one suspension in ninth grade doubles the risk for dropping out, and Rumberger and Losen calculate that overall, being suspended once is associated with a 6.5 percent decrease in the likelihood of graduating from high school.[3] Someone with a sense of powerlessness or indifference might react to that data by saying, "Well, the trouble-makers who are suspended are highly unlikely to become model citizens, so that should not be surprising." However, a trauma-informed response (suggesting a structural ideology) might lead someone to say instead, "It sure seems that out-of-school suspensions are not helping students meet the needs to develop into productive adults." In essence, out-of-school suspensions destroy the sense of belonging that is so important to the trauma-sensitive school culture. Students are temporarily removed from the school and placed into the darkness of environments unknown to the school administrator. Suspended students are beaten, ridiculed, and often spend their idle time engaging in activities that contribute to their delinquent behaviors. Educators might be making it easier to educate the remaining children, but they are not serving the child whose needs are most demanding of attention. Instead of reaching out, schools are kicking out—but calling it *dropping out* because it creates distance that absolves them of responsibility for children's failure.

In a trauma-sensitive school, there are productive alternatives to the ineffective and methodical banishment of the students that need interventions the most. Instead of a punishment that leads to increased levels of disruption and higher dropout rates, perhaps school leaders should target the students in that population and attempt to eliminate the issues, not the students. School personnel cannot establish a sense of belonging with punitive behavior-modification policies. One hundred years of failing children should be enough proof. A carefully planned, in-school suspension process linked to the school-wide positive behavioral interventions and supports (SWPBIS) and the multi-tiered system of support (MTSS) is a key component of the most effective trauma-sensitive school culture. While there are many variables, such as financial resource commitment and human capital attitudes and training, the cost is a minimal investment considering the long term bill. As mentioned before, every dollar spent on social-emotional learning investments saves the community $11 in the long term. An effective SWPBIS with an active MTSS saves even more; in fact, according to one study, "Every $1 invested in SWPBIS resulted in a fiscal savings of $104.90."[4]

The Hospital Model of Therapeutic Behavior Intervention

Imagine that Bob's teacher is not successful and his frustration leads to increasingly disturbing behaviors that blatantly violate the code of conduct while making teaching and learning impossible. Restorative justice strategies are not effective. The teacher has no choice other than to call someone to escort Bob to the office. Traditionally, Bob would then be sentenced to a one-day, out-of-school suspension. His mother would be called to pick him up. She is already upset with him for having to drive him to school because he missed the bus, and now she will have to immediately return. Bob's day keeps getting worse.

But Bob is not sent to a traditional office; he is in a trauma-sensitive school. Sure, he is still a bit upset, but everyone has been extremely nice and supportive to Bob after his "meltdown." Bob's mother will not get a call to return to school to pick him up because he has been suspended. She may get a call, but the school needs to get to work first. In the trauma-sensitive, therapeutic suspension model (the so-called hospital model), the out-of-school suspension is always a possibility, but it serves as a last resort. In the trauma-informed school, the object is to help Bob cope with his stressor more effectively and return to the classroom as quickly as possible, not to punish him. Yes, he could have demonstrated better self-regulation, but the inability to regulate the self needs attention, not isolation. This is where the temptation to punish (the punitive or prison model of rehabilitation) is powerful, which is why training, supportive coaching, and oversight is strongly suggested. From the office staff to the teacher and now to an administrator, the focus remains on the treatment of the root cause of the anger, not the punishment of it. Teachers and staff do not seek revenge or justice; they trust one another and the process. They know that revenge or justice-seeking punitive retaliation is basically quitting on Bob, tactics that either exclude him or kick the can down the road (prolong the inevitable), or both. It will not work, and they know it. They also know what does work, because they have seen it in action. The following is an explanation of the recommended alternative approach, the therapeutic method. It is merely one example, and we will use Bob again.

Bob is referred to a school administrator, who completes a quick electronic assessment of the observable behaviors witnessed during a chat and those reported by the teacher following her restorative justice intervention. He explains to Bob the consequences according to the handbook, and checks Bob's referral history. He then gives Bob a choice. Bob can accept the consequences detailed in the handbook or he can accept a therapeutic intervention. Bob selects the latter. The administrator assigns Bob to what is currently called in-school suspension (ISS) and walks Bob to the ISS room. It should be noted that everyone encountering Bob has been supportive and pleasant, by design. The assessment is electronically shared with the ISS coordinator and media specialist, counselor, social worker, resource officer, and all of Bob's teachers. They all know what to do. Bob's teachers are now aware that he is in ISS, where the coordinator has electronically downloaded the teachers' lesson plan, handouts, and assignments. Within minutes, the student is pre-assessed (i.e., SEL skill areas to improve are identified) by the administrator and given SEL competency supportive videos (from the media specialist, based on the needed positive reinforcement indicated on the administrator's report), and Bob is assigned a work station. Once Bob has completed the supportive videos about his deficient behavioral response, the ISS coordinator sends his class assignments to Bob's workstation computer. Bob begins his coursework, understanding that several members of the support team will be visiting throughout the day. Since members of the support staff were notified, they add Bob to their schedules, and at some point during the morning, visit Bob to counsel him. The counselor and social worker may decide to meet with Bob together or have him join a group session. They may decide to speak to him privately and separately. The social worker is concerned about the family dynamics while the counselor is concerned with internal matters, so they might work together to assure that all avenues of Bob's support group are analyzed. The resource officer may drop by ISS to discuss an issue with Bob, if applicable. All record their interactions electronically in Bob's file. Toward the end of the school day, the administrator revisits ISS, reviewing all of the data with the ISS coordinator. The decision is made to either return Bob to classes the next day, add another day in ISS for therapeutic interventions, or issue the out-of-school suspension detailed in the conduct code. It should be noted that Bob understands that returning to the classroom will be based on the feedback provided by the support team. He knows that it is under his control, and giving Bob control over his consequences after an incident is empowering.

Making the Rounds

Bob encounters several professionals who are trained to get him back on track. Together, these form a team whose members serve the student in different ways, each adding their diagnosis to the overall report to be analyzed by an administrator at the end of the ISS process. The support team

Figure 4. An Example of the Hospital Behavior Intervention Model

includes several individuals with different areas of expertise, and they function something like a pit crew that works together to repair a race car and get it back on the track as quickly as possible. While the hypothetical situation just shared briefly explains the roles of the support staff, the following list provides more detail.

- **The school administrator.** Once the student is referred to the school administrator, the administrator determines whether the student needs an immediate, emergency intervention or qualifies as a candidate for the ISS therapeutic model. If so, the administrator talks with the student to determine the source of the issue and what needs to be done to support his or her deficiency needs. He explains to the student the reason he or she was sent to the office and the consequences prescribed in the code of conduct. He also explains that the ISS therapeutic model is an opportunity to address the weakened SEL competencies, talk to the support staff and get positive momentum re-established. Once the student is informed, the administrator completes an ISS form and checks the boxes beside the support personnel who need to see the student. For example he checks media specialist (to provide SEL videos to watch in competency areas), ISS coordinator (person who hosts ISS and facilitates the process), social worker, counselor, resource officer, and the classroom teachers. The administrator also decides who is to contact a parent or whether that is necessary. If this occurs during the middle or end of the school day, the student reports to ISS immediately and again in the morning if the evaluations and processes are incomplete.
- **The ISS coordinator.** The ISS Coordinator facilitates the therapeutic model by setting up the student in a workstation and downloading the assignments from the student's teachers. He or she is welcoming and helpful. The coordinator also prepares the reports for the administrator to review and informs the students of those decisions. In addition, the ISS coordinator keeps records and has access to MTSS interventions and the SEL survey instruments. He or she may call parents if the administrator checks that box. The ISS coordinator also discusses the support material sent by the media center and coaches the student or answers any questions. In addition, he or she observes the student and adds any unusual behaviors to the student's electronic referral sheet. At the end of the student's ISS assignment at the end of the school day, the ISS coordinator is responsible for presenting the data and discussing the student's progress with the assigning administrator.

- **Social worker.** The social worker visits the student at some point during their ISS experience, counseling the student about family and community issues that may have triggered the undesired behavior. He or she may decide to call in other professionals, such as the school psychologist, nurse, or resource officer. He or she is focused on the external stakeholders and influences outside of school, as a general rule, and may contact the parent if needed. He or she could and should team with the counselor on occasion.
- **School counselor.** The counselor helps with matters inside the school and inside the student's head, but that is an oversimplification. For the sake of this example, the counselor may resolve a conflict between the student and a teacher or another student. He or she may counsel the student individually or host a group session with other students, depending on the student's MTSS level. They may help students with things such as anger management or grieving the loss of a relative. The counselor addresses the trauma, not solely the behaviors that led to the intervention.
- **Media specialist.** The media specialist maintains a repository of supportive materials designed to train staff or assist in therapeutic interventions. These resources are designed to help students strengthen competencies and overcome obstacles and barriers. When the media specialist checks his or her messages in the morning, he or she sends prescribed materials (videos, audio recordings, articles, and so forth) to the student's ISS work station that are aligned with the SEL competencies that need attention. Once the student completes the material, the media specialist may be asked to meet with the student to explain the significance of the content or recommend extension materials.
- **Resource officer.** The resource officer may have any number of reasons for becoming involved. It could be a case in which the student is being pressured by a gang or has used drugs. It may be that the trauma is caused by threats or bullying that crosses the legal line. A student could be experiencing harassment, meaning that the resource officer needs to gauge the seriousness of the threat. A student may have shown signs of coping with drugs or alcohol. The social worker might involve the resource officer because the student has pertinent information that law enforcement may appreciate.

In essence, the student is admitted to a room where he is exposed to materials designed to help him or her overcome barriers and build resiliency.

He is counseled, provided effective interventions, supported, and coached. The student is empowered because the extent of his exclusion is determined by his responsiveness to the interventions. Students in trauma-sensitive schools soon realize that they have some control over the process. Not only can the student choose the hospital model over a suspension, they can regroup and minimize the consequences by cooperating. The student is returned to the school culture as soon as possible, but only when he or she can demonstrate readiness. If in Bob's case a similar incident were to occur within a few weeks, he would undergo the same process, only given level-three interventions on the second occasion (based on the MTSS model). Level-three interventions differ in that they can entail a private counseling session with the student that could result in parental involvement or referrals to professionals, such as the school psychologist or social services. The interventions are suggestions; schools need to build their own processes. Again, the process is never about punitive exclusions based on blocks of time (the same approach prisons use, which have been ineffective reformative strategies); it is a process designed to address the central problem, develop coping or resiliency skills, and return the child to the environment that builds belongingness and self-esteem. Table 3 demonstrates some key differences between the traditional (punitive) and hospital (therapeutic) intervention models.

Table 3.
The Punitive ("Prison") vs. the Therapeutic ("Hospital") Intervention Model

Punitive (Prison) Model	Therapeutic (Hospital) Model
Unacceptable behavior is an action that warrants disciplinary (punitive) consequences.	**Undesired behavior is a reaction** that warrants supportive (therapeutic) attention.
Law Enforcement: Inappropriate behavior is punished as mandated in the code of conduct (which is a set of predetermined laws that establish order and align deviations to consequences).	**Needs intervention:** Behavior, within the framework of the code of conduct, is addressed through a series of interventions designed to help students cope with the actual stressors behind reactive behaviors.
Sentencing: Punishment is issued in "days" in most in-school (ISS) and out-of-school (OSS) suspensions. Students "do time" as in the penal system.	**Diagnosing:** Support is prescribed based on interventions, which help students develop the resiliency and self-esteem needed to cope with the stressors triggering undesired behaviors. There is no predetermined amount of time for returning to the school population; the student returns once the team feels he or she has been empowered to overcome the central issue.

Punitive (Prison) Model	Therapeutic (Hospital) Model
Removal from the Main Population (isolation): Placing students in ISS and OSS is akin to assigning offenders to a cell in the judicial system. The object is to remove the problem from the school, using the revocation of inclusion as the consequence.	**Surrounded by a supportive team (individualized support):** Once the undesired behaviors have been addressed, a process begins that includes visits (in ISS) from the school administrator, ISS coordinator, counselor, social worker, and teacher.
Punitive Rehabilitation is based on a belief that the student's fear of being punished or ostracized again, since the consequences increase as recurrences occur. In other words, belittlement and isolation are at the core of the concept, a common practice in an authoritarian environment.	**Healing** is based on a belief that problems can be addressed with interventions targeting the underlying cause of the problem. While this may necessitate removal from the normal population, the student becomes more of a patient than an inmate. While assigned to ISS (instead of OSS), the support staff make their rounds, providing information, counseling, coaching, and other resources as necessary.
Repeat Offenders: While the likelihood for repeat offenders is high, consequences escalate, even if the severity of the violation does not. The intent is to dissuade inappropriate behavior by increasing the intensity and duration of the isolation.	**Recurring symptoms:** The likelihood for recurrence in the hospital is much lower than in the punitive model. However, if the healing interventions are not effective the first time, the team must consider more effective internal and external options.

12

Support Staff Leadership

Be great in act, as you have been in thought
—*The Life and Death of King John*, 5.1.46

The trauma-sensitive culture depends on non-instructional support staff to be effective, so that population needs empowerment and oversight. Changing the culture requires commitment from every adult in the building. If all it takes is one condescending or belittling comment to derail a child, it's also true that one kind or supportive comment is sometimes all it takes for a child to reclaim the rails. Bus drivers, for instance, are the first adults to see many students each day; they should therefore be included along with the teachers in training related to greeting children before entering the classroom. There are several reasons why this is important for the school leaders tasked with developing, implementing, and maintaining a trauma-sensitive school culture. First, the entire school interacts with children in some way and should demonstrate an awareness of trauma and its impact on children. Second, these personnel are vital to the supportive procedures that are critical to the culture's effectiveness. Third, many of these individuals have roles that are not always clearly defined or strategically aligned to a common vision. They are often outliers whose gifts are not always fully utilized by the school administrator. A collaborative redefining of certain roles can lead, therefore, to the discovery of a powerful human resource in an underappreciated and rarely utilized position, without adding to the expenses. It should be noted that the leader has the flexibility to reasonably expand or alter job responsibilities of these employees. Most contracts contain this statement (or something similar) after detailing a job description: "Performs any other related duties as assigned by the Principal or other appropriate administrator." While conversion to a trauma-sensitive school culture should not mean more of a time commitment for any employee, there are some staff members who could see an increase in responsibility that necessitates greater specialization.

ISS Coordinator

The in-school suspension (ISS) coordinators across the nation have a rather solitary purpose, which is to oversee most processes and reports relating to the traditional model of student isolation in some form of solitary confinement. Essentially, they are paid to segregate the students with behavior problems in a room or area of the school that is separate from the mainstream activities. The ISS coordinator, in other words, is a salaried employee dealing with students who are being punished for their lack of self-regulation and coping skills. These workers are often underutilized, underappreciated members of a staff that does little to change lives. There is no reason the role of the ISS coordinator cannot become one of the most important staffers in the school. The new position should not carry the ISS label, but by referring to ISS and the ISS coordinator for a time, the position is more clearly aligned with the current structure and will make the transition as clear and simplistic as possible to visualize.

The trauma-sensitive school culture opposes out-of-school suspensions because they are ineffective, recurring attempts to punish undesirable behavior until the student learns a lesson. Researchers at the University of Virginia concluded, "out-of-school suspension is ineffective as a tool to improve behavior in students—and often has a negative effect on the students who receive it."[1] Additionally, researchers from the University of Pennsylvania found that "suspensions for any reason are tied to lower scores in math and English language arts tests" and that "the negative effect increases with each additional day of suspension."[2] That research also revealed a negative relationship between suspensions and attendance. It seems likely, then, that any defense of out-of-school suspension would include some traditionalist's explanation of the norm. Of course, it is the norm that needs fixing. A bad idea is one thing, but accepting and practicing that bad idea because the leadership lacks the courage and conviction to challenge it is another. That acceptance of the status quo is in fact blind conformity, and conformity is the opposite of both creativity and leadership.

As described in chapter 12, the ISS coordinator is a central figure because the intent is to eliminate the practice of out-of-school suspension (OSS) by overhauling what is currently called ISS. While OSS may still be needed in some situations, it is abused and is frequently a statistical beacon that reveals the school's social injustice and inequity. As mentioned, the ISS coordinator is the school employee who takes the SEL data from the administrator and develops a support plan to get ISS-confined students back into the classroom as soon as they have demonstrated readiness. Instead of the administrator being the suspending party, he or she simply analyzes the situation and notes areas of social or emotional deficiencies that need to be reinforced before the child returns to classes. The ISS coordinator takes the administrator's assessment data (checklist) and aligns the recommendations with the support personnel and prescribed resources. He or she alerts the social workers, teachers, and counselors so they can schedule a visit during their daily rounds. He or she records the interventions into the student's file, working within the framework of the RTI or MTSS support structure. During this time, the ISS coordinator, who is also trained in trauma sensitivity and social-emotional learning, coaches the student and discusses the prescribed videos, articles, and other materials assigned after the administrator's pre-assessment. By keeping records, coaching the students, organizing individualized intervention programs, and alerting other support personnel, the ISS coordinator performs a critically important role within the trauma-sensitive school culture. It is a huge, challenging job that requires an organized, optimistic person who is capable of positive interaction with children facing challenges.

Bus Drivers

Bus drivers spend as much time with students as many teachers. More than half of all public school students in the United States ride a bus to school. Most are on the bus for an average of one hour per day (30 minutes each way), although some students have combined morning and afternoon rides that surpass two hours each day.[3] Driving a bus has to be one of the most challenging jobs in education, as the adult has to operate a huge, noisy vehicle and monitor safety both inside and outside the bus. Imagine a classroom teacher with no lesson plans monitoring a room full of children with his or her back to the class, watching them through a mirror. Now add the fact that the classroom is traveling 50 miles per hour and that the teacher must also navigate traffic.

The bus driver is the first and last employee that most children talk to every day. They should not be excluded from trauma-sensitive training, nor should their roles in the lives of each child be trivialized. Bus drivers have the opportunity to set the tone for that child's day. They hear and see things, and they are the only adult in the vicinity when problems arise. Cameras should be operational on all buses, of course, but the hidden filming is not much of a deterrent or help when intervention is needed. A school bus is a prime setting for a bully, especially if only one adult is monitoring some 50 children while driving. The bully can trap the victim very easily, so all students must be protected from the time they leave their doorsteps to the moment they step back on it. If students are repeatedly traumatized on the bus coming to school and then again leaving it, the trauma-sensitive culture is probably not going to be much help. Imagine the impact of being trapped in tight confines with a bully who torments you up to two hours each day. Since not all bullying is effectively deterred by glancing into a mirror for two seconds every so often, drivers need empowerment and skills to minimize these occurrences. There seems to be a shortage of qualified school bus drivers in many areas across the nation, so anything the school leader can do to maximize job satisfaction and include the drivers as part of the trauma-sensitive team will help develop a sense of belonging and ownership. Drivers need to be invited to staff events, awards ceremonies, and celebrations if and when possible. They need to be given school shirts and hats and recognized for their efforts. If the leader cannot pay them what they deserve, they can embrace them and recognize their importance. Bringing the bus drivers into the culture (family) is one of the details that could reap the biggest rewards.

While bullying is not the only concern, it is a place to start. Drivers and schools must do more to safeguard the emotional wellness of the students. Aside from educating all students about trauma and teaching them compassion, empathy, and other social-emotional skills, leaders need to help students develop civic responsibility. The best people to end bus bullying, for example, are the passengers. By developing a trusting relationship with the driver and other members of the school, they will understand that it is their duty to report verbal and physical bullying. Drivers need to be informed when a parent reports sudden changes in their child's behaviors at home, such as seriousness or increased irritability.[4] The driver may be able to provide helpful insights not observable in the school but obvious on the bus. There needs to be a process in place that protects individuals involved in the reporting process. In summary, the bus is an extension of the school and children should be offered the same reassurances there that they receive in the building. Leaders who exclude the adults who are with students several hours per week are missing an opportunity to prevent trauma from being triggered moments before students enter the building.

Media Specialist

The media specialist can play a role in the ISS therapeutic approach to self-regulation. Once the administrator delivers the student to the ISS coordinator, and identifies which SEL competency areas are in need of development, the media specialist will provide resources for the first stage of the ISS process. Having established a repository of interactive resources directly aligned with aspects of each SEL competency, the media specialist prescribes age-appropriate materials for students, based on their deficiency. These resources include interactive software, audio recordings, video clips, discussion questions, or extension activities designed to personalize the learning and provide opportunities for demonstrations of the student's understanding. The media specialist works to increase the variety and depth of these instructional activities, and can make them available to teachers, parents, and other staff members who are interested in the materials related to SEL objectives. The media specialist may opt to make technology available if necessary. In addition, the media specialist is encouraged to stay current in the areas of trauma sensitivity and SEL program upgrades and should be added to the faculty meeting agenda if he or she deems new developments to be newsworthy. While developing and maintaining a repository for student-centered SEL resources, the media specialist will assist the instructional coach design staff development to help train teachers. He or she will coordinate with the instructional coach, counselor, and social worker to suggest topics, support concepts, and align resources with the faculty development timeline. Essentially, the media specialist maintains the repository for supportive resources and current developments in the areas related to the culture of the school.

Finally, the media center is where the school marketing plan can be created and maintained, with the specialist overseeing this very important work. Most of this can be done through the website in cooperation with school administration. Morning announcements, SEL and school improvement data, videos from field trips or events at the school, athletic schedules and photos, celebrations such as teacher of the month or student of the week, informative videos that educate the public, and so forth are some of the items the web site might promote. As the job title implies, the media specialist is responsible for critical information and media content. It should be noted that much of this work can be done by parent volunteers, students, assistants, and others since there is not confidential data involved in most functions.

Office Staff

While teachers are the trauma-sensitive soldiers on the front lines in the classrooms, the office manager and staff are the people who serve in the same capacity on the front lines of the school. "In a trauma-sensitive school, all staff share a common understanding of trauma and its impact on students, families, and staff and a joint mission to create learning environments that acknowledge and address trauma's impact on school success," according to the National Center on Safe Supportive Learning Environments.[5] The front office of the school is often where the first contact is made between a school employee and a visiting external stakeholder. It is probable that there will be questions about trauma-sensitive approaches to child development and SEL strategies, especially in the beginning. An informed office staff can answer basic questions and develop skills to identify potential threats to the school culture. Should a student be referred to the office for any reason, the interaction between office staff and the student is rather powerful and can often have a calming influence, but it is also potentially explosive if staff handled the student carelessly. Office staffers are also likely to receive phone calls from stakeholders; they need to understand the culture and the marketing plan to help members of the community interested in learning more about the school's new vision. In addition, office workers often interact with all of the stakeholders in the student's orbit, and may notice things that need to be addressed, which they can share with school leaders.

Custodian

The custodian is perhaps the most underappreciated person in the school, but he or she can play an important role in the SEL school culture. The custodian's primary responsibility is cleanliness and safety, obviously, but it goes beyond clean floors and locked closets. That is not to discount the importance of cleanliness or belongingness; a clean school is related to positive moods and attitudes. The custodian should model TSSEL behaviors, such as welcoming visiting stakeholders or pleasantly greeting students and teachers in the hallway. "It doesn't matter if it's a custodian, a security officer, the principal, a parent—whoever it is," according to an article in EdSurge. "There's an acknowledgment and eye contact."[6] The custodian is an extra pair of eyes around the school and should feel empowered to alert the administration if threats to the culture are observed. He or she should be on the lookout for suspicious activity in parking lots or areas of the building not recorded on video tape, for example. In relation to the marketing plan and external stakeholder relations, the custodian is often the person who prepares facilities and can oversee the important details, so it is recommended that custodians serve on committees that require their services. In addition, every person in the school needs to appreciate the contributions of the school custodian, starting with the administration.

When the school leaders model respect for the custodian, it teaches important values to all staffers and students. It also motivates the custodian to serve the school with a sense of purpose and pride. In turn, students will be taught to respect the custodian and appreciate the significance of his or her contributions.

Resource (Police) Officer

The school resource officer can play a critical role in the school, especially in the hospital model described in the previous chapter. The resource officer may not be involved in every situation concerning ISS, but he or she plays a key role in developing positive relationships between youth and law enforcement. The social worker and the resource officer should partner in the event that there is concern that external influences may be illegal in nature. For example, if a student believed to be affiliated with a gang were sent to ISS, the resource officer may need to be brought in, not as a threat but as a listener who can help build a relationship between the law and the child. If alcohol or drugs are involved, the resource officer may meet privately with the child. In addition, the resource officer may have access to criminal records that he or she can research names provided to the social worker during conversations with the child, to gauge the extent of his influence in the community. Finally, there could be signals or signs that the student projects that others may not catch; involving the resource officer could prevent escalating violence in the school. The resource officer can be a valuable asset and should be part of the MTSS and ISS processes as needed. The officer should also contribute to the school marketing plan by sharing videos, notes, and information for parents.

Athletic Director

Since extracurricular activities are extensions of the school day and its culture, the athletic director is in many ways an extension of the principal and should oversee the athletic programs with similar diligence. Social-emotional competencies, after all, need also to be embedded in the values of the athlete, the team, and its coach. During competitions at home and on the road, student athletes and coaches are expected to model these skills, values, and virtues. In many cases, the only contact a school has with certain external stakeholders and family members is during athletic contests, so it is incredibly important that trauma-sensitive approaches to child development are practiced at all times. In some cases, coaches have been known to angrily argue with umpires and referees; players have been known to humiliate or taunt opponents. The SEL competencies, on the other hand, require composure, empathy, and many of the same traits attributed to sportsmanship. Frankly, students with higher levels of self-esteem tend to have more self-confidence and be more competitive than those with fragmented deficiency needs. Players and coaches should understand that they are ambassadors of sorts, and that the school is judged by their work ethic, success, and composure. It is suggested that the athletic director serve on the committee that addressed external relationships and school marketing.

Cafeteria Staff

While the cafeteria workers' encounters with students are brief, it is important that their interactions be in harmony with the aims of the school. Communications with children should not be threatening or intimidating, and students are not to be embarrassed or shamed for having no lunch money. The reason the child is behind is likely not his or her fault. What does a trauma-informed cafeteria worker look like? One who, when the child's debt is excessive, pleasantly hands the him or her a form letter for the parents and does not scold or belittle him. Targeting the child is not addressing the source of the problem. Cafeteria workers should be supportive, kind, and professional. Most of the time, this is not a concern, and cafeteria staffers understand protocols and confidentiality (as when dealing with food allergies, for instance). They simply need to be informed so that they can support the process. In turn, students will learn to demonstrate emotions such as gratitude when being served by the cafeteria staff.

School Nurse

While not all schools have a full-time nurse, the nurse assigned to a trauma-sensitive school should be knowledgeable about the health risks associated with the adverse childhood experiences research findings. Knowing the effects of traumatic stress on blood pressure and cognitive processing disorders, for instance, is essential in the whole-child development framework. In addition, traumatized children often self-medicate to ease the anxiety, often starting with prescription drugs or intoxicating stunts that involve household chemicals such as aerosol cans. The nurse needs to be aware of such behaviors, and to make others aware. Furthermore, there are tips the nurse can share with members of the faculty that help things such as elevated heart rates or blood pressure, which can be triggered by stressors that cause panic attacks. The blood levels of cortisol and dopamine, for example, can be decreased or stabilized with simple tricks such as supportive touching or drinking water. These seemingly insignificant acts can have a rather significant impact on the school culture over time. Finally, the nurse, along with the social worker and counselor, serve as the liaison between need and community resources.

Social Worker and School Counselor

These positions are combined because both roles serve to counsel and coach children who are experiencing problems. The school counselor's focus is on the psychological and emotional well-being of the child and the improvement of conditions within the school to assure that child's success; the social worker addresses issues more globally, considering the impact of family and community on the student and advocating for resources external to the school setting. Those are over-simplifications of their separate responsibilities, admittedly, but the suggestion here is that they work as a team, at least until the problem has been identified and the intervention strategy designed. Often there is overlap, depending on the complexity of the situation. The difference between the two may be subtle, but an effective social worker–school counselor combination has the power to help remove barriers and facilitate healing and growth for needy students. They may assume similar roles and share tools in several key areas of child development:

- **Assisting teachers with behavior management techniques.** Here, the instructional coach should team with the counselor and social worker to develop effective classroom and behavior management approaches that are congruent with SEL strategies.
- **Counseling students.** Both counsel students, but the approaches and formats are a bit different. The counselor is effective in an intervention for individuals or small groups following a disciplinary episode or matters concerning the child's future. The focus in these scenarios is on the individual student's personal ability to learn and reach goals. These sessions could lead to areas of concern better suited to the social worker or necessitate inclusion of the social worker in a supporting role. The social worker also counsels students in small groups, individually, and with families, but his or her focus is generally on systems of support. The social worker may advocate for students during special education assessment meetings and in the development of individual education plans.

- **Developing supportive networks.** The counselor may support students by maintaining current and accurate records while keeping the administration abreast of student issues, needs, and problems. The social worker supports students beyond the walls of the school by working with families, social and mental health agencies, and advocating for community and school services to help meet the needs of students.
- **Meeting with students during therapeutic interventions.** In the new and improved ISS process, both the social worker and the counselor meet with the students in ISS. They may do so together or separately, but the intention is to see the same problem from different perspectives. After the meeting, each seeks support for the child, but in different ways.[7]

The school counselor should assist the instructional coach in the development and training of teachers to incorporate the SEL curriculum into the required curriculum. The social worker, on the other hand, may contribute in the area of trauma sensitivity, explaining the adverse childhood experiences study and how domestic trauma contributes to social, emotional, and cognitive impairment and health-risk behaviors. It is strongly encouraged that these support staff members find ways to unify as a team, and that leadership develop an understanding of the different areas of expertise needed to succeed. While individual needs and demands are too numerous to detail here, the counselor and social worker should work interchangeably and together when needed. If the concerns include events in the classroom, such as curricular or management issues, the instructional coach may need to become involved as well.

Some readers may be wondering, "Why is there no mention of a school psychologist?" That is a good question, and the omission of that resource from the foregoing discussion is not an oversight. The plan advanced in this book is for schools that may not have such a psychologist in the building. All schools and students are required to have access to a psychologist as needed, but the reality of their scarcity is something that should be addressed. While it seems the benefit of having a psychologist, counselor or two, and a social worker would be well worth the investment, an accounting for the long-term savings to society has yet to influence many budgetary decisions. Instead, leaders choose to save a salary now and kick the can down the road, perhaps until it takes five salaries to repair the can and the damage to the foot, seems to be the strategy. The National Association of School Psychologists (NASP) recommends that districts employ one school psychologist for about every 600 students. Few do, however. As the association reported in a 2017 research summary, "In many states, that ratio is more in the neighborhood of one to 2,000, though in some states it goes as high as one to 3,500.... We certainly don't have the number of personnel we feel is necessary."[8] With that in mind, the psychologist will be considered a luxury, more of an external resource than an internal one. It is assumed that a school with access to a psychologist will not feel slighted by the omission of that resource from the discussion here, whereas the school without access might consider this plan unrealistic or written for only the better-funded schools. It should be noted that a school psychologist shared with the other schools in the system could be scheduled to visit one day per week for several hours to meet with students in need of their services, but unless the psychologist is in the building, it is difficult to schedule or plan. School psychologists are tremendous resources, but until their numbers meet the demand, it is helpful to devise a plan that has limited access to them, empowering the counselor to facilitate any psychologist interventions.

Instructional Coach

Needless to say, instructional coaches are critically important to the development of trauma-informed teachers who have the capacity to fuse social-emotional learning strategies into classroom instruction. The instructional coach should be prepared for the challenge; their effectiveness requires deployment of andragogic strategies (that is, strategies for teaching adults) and a deep understanding of the relationship between the SEL competencies and best practices that enrich the content curriculum mandated by the states. It is important that the instructional coaches and teachers realize that although there will be a steep learning curve, the SEL lesson implementation is not merely "something else to do"; it is a new, more effective and strategic way of personalizing the required content. Instead of developing and assessing the knowledge of stuff, teachers will be focused on using the stuff to better understand the self. The instructional coach will be responsible for heading the committee that develops training and procedures that direct instruction. He or she will work with the principal to realize the vision, seek funds, develop timelines, and approve assessment and feedback protocols. However, the committee that supports the development of trauma-sensitive instruction and social-emotional learning must be a functional pit crew of sorts for the teachers in the school. That committee and the roles are recommended as follows:

- **School counselor:** Based on an understanding of the psychological and emotional needs of students, the counselor provides insights useful to the instructional coach, who in turn develops training sessions that will ultimately help children overcome the trauma that impedes cognitive development. For example, teachers might need to know strategies from brain research that have proven to calm anxieties and increase attendance rates. As the program develops, counselors can introduce new strategies that separate the detail-oriented professionals at successful schools from the routine-blinded creatures of habit that roam the halls at underperforming schools. .

- **Social worker:** The social worker and counselor will often drive in one another's lanes and that is usually acceptable, if not encouraged; but one area in which the social worker can really contribute is lesson development that incorporates strategies to help students cope and develop relationships with family members and groups within the community. The social worker helps the instructional coach devise strategies that will strengthen areas vulnerable to familial or societal toxins that he or she knows to be unique to the population of students.
- **Media Specialist:** The media specialist serves as the resource behind the curtain, constantly researching and creating new materials to be used to effectively train students and teachers. Much in the same way the cafeteria manager orders food within the specifications of government nutritional requirements, the instructional coach is constantly sharing training and one-on-one topics with the media specialist, who becomes the refrigerated truck driver in this metaphor, the person who backs up to the loading dock and fills the freezers and cabinets with ingredients to be used later.

Of course, others could be part of this committee. The new and improved ISS coordinator, for example, might want into the fold. A teacher or two may express interest. An administrator should always be involved in some manner, but if that isn't possible, the instructional coach must keep administrators fully informed at all times to assure consistency and fluency of meaning.

This professional learning committee is to be one of the most important in the school; the success of the academic program and its alignment with whole-child development is critical. It is the heart of the trauma-sensitive school culture and its directives are to be respected by everyone, including the administration. A suggestion would be to have one member represent the instructional coach's committee at grade- or subject-level meetings. While this may seem a bit time consuming, dropping in to answer a few questions at the beginning or end is a wise investment of time.

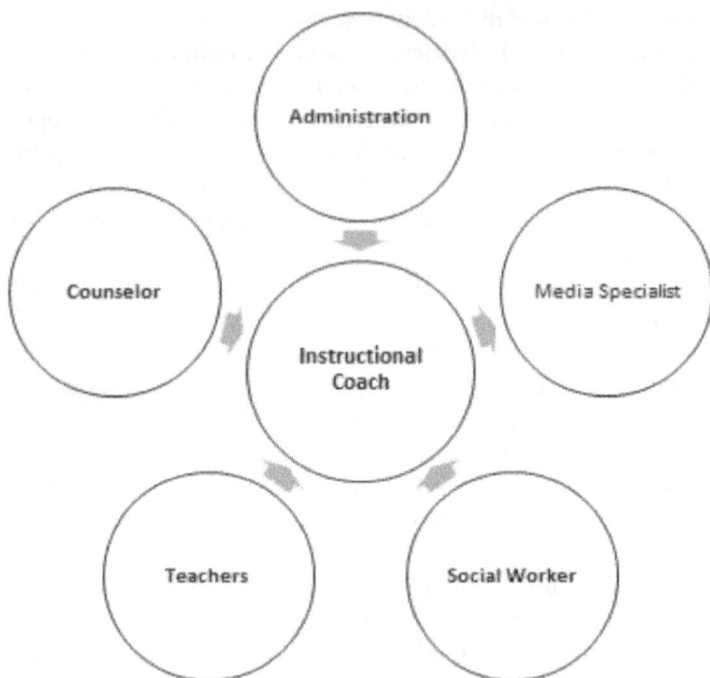

Figure 5. The Instructional Coach's Spheres of Influence

Finally, the instructional coach will have to share the SEL curriculum with teachers and demonstrate how both it and their use of it is to be assessed. The instructional coach needs to focus on two very basic concepts: (1) keep it simple and (2) improve efficiency. Assessment is not restricted to the teacher when it comes to social-emotional learning; parents, support staff, and administrators will all have opportunities to provide feedback. Print a report every nine weeks, and send SEL progress reports home with the report cards. This is important because students value what is assessed. As Jennifer Crocker notes in an article published in *Monitor on Psychology,* "When students were asked about what they base their self-worth on, more than 80 percent said 'academic competence (grades).'"[9]

Eventually, stakeholders will be able to see parallels between social-emotional growth and academic growth. But student academic performance should not be the only indication of success. In fact, the same indicators that the school already has in its database provide solid evidence for the TSSEL influence. Note that these measures need to be entered into the school database so that subcategories such as gender, race, grade level, and economically disadvantaged status can be easily norm-referenced. In one fictitious example, Wildcat Elementary has decided to measure the impact of SEL using these measures:

- Standardized test scores
- Attendance (student and teacher)
- Disciplinary referrals and suspensions
- SEL assessments
- End-of-year teacher surveys

Some of these indicators can be evaluated throughout the year to monitor progress. In October, for example, Mrs. Jones, a first grade teacher at Wildcat Elementary, is provided a report that indicates her students' attendance is higher than it was last year but slightly behind this year's schoolwide average. Her disciplinary referrals are down 3 percent from last year, but she has sent more children to the office than any other teacher so far this year. Her first quarter SEL survey results reveal that many of her students exhibit deficiencies and about 12 percent will be moved to level two of the RTI/MTSS support structure, about average when compared to the school-wide percentage for teachers. She is upset and claims that the information is not fair. The instructional coach decides to meet with her. Mrs. Jones explains that she cannot control which children are assigned to her. She adds that most of her children are on free or reduced lunches and starts to go into another rehearsed excuse. The instructional coach, armed with the data, needs to set Mrs. Jones straight, right?

Nope. The instructional coach asks Mrs. Jones to share her lesson plan notebook. She examines a few lessons, asking Mrs. Jones questions such as, "How did this activity reinforce your SEL objective? Your class, as you state, is impacted by poverty, so how are you addressing the impact of poverty on trauma? We have been in school for nine weeks; which parents have you not met yet? Are their children those with the lowest grades?" These are all valid questions. The data suggests that there are issues that need to be addressed, especially in light of Mrs. Jones's excuses, which should be perceived as opportunities to open the discussion. Is there an issue with cultural competence? Is there evidence of cultural relevance in the lesson designs? Is there another teacher with similar challenges who would be willing to meet with the teacher? The instructional coach notices that Mrs. Jones struggled to convincingly align the class activity with the SEL objective stated on the lesson plan. Perhaps that needs to be considered as well and should determine the next few questions. Even though there are other things that the instructional coach notices that could be addressed, it is probably a good idea to identify the most significant issue and address it first. In this case, culturally relevant instruction could solve one problem, but the coach decides to focus on the instructional strategy and align it with SEL competencies related to more pressing needs. It is the coach's assessment that fixing this issue might make the other disappear. Perhaps later, the culturally relevant instruction will be an issue that needs addressing. If so, there is probably growth occurring, since the smaller problem would then become the most pressing.

There is no blaming or shaming in the trauma-sensitive school. The coach is just that, a coach. His or her success depends on the success of the team. However, the coach needs to make a prescription, like a doctor. For example: "Mrs. Jones, here is what we should try: First, I want you to see a great video about differentiating instruction for SEL growth. I forget what it is called, but I will have Mr. Books (media specialist) send you the link. Take about 30 minutes to watch it and let me know what you think." The instructional coach makes note on agenda to follow up with Mrs. Jones about the video in three days. The coach continues: "Then I want to see a lesson you have designed with that in mind. By the way, Mrs. Smith in fourth grade is great at this and I am sure she would love to show you her secrets. You are improving, Mrs. Jones, and that is what this is all about; however, some of your concerns are, in my opinion, just a tweak or two from being strengths. Let's see how it goes. I will follow up on Friday, after you have seen the video. See you then!"

Again, there are other concerns about Mrs. Smith's class, but the problem identified is probably bigger than the others. It is demoralizing to have three or four concerns addressed at one time; the coach needs morale to be high. In fact, Mrs. Jones may have a strength, such as questioning techniques, and the coach may ask her if she can send teachers who struggle in that area to observe her in action. She learns that she has strengths and weakness and that there is support for her to improve her feedback in October, well before the summative evaluations and the standardized final exam.

13

Changing the Culture

Be not afraid of greatness.
—*Twelfth Night*, 2.5.148

Obviously, the principal of the school faces a monumental yet reward-ing task, one that must be executed carefully, patiently, and methodically. The depth and breadth of the problems must be fully understood; the fac-ulty must not only share the vision but have faith that it will effectively rem-edy a majority of the ailments plaguing the school. Everyone must become introspective, reflective, and willing teammates, trusting in the research and having faith in the outcomes. The staff must feel their own strong sense of belonging and feed on the self-esteem needed to realize their full poten-tial. Each must define his or her role by expanding the spheres of influence and commit to doing more than what is required. It can seem impossible, especially in schools where massive transformation is sorely needed. Peo-ple will doubt. Some will laugh and shake their heads. The leaders, how-ever, realize that great achievements take a certain amount of courage. The doubters and skeptics, whether they are internal or external stakehold-ers, need to be shown that their attitudes are the reason change is needed. Because there have been great leaders who did not veer away from an opportunity even when all others before them did, we now know the world is not flat and that the moon is not really made of cheese. These daring individuals defied the ignorance of our forefathers while embracing their wisdom and blazed new trails of inquiry and discovery. Building trau-ma-sensitive schools is that new challenge, and it requires leaders who do not flinch under pressures from influential forces that threaten children. The approach describe in this book works, and if leaders believe it, they will do whatever it takes to make sure it thrives.

After the awareness stage, beyond the establishment of motivation and a shared vision, comes action. Remember the dogs of leadership from chapter 7? The sheepdog now begins the journey, leading the herd from the rear, empowering those that share the vision to lead, collaborate, and follow when necessary. The sheepdog knows the depths of the rivers and where they must cross, and chases away the wolves and bobcats as necessary. He or she empowers the leaders and runs with those at the back of the pack, modeling courage and stamina while nurturing the weak and the young. This servant leader understands the best position from which to lead and keeps both the vision and the team in sight.

The leader must establish trust before he can empower; he must instill a sense of belonging before selfless teammates develop the chemistry known to the greatest teams, armies, and families. The leader makes sure that every person in the school, from the substitute teachers, custodians, and bus drivers to the support staff at central office, is given the opportunity to build something so great it has the power to save lives. There will be those whose primary purpose seems to be to preserve mediocrity or worse; they are the weak sheep at the back of the herd. Run with them, offering support and encouragement as long as there is hope.

Understand, before moving into specific ideas, that there are literally dozens of ways a leader might design the TSSEL school model. To do it correctly, considering the enormousness of the endeavor, ask for three years of support. Once everyone's expectations are tempered, the principal should develop a timeline, one that includes strategies to realistically develop systems of support, networks, resources, and benchmarks. The sheep need to know what to expect and the farmhands at the corral gate need to know when the herd will arrive. The sheepdog knows that some will get tired and lose focus; others will need hope and encouragement along the way. Some days the herd will cover miles, but there will also be nights that seem to last forever.

Professional Learning Communities (PLC)

A school transitioning to the trauma-sensitive model faces substantial change. Consider the following example. A principal chooses to develop five professional learning communities, each led by a support staff member considered an expert in the area where his or her strengths are most advantageous. Most jobs will be redefined, expanding each individual's sphere of influence as a key aspect of their empowerment. Ideally, these five individuals will be trained and supported over the summer prior to the launch date in year one. In this transitional model, one that implements trauma-informed instruction using social-emotional learning strategies, the five pillars (TSSEL committees) and the chairs of each committee are as follows:

- **Instruction and Assessment (Instructional Coach, Chair).** This committee oversees the development and maintenance of SEL–content curriculum instruction, assessment, and data analysis. In addition, this committee will work with the principal to identify areas where training and staff development in SEL strategies are needed. Beyond the chair of the committee, it is recommended that the principal require certain other personnel to serve. They are the department or grade-level teacher leaders, beginning teachers (first three years), and a special education teacher. The remaining seats are voluntary but must be filled by school personnel directly involved with classroom instruction. Consultants are people who do not serve on the committee because they bring experiences and awareness from other committees to assist the chair. In our example, the consultants are the school counselor, social worker, and the media specialist. These consultants will assist the committee by providing expertise and resources as needed.
- **Developmental Resources and School Marketing (Media Coordinator, Chair).** This committee oversees the development, maintenance, and enrichment of a repository of resources (including developmental videos, interactive software, articles, and so forth) to support teachers as requested by the teacher or instructional coach and to reinforce competencies as part of the ISS program. In addition, this committee will develop and maintain the school marketing plan and promote it on the school website. Since athletics are one of the most visible ways a school markets itself, the athletic director (if applicable) is required to serve on this committee, along with the office manager, interested teachers, and parent-teacher organization volunteers that can assist with technology requirements and promoting the school marketing plan. The consultants are the school counselor, the social worker, and the instructional coach.
- **Behavior Modification and Self-regulation Program (ISS Coordinator, Chair).** This committee is designed to eliminate most out-of-school suspensions by implementing an in-school, therapeutic ("hospital") system or network of interventions with key support personnel involved until all behavioral experts approve the student's return to the classroom. The traditional ISS coordinator's responsibilities are tremendously increased, as he or she schedules prescribed resources and communicates with experts qualified to counsel and develop professional interventions to address deficiencies and build SEL competencies. The committee

includes an administrator who oversees suspensions and is assisted by interested teachers. In addition, the chair is supported by key consultants, including the school counselor and social worker, both of whom can counsel students and advocate for internal and external resources, and the media specialist, who aligns documented deficiencies with resources to strengthen related SEL competencies.

- **Counseling and Trauma Management (School Counselor, Chair).** This committee examines the impact of trauma on individuals in the school setting, offering support services for students, teachers, and all staff members requesting an intervention. The counselor provides a number of key services, including private counseling sessions, referrals for professional services, supportive mentor pairing, big brother / big sister program oversight, and student-student or student-teacher conflict resolution. In addition to specific services for individuals, the committee works with the principal, instructional coach, and counselor to provide workshops and training. The primary consultant is the social worker.

- **Counseling and Social-Emotional Support (Social Worker, Chair).** This committee supports students by developing stronger relationships with families and communities. Understanding Maslow's basic and emotional needs (deficiency needs), the committee works to mitigate the external factors that impede the whole-child development of the students. For this reason, this committee might collaborate with the instructional coach. This committee is also charged with explaining to the staff the significance of Maslow's needs, ACE findings, equity, social justice, cultural competency, and culturally relevant instruction. In addition, the committee plans events that involve external stakeholders such as pediatricians, politicians, members of the clergy, and parents (to name only a few) and conducts informational workshops, town hall discussions, and so forth. The custodian, office staff, interested teachers, and volunteers are encouraged to participate on this committee. The social worker also works with the ISS coordinator and the school counselor to provide interventions and maintain documentation of interventions as mandated in the MTSS for each student in the therapeutic intervention process. The primary consultant is the school counselor.

Measures of Success

Obviously, emphasis on the measures of success is critical. The school leader in our example will rely on the leaders of the aforementioned TSSEL committees for formative feedback, but he or she will also rely on observation and formative data to monitor progress. Still, there should be goals based on the available data from prior years to demonstrate growth to all stakeholders. During the first year of the program, data is collected in areas that will be measured, and much of the program's progress will be monitored by the feedback these variables provide. For example, the following could be areas used to demonstrate the impact of the TSSEL culture:

- **Attendance.** One of the key indicators of a successful school is measured in terms of attendance. Since attendance is mandatory for most students, it may seem remarkable that the difference between, for instance, 94 and 95 percent attendance rates can be dramatic discrepancies in academic achievement and dropout rates. Teacher attendance rates tell a different story, one that reveals the levels of morale and job satisfaction.
- **Teacher, student, and parent surveys.** Attitudinal surveys about every aspect of the school culture reveal many potential areas of inquiry that could influence decisions. Teachers are the most qualified observers on the inside, while parents are often the best sources of feedback from the outside. Likert scales, for example, show growth or decline in the areas of inquiry.
- **Test Scores.** It is easy to use test scores to measure progress from year to year, and easy is good. Leaders can add SEL measurements to the mix, complementing those related to academics. It is reasonable to expect development of social-emotional competencies to support improved academic performance, so the comparison of these scores is a key part of the data analysis. Since training and staff development will be ongoing, the effect of the SEL influence should be noticeable as teachers and support personnel become more familiar with the process and convinced of its effectiveness. Gaps between subgroups should be examined to see if, for example, the process is culturally sensitive.
- **Disciplinary referrals and suspensions.** Just as integrating SEL strategies that support content objectives into lesson plans is expected to improve academic performance, the therapeutic ("hospital") disciplinary model is expected to minimize absenteeism and develop social-emotional deficiencies. If the research is accurate, this process should decrease recurring

undesired behaviors and improve self-esteem and belongingness. Over the long term, suspension recurrences should likewise decrease rather significantly.

- **External Interest.** There are ways as well to monitor parental and community involvement. For example, the school marketing plan can count visits to the website, demonstrating that there is increasing traffic or interest. Other indicators, such as PTO or PTA membership and attendance at meetings, athletic contests, and annual events, can reflect increasing interest on the part of external stakeholders, as well. Most of this can be reduced to common sense and human nature: If adults feel invited and welcomed, and if they see the great things the school is doing, they will want to come to events.

The Field of Dreams *Metaphor*

Before and perhaps after reading the remainder of this text, the leader should watch the 1999 blockbuster film *Field of Dreams*, a movie that has so many great lessons for this concept. Motivation (or calling) and vision are provided by a whispering voice at first heard only by main character Ray Kinsella. While the source of the voice is unclear, it offers three bits of advice throughout the movie, advice that at times makes Kinsella seem a bit crazy to others. An outsider facing the daunting task of learning to farm in a community that has done it only one way for decades, Kinsella soon comes to understand that he has a different purpose.

"If you build it, he will come," whispers the disembodied voice on the first occasion Kinsella hears it.[1] Life takes us many places, and it becomes clear that circumstances landed Kinsella on a farm in the middle of the nation's heartland before he heard his calling, forcing him to choose between what he must do to survive and what he must do to live. For educational leaders, as for Kinsella, the voice offers its lessons, especially for one determined to start meeting the needs of every child in his or her school. "He" (from the quote) is at first unidentifiable to Kinsella, but for the teacher or other school staffer, it could represent the traumatized child, a lost and wounded soul searching for a place where his dreams can come true. Kinsella even tells his wife, "I never did one spontaneous thing in my life,"[2] summoning the courage to follow the directives this voice was suggesting. To an educator, answering a calling is hardly spontaneous, but his decision required courage and conviction, requirements for all transformational leaders. Kinsella plows his crop under to build the field, criticized by the townspeople who mock the newcomer's antics. But Kinsella sees the sacrifice as potentially more important than corn, because there is more to life than feeding the stomach with bland grain year after year. He knew it would be risky and there would be doubters, but the calling and the vision were stronger, growing louder in his head. Although there were times he doubted himself, he believed that the greater good would be served; he just did not know how or for whom. Principals do. In education, how often do leaders follow the wisdom of their inner voice in lieu of the procedural, dogmatic, parroted chants of the status quo?

For the transformational school leader that is determined to meet the needs of the whole child, the voice and vision are what the first year is all about. It is all about becoming informed and developing the infrastructure and systems. He or she must convince the internal stakeholders (the real-life counterparts to Kinsella's wife and brother-in-law) to share the vision and trust decisions as you labor to help them see it. The leader must also educate the external stakeholders (in the film, the townspeople, Terrence Mann, the author and civil rights activist who has lost his dream), who are either blinded by habit or exhausted from championing a different cause; they have no faith in new, radical ideas. They are non-believers. But Kinsella follows his calling alone at first, knowing that others will gradually hear the voice or share the vision and rally to support the effort. Many things we now call genius were once thought of as lunacy, at least in part because they were radical thoughts and ideas that disrupted habit. There are many reasons the traumatized child (for our purposes, the real-world version of the inspiration for Kinsella's actions) needs advocacy. "He" needs someone with the vision and courage to set a radical new course, even at the risk of failure. Frankly, the skeptics and protectors of routine are the reason "he" needs a "field of dreams." It seems most people find their lives unsatisfying but lack the guts to do something about it. Instead, they go to the movies and urge protagonists to do the things they would never do. That is rather sad, but it does not have to be the case.

"Ease his pain."[3] Just when Kinsella thinks he has honored his vision and appeased his inner voice, the voice returns and calls on him to take further action. So too the leader needs to realize that there is more to this program than building the foundation. Unsure of what this new message means or how to do it, Kinsella travels to see the writer Terrence Mann and then on to find Archie "Moonlight" Graham, a former baseball player who has become an old physician. Graham, referring to the small town where he lives and where he discovered his true calling, tells Kinsella, "This is my most special place in all the world. Once a place touches you like that, the wind never blows so cold again."[4] Graham surprises Kinsella, who had assumed that Graham spent a lifetime considering himself a failure because he did not realize his dream of facing a major league pitcher. Instead, he answered his own voice and became a doctor in the place he belongs. Later, when the magic of the Iowa baseball field extends an opportunity for a younger, cockier version of Archibald Graham to face that major league pitcher, the fantasy is interrupted by a choking child in the makeshift bleachers. Graham, being true to himself and making the ultimate sacrifice for a child in need, steps out of his fantasy and into reality. As Kinsella realizes that his calling is not farming, Graham demonstrates why his calling was not baseball. He saves the child and disappears. One might recall his words earlier in the film when he prophetically explains to Kinsella, "You know we just don't recognize the most significant moments of our lives while they're happening. Back then I thought, well, there'll be other days. I didn't realize that that was the only day."[5]

How many children are we going to lose before someone summons the courage to step out of their illusions and into the realities facing today's child—to do something to "ease his pain"? Year two is a process of reflection and tweaking, continued training and celebrating in the successes that are already noticeable. "Trauma-informed" becomes "trauma-responsive," and all teachers and support staff are fully trained in social-emotional learning and the systems of support surrounding the child. It is the year in which all teachers should be on board and everyone understands not only their spheres of influence but what colleagues have to offer. In the movie, Terrence Mann (played by James Earl Jones) reluctantly commits to Kinsella's seeming crazy odyssey when he admits that he hears the voice too and agrees to travel back to Iowa with him. In Iowa, after Graham helps the choking child, Ray's brother-in-law (awkwardly, also the banker holding the farm mortgage), who has been trying to convince Kinsella to sell the farm to avoid foreclosure, suddenly sees the players on the field, finally sharing his vision. Instantly, the brother-in-law sees the reward over the risk for the first time, and changes his previously skeptical position. Some have to see the evidence before buying-in, so his late arrival to the party is understandable. It should be noted that the only child in the movie, Ray's daughter, Karin, has always seen the "field of dreams" and the magical ghosts that playfully dance atop the blades of grass every evening. Children are all about dreams and fantasy, which is a quality adults seem to lose. Once Kinsella's calling and vision are understood by his internal and external stakeholders, everyone starts believing in the cause. In the same way, while year one of the transformation to a trauma-sensitive culture is focused on sharing the vision, developing the network, and training the staff, year two should bring the awakening, when all stakeholders stop thinking the leadership is crazy and start wanting to become a part of the movement.

On a side note, the image of a doctor smacking a child on the back to dislodge a hot dog can be useful metaphorically, since in a sense it illustrates the therapeutic or hospital approach to whole-child development. Figuratively, adults feed the child something that has no nutritional value and she chokes on it. As she is choking, the adults, including those who fed her the hot dog, stand helplessly watching without taking action. They are powerless because they do not know how to help. Perhaps they might blame the child for not chewing the hot dog as they told her to do. Who knows? They do not appear to understand why she is choking, even though they gave her the hot dog and half of it is lying next to her on the ground as she gasps for air. There is one person who understands because he is trained to address the central problem and not react to the symptoms. He steps out of the past and into the challenges facing the children during the moment. In doing so, he honors the voice that guided him into the medical profession and off the diamond so many years ago. He has lived a life of no regrets, demonstrated by the fact that he is given a second chance and makes the same choice. Graham becomes the child's hero, taking action that earns the respect of everyone present and confirming his decades-old decision to follow his calling. As Graham explains to Kinsella, "We just don't realize the most significant moments of our lives while they are happening."[6]

"Go the Distance," the last directive issued by the persistent and seemingly difficult to satisfy voice in Kinsella's head, is applicable to the theme for the third year of the trauma-sensitive, social-emotional learning school. The third year is when the school transitions from a trauma-informed and trauma-responsive school into one that is trauma-sensitive. What appears to be a wild goose chase in the beginning becomes a fulfilling journey of discovery, one that in the film might be represented by Kinsella's reunion with his deceased father. Kinsella's journey, thought to be one of sacrifices for others so they could fulfill their fantasies and dreams, ironically makes him whole. He finds peace and closure with his father, burying the guilt and misunderstanding of a lifetime, during a simple game of catch. In going "the distance," leaders extend whole-child approaches to whole-school strategies, which leads to a realization of the kinds of idealistic goals most educators have upon entering the profession. There are few professions like education, and in particular educational leadership, where the only way to become whole is to support and build the capacity of others to fulfill their obligation to children. It is pure servant leadership. The smallest gestures, like playing catch with a child or complimenting a new haircut, have the power to heal and mend beyond what most people realize. There is an inner child in each of us, the one whose voice is always leading us in the right direction. Once again, children have dreams that are more than "vain fantasy"; they are the fuel for motivation, hope, and growth.

Distance, a word that has been mentioned throughout the text of this book, now comes full circle, but seems to have a different meaning than before, yet one equally applicable. Earlier, the reference was to professional distancing, something educators do when results are not they had hoped and the gap between success and failure is determined to be the sole responsibility of the student. The gap between what was done and what could have been done is rarely considered. *Distance*, in this definition, is the removal of emotional consequences attributed to the custodial decisions that impact children. The only time distance is needed in education is during the process of reflection, when the individual objectively steps back to analyze what he or she could have done but did not. This is not to suggest that the solution is better teaching, but teaching is a factor. There are literally hundreds of potential variables that could have hindered the child, and the teacher needs to understand how he or she might have facilitated more effective relationships, climates, or supportive resources, for example. Leaders must distance themselves not from what are hired to do, which is to develop every child, but from the ego, bias, and naiveté that stunts objective reflection. The student should never accept blame for failure without the person hired to make that child successful shouldering at least an equal share. The distance here is an understanding that whole-child development requires whole-educator commitment. Essentially, healthy ethical codes require introspective honesty. In other words, "going the distance" means doing whatever it takes to make a child succeed, even if that child is afflicted by problems beyond the walls of the school. Imagine a hospital that did not go the distance with a patient brought into the emergency room after a tragic automobile accident. The hospital staff do not question the make of the vehicle or debate the rules of highway safety in the analysis of the patient; they get to work and save the patient. There is no gap between what they could do and what they do, regardless of the outcome. Imagine how the patient's family might feel if the doctors could not save the patient but blamed him for not being a good driver or for not having the right blood type. *Distance* in that case would be a form of depersonalization and denial. It would be malpractice—and it happens in schools every day.

While some readers might expect this book to provide an elaborate timeline for the transition to trauma sensitivity, that is up to the leadership and must be based on individual circumstances. There are no recipes or blueprints that solve all problems, which is why schools need to be governed by municipalities. However, there are some commonalities between schools, and it might be instructive to look again at *Field of Dreams*. To summarize:

1. **Year one: "If you build it, he will come."** In this case, consider "he" to be a reference to today's student, especially the traumatized child in

need of a whole-child, social-emotional, trauma-sensitive culture where learning is based on brain research and a thorough understanding of things that inhibit learning, not blind tradition or unchallenged assumptions. Build it, train the staff, empower the leaders, and make use of the data. Share the vision and develop the plan, two things Kinsella did not do. But, like Kinsella, listen to the voice and trust it. In terms of the sheepdog leadership style discussed in chapter 7, this is the act of beginning the journey, monitoring the sheep, allowing for some to lead, but standing behind the group to make sure everyone is heading in the right direction and staying together. Going the wrong way or allowing for cliques to form that cause the sheep to move in multiple directions is not advisable. Staff education, training, role definitions, TSSEL committees, parent and community education, assessment and disciplinary models, the marketing plan, and SEL pedagogical development are areas that one might consider in year one.

2. **Year two: "Ease his pain."** After a year of growing pains, this quote is applicable to the school leader as well as the child, but let's focus on the child. Year one, although probably awkward at times, should have developed the strategic teams, roles, and expectations. In addition, it should have provided data that can lead to growth. It may have been fraught with experimentation, coaching, training, and even resistance. There will be favorable results if there is a sincere effort, but these results are not indicative of what the trauma-sensitive school can become. Year two is launched with a more concrete, experienced, strategic, whole-school strategy, where staff members are more empowered and interactive. It is the year the program needs to be tweaked, personnel need to be strategically positioned and developed, and new people need to be trained. Systems of support for teachers and staffers need to be put in place, if that has not already been done. They, like the children, are probably sensing a greater sense of duty and purpose because they work in a positive place where great things are on the horizon. They have seen powerful glimpses of how the school eases pain, and with a year of staff development that coincides with a year of trial and error, they are ready to focus less on their own development and more on the development of the child, whose pain is now something the school is qualified to address.

3. **Year three: "Go the distance."** In the third year of transition, it is time to develop long-term goals and expand resources and opportunities for increased involvement and leadership. Reflect, refine, and celebrate the results, but become a leader in the area of trauma sensitivity and social-emotional development. To inform long-term goals, measures should be put in place to gauge the number of students

exiting the program. Ideally, once the school demonstrates success, you can also expand the program into the community. Help other schools in the attendance district, youth league coaches, scout leaders, parents, day care workers, and others to develop the skills that now have yielded results. Invite clergy, lawmakers, state educational leaders into the school for town halls and roundtables. You have served the children in your building, and you have served the community. Become a model school or school system, providing an example that others will follow. Consider the long-term impact on the child and strive to make things better beyond the child's time in the school. Lead the movement and start helping others save their children. Develop a long-range plan with goals and a new vision to maintain and develop what has been established.

Raising Test Scores

While there are many reasons to implement the TSSEL program designed to develop the whole child, there are few if any reasons to wait to implement it. Aside from training and a few resources (such as a uniform assessment process), the program is relatively inexpensive, well worth the investment of time and money. In 2008, a mega-study that involved nearly 325,000 students determined that test scores for elementary and middle school students increased between 11 and 17 percent, leading the authors of this study to conclude that "SEL programs appear to be among the most successful youth-development interventions ever offered to K-8 students."[7] While SEL programs continue to boost test scores and academic performance, and to dramatically decrease suspension and expulsion rates, that is an expectation more than a goal. The SEL and trauma-sensitive cultures target results that are permanent. In 2011, a team of researchers concluded that there were substantial, positive correlations across the board after schools implemented SEL strategies in all three of the key areas measured: attendance, behavior, and academic performance. In 2017, CASEL provided results from a meta-study at 82 sites that included 97,000 children, concluding that "3.5 years after the last intervention the academic performance of students exposed to SEL programs was an average 13 percentile points higher than their non–SEL peers, based on … eight studies that measured academic performance."[8] Note that this information reflects lasting, permanent improvement in academics alone. That suggests that the learning is social, experiential, and intrinsic, unlike the drill-and-practice methods that yield only short-term retention. Some teachers resort to the latter when they feel the pressure that comes with standardized testing. Imagine a program that reassures them that the test scores will come naturally if they adopt a few simple methods. According to the meta-study, attendance and behavior in SEL populations are also improved when compared to non–SEL groups: "At other follow-up periods, conduct problems, emotional distress, and drug use were all significantly lower for students exposed to SEL programs, and development of social and emotional skills and positive attitudes toward self, others, and school was higher."[9] The program suggested in this book combines two strategies that have led to similar results when applied separately. Trauma sensitivity is focused on educator awareness that develops empathetic approaches to learning, discipline, and assessment, while social-emotional learning strategies involve cultivating emotional intellingences needed for resiliency. While trauma-sensitive schools are more focused on overcoming the effects of trauma, they too can boast that their programs increase academic performance and significantly reduce student suspensions.[10] But while both SEL and trauma-informed schools address deficiencies and build resiliency, only one of them informs teachers' sensitivity and motivates them to develop empathy and understanding. Trauma is one of the reasons to implement an SEL model, but not the only reason. The trauma-sensitive school culture develops children beyond the walls of the classroom and involves all stakeholders; social-emotional learning develops skill sets that are also important in establishing resiliency.

The research suggests that there are strong "teeter-totter" effects related to the some of the data mentioned here. When suspensions decrease, for example, assessment scores improve. Traditionally, support staff and some teachers who do not offer instruction in tested areas have been of the mindset that they have nothing to do with end-of-year examination data, which is probably the most significant indicator of success. That is not the case in the trauma-sensitive school, where everyone plays a role because the focus is on meeting needs through social-emotional learning and awareness, which are intermingled with the taught curriculum. For example, the bus driver might compliment a child who exits the bus in the morning. The custodian greets him and the teacher gives him a knuckle bump at the door. Before he enters the classroom, the baggage he brings, whatever it is, has been lightened or eliminated. That child is much more likely to be engaged and confident than a child who has been ignored, barked at, and threatened before arriving. Not only do these small gestures increase engagement in the classroom, they are contagious. And they cost nothing. In addition, they can replace rejection and anger with a sense of belonging that is tremendously therapeutic for a child. Of course that child learns more and acts out less. If a teacher's greeting at the door can increase engagement 20 percent, then there is a connection between "Have a nice day, Brad!" and academic achievement. Brad knows that he has options, people in the school to help him calmly overcome adversity. He is not tense in anticipation of the next confrontational adult. That means he is triggered less and may need to be disciplined less. This really is not rocket science. It is human nature and common sense.

Despite the best intentions of every adult in the school, there will be occasions when traumatic demons break through the perimeter of the school culture and find their victims. While the child's reaction is likely to be less severe in school than in other settings, that is not always the case. In school, the audience is usually larger and the embarrassment factor could magnify reactions. Inappropriate behavior is not what needs to be corrected; it is usually the child's reaction to what actually needs to be corrected. Punishing behavior issues without proper intervention only increases the levels of frustration, which leads to recurrence much more often than to reformed behavior. In the TSSEL culture, the student is sent to ISS, where the coordinator greets him. This new form of ISS is not where students are placed in solitary confinement as before; it is a place where they are given individual attention such as counseling, developmental resources, and a voice. The object is to return the student to the classroom as soon as possible. Since being in class tends to improve academic achievement, it is logical to credit the ISS coordinator, the counselor, the social worker, and the media specialist for doing their part to improve the test scores of this particular student. Traditionally, a student with behavior issues is given an out-of-school suspension that serves no productive purpose beyond punishing and labeling him as either unworthy or unable to function in public. He returns three days behind the others, lacking the motivation to close that gap. There is no attempt to repair the child, simply an order to contain undisciplined reactions that cause disturbances or endanger others. So while other schools may have stronger disciplinary policies, they also have many broken children taking the standardized tests. It is cyclical nonsense—time and energy dedicated to negative energies that do not build, they destroy.

Instead, the school should be asking, "How can we help you overcome the trauma that is related to your undesired behavior?" The objective is still to create a safe, orderly environment, but some attempt to therapeutically address the central problem has always been more effective than punishing the symptoms. Since the school rarely asks this question, the student returns in three days, along with the other rejected children coming off suspension, more confused than before (over the missed time and content), and an overwhelming shadow of doubt. It is a sadistic, cruel joke, one that often leads to a literal punch line at home, one that might be the biggest problem in education. Once the staff and administrators learn how to develop the whole child using the content and the culture, test scores will increase.

Relationships are much more important than content acquisition. While measuring whole-child development with test scores is ludicrous to some, there is a correlation between the scores and whole-child development that should be respected. This in no way suggests that the reason for developing the child is to get test scores up; however, better scores are a side effect that will appease the people who need bar charts and line graphs to justify their positions. But the school administrator that allows the tests to run the school, that piles resources into the tested areas while starving the arts or courses that stimulate personal interests in the students, is on a fool's errand. Remember, the school was not built so that administrators could have jobs. Tests are not administered so that leaders can bend rules and slide through loopholes. Manipulating the educational system for such purposes is not what develops children into self-actualized adults. It could be what keeps them from becoming so, however. If any educator feels a need to put his or her thumb on the scales to distort assessment figures in order to get another contract, it is possible they heard the wrong calling.

The program described in this book, however, generates better results than all of the shell games and clever card tricks combined. When attitudes, attendance, and awareness are up, test scores follow. When disciplinary referrals go down, everyone begins to see the field of dreams. Instead of weaponizing the curriculum, build the village. So if the best way to improve those sacred test scores is not practicing and drilling, could it be that focusing only on certain classes, subgroups, and those with the most growth potential is not as effective as we thought? One teacher in a content area can do only so much, especially if the child has to run the gauntlet before coming to class every day or is constantly catching up after suspensions. Everyone in the school affects attendance in positive or negative ways. Everyone in the school helps or hinders in developing a sense of belongingness and self-esteem. Everyone encourages or discourages student engagement, even after the teacher closes the door and the children disappear. Everyone in the school has some impact on the number of teacher referrals and suspensions. The difference between what an educator is willing to do and what he or she is able to do is the gap leaders should target. Imagine the impact of an entire school going above and beyond the job descriptions to help children overcome trauma and become self-actualized adults. That is the measure of a great teacher, great school, and great leadership. All it takes is some training and a determination to make the biggest impact possible on a child's life.

The Marketing Plan

While the field of dreams in the film seemed to need no marketing plan before the masses jumped into their cars and headed toward its soothing, fantastical blades of grass, the TSSEL school will need to market its magic to an indifferent or even skeptical public. The school will at first struggle to shed its reputation or convince the public that this latest approach to education is better than the rest. A reputation, like a culture, is a challenge to change. The school marketing plan attracts attention to the program that everyone has labored so diligently to build. It is a chest-pounding, self-promoting, people-recruiting, pride-instilling, aesthetically pleasing, data-supported celebration of all that makes the school unique. Educational leaders need positive publicity to encourage support on all levels, and the marketing plan is the preferred window into the heart of the school.

Public schools are fighting for their lives in this age of choice. Students want to attend the best schools, and their parents want them to, as well. The marketing plan should inform all stakeholders about the TSSEL concept through data, testimonials, and other celebrations that help outsiders share the vision as it is actualized. Teachers in search of a place to work should be able to view the marketing plan and understand what kind of instructors thrive in the trauma-sensitive culture. And do not underestimate the importance of the marketing plan on teacher retention.

Often the school's reputation is the reason the transformation to a TSSEL model is needed, but it will not change the minute the program is launched; reputations can take time to overcome. Therefore, people need to know what the school is about, how things are going to change for the better. The school marketing plan, then, is something that needs more attention. What follow are suggestions, a couple of which overlap with those in an article by Erin Balsa:[11]

- **Promote the school's niche.** This should be obvious. The first step is to promote the TSSEL concept and why it is needed. These reasons need to be not only spoken about but shown. Present pie charts and line graphs, for instance, that depict the data behind the research. Focus on the expected outcomes that are relevant to outsiders, such as expected graduation rates and improved self-awareness. If the administrator has data that identifies parental and community concerns, review strategies that might address them.
- **Build the brand.** A brand is a visual or a concept that briefly demonstrates what sets the school apart. In the TSSEL school, this should not be difficult. However, the challenge for the school

marketing TSSEL committee will be to create a brief, interactive program that promotes the vision of the school so thoroughly that any reference to the school triggers in stakeholders an instantaneous, positive association with that vision. A parent might think of whole-child development and its increased likelihood of college admission, while a prospective student might envision a collaborative, fun place where "everybody knows your name." Staff members might swell with pride and start thinking of ways to improve the improvements. The first step is to identify what people currently think and then design a process that leads them to what they should be thinking. Remember that marketing is not about selling the school; it is about helping people see the qualities of the school that set it apart from others.

- **Prove it.** Using social media, embedded videos, blogs, student and parent testimonials, and other evidence that shows outsiders that the school has achieved, or soon will, all that you promise. Consider all aspects of the process—the need to see the purpose from every perspective is precisely why the professional learning committee is so critical—and how this might inspire them. For example, if you want to emphasize a whole-school culture, make sure videos feature a kind gesture from a cafeteria worker or a comment from a custodian and bus driver. Inclusion is important. In addition, make the presentation of evidence constructive and informative. Have the ISS coordinator, media specialist, counselor, social worker, resource officer, and a teacher explain the therapeutic or hospital intervention model by compiling clips of each person discussing it.

- **Reach out.** Placing the school marketing plan on the website and adopting the if-you-build-it-they-will-come attitude is limited thinking. Imagine what companies do after creating a commercial. They target audiences, decide what media outlets will be used, select effective timing strategies, and so forth. The PLC may want to consider electronic strategies to spread the word—whether it's emailing the link, creating a Facebook page, or setting up audio-visual booths at community festivals. Perhaps the local public access television station will play video documentaries or a radio station will donate a few free 30-second commercials.

- **Become spokespeople.** The most effective means of promoting is through word of mouth. When word starts getting out, people will be curious. Staff members are also part of the community, and people are going to ask them about this new approach to educating their children. An uninformed or negative staff member testimonial is problematic, but a positive response will generate interest and create an ally. One strategy is to have employees develop an elevator pitch, an honest statement about the school culture that can be delivered in approximately 30 seconds. Each employee can develop their own during a collaborative workshop, but all employees need to know that they might be approached at the grocery store, church, at ball games, and other gatherings, so a heartfelt, planned response might help them avoid being blindsided.

An Elevator Pitch

The trauma-sensitive school promotes a whole-child approach to education through the development of a supportive culture that includes all stakeholders, regardless of cultural, racial, or economic differences. It is a school for all children where the focus is not on grades and discipline but on a strategically designed curriculum enhanced through building resiliency and helping all students reach a state of self-actualization. It is a place of rigorous growth inspired by solid relationships, where critical thinking, creativity, and problem solving are mastered in a supportive, collaborative environment. Children from all walks of life have been extremely successful in every aspect of this model, but those who need it the most benefit the most. It is a school dedicated to removing the barriers and obstacles that impede learning so that all children reach academic, social, emotional, and psychological goals designed to help them become well-rounded, happy, successful adults. At the trauma-sensitive school, the whole staff understands trauma and is trained to handle it in an effective, productive, nurturing manner. Teachers know the brain science related to the learning process and how to overcome stressors that are known to hinder children. It teaches children how to love themselves and be confident, how to trust others, and the reasons they need to build supportive networks. It strengthens the relationships with the family and develops strong alliances with the community. Frankly, there are few schools like it right now, but once others start noticing the results, there will be more of them.

Reality

Most educators feel as if the profession is their calling, as if a voice like the one in *Field of Dreams* has summoned them to serve children. A state-mandated curriculum and teaching for test scores are no one's idea of a calling. Floating through a career filled with uneventful classrooms, numerous meetings and boring conferences until thirty years of service becomes as memorable as yesterday's bagged lunch does not means that the calling goes unheard. Some hear it but never answer. How tragic. The voice behind the calling is not that of a career counselor or hiring principal; it is and was always that of a child. Educators are lured toward it because they have the compassion and the self-confidence to know they can make a difference, like those few teachers who influenced us all when it mattered most. Taking a job as a teacher and putting up bulletin boards and classroom rules does not make you a hero. Most children do not need another adult boss, but they need an advocate. To answer the calling, one must embrace the challenge and work hard until there is no gap, no crevice of separation, between what could have been done and what was done. The process described in this book can turn a fragmented group of adults who once heard that voice call them into a group that dares to challenge norms, traditions, and antiquated, sacred logic. It takes calculated boldness, but it also may require that the sheepdog leader help the herd to stop long enough to become reacquainted with the voice. It is always calling. Perhaps the answer will put everyone back on the right path and re-energize the weary. There are so many children whose fates depend on that decision. "Go the distance."

The Last Word

"Parting is such sweet sorrow"
—*Romeo and Juliet*, 2.2.188

This book was inspired by my child self, the scared and battered little boy who had the presence of mind to make promises on behalf of the adult he would become. It is for the traumatized and voiceless children lost in a sea of reform efforts scanning the empty offing for an approaching rescue ship. It is for educators who are willing to change course to save the young faces held hostage by the bad habits of human history. It is to honor my little brother Freddie in a tribute characterized by remorse for not understanding how I could have saved him until now. I stood beside the others and watched him absorb the blame for reacting to a world not ready to understand its role in his demise. His face is the one I see, the personification of the masses he now represents. Today, I am no longer the onlooker, ignorant and weaponless against the invading armies that march into our homes, communities, and schools and make casualties of children. I now know how to defeat them, but cannot do it alone.

Throughout time, there have been people, real and fictional, with the courage and vision to challenge social injustice. History calls them heroes, but their contemporaries did not. Romeo and Juliet died in order to awaken Verona from its nightmare. Jesus and Abraham Lincoln were killed by those loyally committed to corrupt ideologies. Martin Luther King, Jr., and Gandhi were shot while peacefully campaigning for love and understanding for the oppressed. How many are going to be martyred for this cause? As a society, we will be barbaric until we learn to nurture, support, and cherish children. Someone should not have to die before we realize the obvious. We are products of the same system we must overcome, where blind tradition and calcified, faulty logic have been the bedrock of our philosophies for generations. We are all, in a sense, the "children of an idle brain" until we learn to challenge the things we were told to value without question. Only then will we have the mindset needed to save our children from the toxic and deadly effects of trauma that have been tolerated for much too long. To Freddie, "Good night, sweet prince." To everyone left, Shakespeare's *King John* offers this warning: "And oftentimes excusing of a fault / Doth make the fault the worse by the excuse" (4.2.30–31). No more excuses; it is time to act.

Chapter Notes

Chapter 1

1. Abrahm Maslow, *Motivation and personality* (New York: Harper & Row, 1970), xxii.

2. "What Is SEL?" Collaborative for Social and Emotional Learning (CASEL), accessed March 03, 2019, https://casel.org/what-is-sel/.

3. "What Is SEL?"

4. "National School Lunch Program (NSLP)," Food and Nutrition Service, December 19, 2018, accessed March 03, 2019, https://www.fns.usda.gov/nslp/national-school-lunch-program-nslp.

5. Jisung Park, "Temperature, Test Scores, and Human Capital Production," *Harvard Education*, February 26. 2017, accessed December 02, 2018, http://scholar.harvard.edu/files/jisungpark/files/temperature_test_scores_and_human_capital_production_-_j_park_-_2-26-17.pdf.

6. Zoe Greenberg, "Is the 'Heat Day' the New Snow Day?" *New York Times*, September 06, 2018, A25.

7. Melissa Allen Heath, Katherine Ryan, Brenda Dean, and Rebecka Bingham, "History of School Safety and Psychological First Aid for Children," *Brief Treatment and Crisis Intervention* 7, no. 3 (August 2007): 206–23, https://doi:10.1093/brief-treatment/mhm011.

8. Madeline, "Bronfenbrenner's Bioecological Model of Development (Bronfenbrenner)," Learning Theories, May 15, 2017, https://www.learning-theories.com/bronfenbrenners-bioecological-model-bronfenbrenner.html.

9. "10 Components of a Successful Education Marketing Plan (Part 1)," Caylor Solutions, February 1, 2018, https://www.caylor-solutions.com/10-components-education-marketing-plan-part-1/.

Chapter 2

1. "America's Children: Key National Indicators of Well-Being, 2017," Table POP1, Childstats.gov, accessed March 08, 2019, https://www.childstats.gov/americaschildren/tables/pop1.asp.

2. *Child Maltreatment 2014*, report issued by the Children's Bureau, Administration for Children and Families, accessed March 08, 2019, https://www.acf.hhs.gov/cb/resource/child-maltreatment-2014.

3. Julie Crandall, "Poll: Most Approve of Spanking Kids," ABC News, November 08, 2018, accessed March 08, 2019, https://abcnews.go.com/U.S./story?id=90406&page=1.

4. Nicholas Yoder, "Teaching the Whole Child Instructional Practices That Support Social-Emotional Learning in Three Teacher Evaluation Frameworks," Center on Great Teachers and Leaders, January 2014, accessed March 06, 2019, https://gtlcenter.org/sites/default/files/TeachingtheWholeChild.pdf.

5. Ron Haskins, Janet Currie, and Lawrence M. Berger, "Can States Improve Children's Health by Preventing Abuse and Neglect?" *The Future of Children* 25, no. 1 (Spring 2015): 1–8.

6. Xiangming Fang, Derek S. Brown, Curtis S. Florence, and James A. Mercy, "The Economic Burden of Child Maltreatment in the United States and Implications for Prevention," *Child Abuse & Neglect* 36, no. 2 (February 2012): 156–65, accessed January 01, 2019, https://doi.org/10.1016/j.chiabu.2011.10.006.

7. U.S. Department of Health and Human Services, *Child Maltreatment 2012*, accessed June 3, 2020, http://www.acf.hhs.gov/sites/default/files/cb/cm2012.pdf.

8. Bill Press, "Bush Cuts Children's Health to Pay for Tax Cut," CNN, April 06, 2001, accessed March 08, 2018, http://edition.cnn.com/2001/ALLPOLITICS/04/06/press.column/.

9. "Child Abuse Stories." Child Abuse Stories. May 07, 2012. Accessed March 08, 2019. http://www.childabusestories.org/factss/2005-2009-congress-cut-federal-funding-states-treat-and-protect-abused-and-neglected-children.

10. Vincent J. Felitti et al., "Relationship of Childhood Abuse and Household Dysfunction to Many of the Leading Causes of Death in Adults," *American Journal of Preventive Medicine* 14, no. 4 (May 1998): 245–58, https://doi.org/10.1016/S0749-3797(98)00017-8.

11. Centers for Disease Control and Prevention, "Adverse Childhood Experiences (ACEs)," April 01, 2016, accessed March 08, 2019, https://www.cdc.gov/violenceprevention/childabuseandneglect/acestudy/index.html?CDC_AA_refVal=https://www.cdc.gov/violenceprevention/acestudy/index.html.

12. Centers for Disease Control and Prevention, "Adverse Childhood Experiences."

13. Felitti et al., "Relationship of Childhood Abuse and Household Dysfunction to Many of the Leading Causes of Death in Adults."

Chapter 3

1. Centers for Disease Control and Prevention, "Adverse Childhood Experiences."

2. Centers for Disease Control and Prevention, "About the CDC-Kaiser ACE Study Error Processing SSI File," June 14, 2016. Accessed March 22, 2019, https://www.cdc.gov/violenceprevention/childabuseandneglect/acestudy/about.html.

3. "Few Consider Spanking Child Abuse." Rasmussen Reports, November 15, 2018, accessed March 22, 2019, http://www.rasmussenreports.com/public_content/lifestyle/general_lifestyle/november_2018/few_consider_spanking_child_abuse.

4. Joan Durrant and Ron Ensom, "Physical Punishment of Children: Lessons from 20 Years of Research," *CMAJ* 184, no. 12 (September 2012): 1373–1377, accessed March 08, 2019, http://www.cmaj.ca/content/184/12/1373.

5. Tracie O. Afifi et al., "Spanking and Adult Mental Health Impairment: The Case for the Designation of Spanking as an Adverse Childhood Experience," *Child Abuse & Neglect* 71 (September 2017): 24–31, https://doi.org/10.1016/j.chiabu.2017.01.014.

6. Afifi et al., "Spanking and Adult Mental Health Impairment."

7. "Anti-Bullying Help, Facts, and More," Bullying Statistics, accessed March 09, 2019. http://www.bullyingstatistics.org/.

8. "Bullying Statistics," National Bullying Prevention Center, updated May 2020, https://www.pacer.org/bullying/resources/stats.asp.

9. "Students with Disabilities and Bullying," National Bullying Prevention Center, accessed September 8, 2020, https://www.pacer.org/bullying/resources/students-with-disabilities/.

10. "Bullying Statistics," National Bullying Prevention Center, updated May 2020, https://www.pacer.org/bullying/resources/stats.asp.

11. Stacey Colino, "Bully-Proof Your Child: How to Deal with Bullies," Parents.com, accessed December 11, 2017, https://www.parents.com/kids/problems/bullying/bully-proof-your-child-how-to-deal-with-bullies/.

12. Karen M. Pert, "Bullying-Suicide Link Explored in New Study by Researchers at Yale," *Yale News*, December 21, 2017, accessed December 11, 2017, https://news.yale.edu/2008/07/16/bullying-suicide-link-explored-new-study-researchers-yale.

13. National Center for Injury Prevention and Control, *The Relationship Between Bullying and Suicide: What We Know and What It Means for Schools*, a report published by the Centers for Disease Control and Prevention, April 2014.

14. Kate Baggaley, "How Being Bullied Affects Your Adulthood," Slate, June 20, 2016, https://slate.com/technology/2016/06/the-lasting-effects-of-childhood-bullying-are-surprisingly-not-all-detrimental-in-adulthood.html.

15. Bruce P. Dohrenwend, et al., "The Roles of Combat Exposure, Personal Vulnerability, and Involvement in Harm to Civilians or Prisoners in Vietnam-War-

Related Posttraumatics Stress Disorder," *Clinical Psychological Science*, 1, no. 3 (February 2013): 223–238.

16. Cindi May, "Bullies Hurt Themselves," *Scientific American*, April 16, 2013, accessed March 27, 2019, https://www.scientificamer ican.com/article/bullies-hurt-themselves/.

17. Joel Schwarz, "Violence in the Home Leads to High Rates of Childhood Bullying," UW News, September 12, 2006, https://www.washington.edu/news/2006/09/12/violence-in-the-home-leads-to-higher-rates-of-childhood-bullying/

18. Lori Soard, "Bullying Statistics," LoveToKnow.com, accessed December 12, 2017, https://teens.lovetoknow.com/Bully ing_Statistics.

18. Alan McEvoy, "Abuse of Power," *Teaching Tolerance* 48 (Fall 2014): 51–53, accessed December 12, 2017, https://www. tolerance. org/magazine/fall-2014/abuse-of-power.

19. Alan McEvoy, "Teachers Who Bully Students: Patterns and Policy Implications" (paper presented at the Hamilton Fish Institute's Persistently Safe Schools Conference, Philadelphia, September 11–14, 2005), accessed December 13, 2017, http://nospank.net/mcevoy.htm.

20. McEvoy, "Teachers Who Bully Students."

21. Betty Lai,"Helping Children Recover from the Trauma of Disaster," CNN.com, September 01, 2017, accessed November 22, 2018, https://www.cnn.com/2017/09/01/health/disasters-children-recover-trauma-partner/index.html.

Chapter 4

1. Bruce Perry, "Traumatized Children: How Childhood Trauma Influences Brain Development," *Journal of the California Alliance for the Mentally Ill* 11, no. 1 (2000): 48–51.

2. Bruce Perry, "Incubated in Terror: Neurodevelopmental Factors in the 'Cycle of Violence,'" in *Children in a Violent Society*, ed., J.D. Osofsky (New York: Guilford Press, 1997).

3. "Memory, Learning, and Emotion: The Hippocampus," PsychEducation.org, December 2014, accessed March 09, 2019, https://psycheducation.org/brain-tours/memory-learning-and-emotion-the-hippo campus/.

4. Bruce Perry and Ronnie Pollard, "Altered Brain Development Following Global Neglect in Early Childhood," *Society for Neuroscience: Proceedings from the Annual Meeting*, New Orleans. 1997.

5. Perry and Pollard, "Altered Brain Development Following Global Neglect in Early Childhood."

6. Peter Gray, "The Decline of Play and Rise in Children's Mental Disorders," *Freedom to Learn (blog)*, *Psychology Today*, January 26, 2010, accessed March 09, 2018, https://www.psychologytoday.com/us/blog/freedom-learn/ 201001/the-decline-play-and-rise-in-childrens-mental-disorders.

7. Jean M. Twenge, "Americans Reporting Increased Symptoms of Depression." NewsCenter, San Diego State University, September 30, 2014, accessed July 09, 2018, http://newscenter.sdsu.edu/sdsu_newscen ter/news_story.aspx?sid=75201.

8. "Dopamine," *Psychology Today*, accessed May 05, 2019, https://www.psy chologytoday.com/us/basics/dopamine.

9. Nadine Burke Harris, "How Childhood Trauma Affects Health Across a Lifetime," TED video, 2014, accessed May 05, 2019, https://www.ted.com/talks/nadine_ burke_harris_how_childhood_trauma_ affects_health_across_a_lifetime#t-430498.

10. I. Mavridis, "The Role of the Nucleus Accumbens in Psychiatric Disorders," *Psychiatrike*, October 25, 2015, accessed May 05, 2019, https://www.ncbi.nlm.nih.gov/pubmed/26709994.

11. Lindsey Layton, "Majority of U.S. Public School Students Are in Poverty," *Washington Post*, January 16, 2015, accessed June 09, 2019, https://www.washingtonpost. com/local/education/majority-of-us-public-school-students-are-in-poverty/2015/01/15/df7171d0–9ce9–11e4-a7ee-526210d665b4_ story.html?utm_term=.b24785fab703.

12. "Nearly Half of American Children Living Near Poverty Line," Columbia University, Mailman School of Public Health, March 02, 2016, accessed May 28, 2020, https://www.publichealth.columbia.edu/public-health-now/news/nearly-half-amer ican-children-living-near-poverty-line.

Chapter 5

1. Madeline, "Bronfenbrenner's Bioecological Model of Development," Learning

Theories, May 15, 2017, https://www.learning-theories.com/bronfenbrenners-bioecological-model-bronfenbrenner.html.

2. Dianne Franc, "How Does Religion Affect Parenting? Here Are the 3 Most Important Things You Should Know," Parent Herald, May 5, 2016, https://www.parentherald.com/articles/41487/20160505/religion-affects-parenting-here-3-important-things-know.htm.

3. Philip Greven, *Spare the Child: The Religious Roots of Punishment and the Psychological Impact of Physical Abuse* (New York: Knopf, 1991).

4. "Religion in America: U.S. Religious Data, Demographics and Statistics," Pew Research Center's Religion & Public Life Project, May 11, 2015, accessed March 17, 2019, http://www.pewforum.org/religious-landscape-study/.

5. "Religion in America."

6. "Religion in America."

7. "Religion in America."

8. "Religion in America."

9. "Religion in America."

Chapter 6

1. Tala Esmaili, "First Amendment," Legal Information Institute, Cornell Law School, accessed May 28, 2020, https://www.law.cornell.edu/constitution/first_amendment.

2. "Same-Sex Marriage Fast Facts," CNN.com, May 25, 2019, accessed June 3, 2020, https://www.cnn.com/2013/05/28/us/same-sex-marriage-fast-facts/index.html.

3. William Shakespeare, *The Merchant of Venice*, ed. Barbara A. Mowat and Paul Werstine (Washington: Folger Shakespeare Library, n.d), accessed September 17, 2020, https://shakespeare.folger.edu/shakespeares-works/the-merchant-of-venice),

4. Davison M. Douglas, "God and the Executioner: The Influence of Western Religion on the Use of the Death Penalt," *William & Mary Bill of Rights Journal*, 7th ser., 9, no. 1 (2000): 137–70, accessed December 24, 2017, https://scholarship.law.wm.edu/cgi/viewcontent.cgi?referer=https://www.google.com/&httpsredir=1&article=1373&context=wmborj.

5. Arthur J. Schlesinger, "Mark Twain, or the Ambiguities," *Atlantic* Monthly, August 01, 1966, accessed March 19, 2019, https://www.theatlantic.com/magazine/archive/1966/08/mark-twain-or-the-ambiguities/305730/.

6. Kristina Otterstrom, "The Legal Rights and Responsibilities of a Parent," Lawyers.com, accessed February 18, 2019, https://www.lawyers.com/legal-info/family-law/children/the-legal-rights-and-responsibilities-of-a-parent.html.

7. Valerie Tarico, "Does the Bible Sanction Child Abuse?" Salon.com, October 22, 2013, accessed December 07, 2018, https://www.salon.com/2013/10/23/does_the_bible_sanction_child_abuse_partner/.

8. "Child Abuse in North Carolina," Waypoint Legal, 2011, accessed January 19, 2019, http://www.waypointlegal.com/index.php/topics/view/child-abuse.

9. "Assault and Battery in North Carolina," Waypoint Legal, February 15, 2011, accessed March 19, 2019, https://www.waypointlegal.com/index.php/topics/view/assault-and-battery.

10. "Cruelty to Animals," NC Gen. Stat. §14-360, North Carolina General Assembly, accessed August 29, 2017, https://www.ncleg.gov/EnactedLegislation/Statutes/PDF/BySection/Chapter_14/GS_14-360.pdf.

11. "Petersen v. Rogers," Justia Law, July 29, 1994, accessed April 19, 2017, https://law.justia.com/cases/north-carolina/supreme-court/1994/427pa93-0.html.

12. "U.S. Supreme Court: Parents' Rights Are Fundamental (Review of Troxel v. Granville)," HSLDA, August 17, 2001, accessed March 19, 2019. https://hslda.org/content/docs/nche/000010/20011210.asp.

13. Emery P. Dalesio, "NC Supreme Court Weighs Corporal Punishment vs. Child Abuse," BlueRidgeNow.com, April 18, 2018, https://www.blueridgenow.com/news/20180418/nc-supreme-court-weighs-corporal-punishment-vs-child-abuse.

14. "14th Amendment," History.com, November 09, 2009, accessed January 19, 2019, https://www.history.com/topics/black-history/fourteenth-amendment.

15. "14th Amendment."

16. "Bill of Rights," Bill of Rights Institute, 2019, accessed March 19, 2019. https://billofrightsinstitute.org/founding-documents/bill-of-rights/.

17. "Child Abuse in the U.S.—Total Number of Reported Cases 1990–2010," Statista, accessed March 19, 2019, https://www.statista.com/statistics/203816/number-of-child-abuse-cases-in-the-us/.

18. "Convention on the Rights of the Child (CRC)," Global Initiative to End All Corporal Punishment of Children, 2018, accessed March 20, 2019, https://endcorporalpunishment. org/human-rights-law/crc/.

19. "Convention on the Rights of the Child (CRC)."

20. "Convention on the Rights of the Child," Office of the High Commissioner for Human Rights (HCHR), adopted September 2, 1990, accessed March 20, 2019, https://www.ohchr.org/EN/ProfessionalInterest/Pages/CRC.aspx.

21. Mark Edwards, "Was America Founded as a Christian Nation?" CNN. com, July 04, 2015, accessed June 20, 2018, https://www.cnn.com/2015/07/02/living/america-christian-nation/index.html.

22. Jonas Fredén, "Smacking Children Banned," Sweden.se, May 21, 2018, accessed August 12, 2018, https://sweden.se/society/smacking-banned-since-1979/.

23. "Compare the U.S. to Sweden," IfIt WereMyHome.com, accessed February 22, 2018, http://www.ifitweremyhome.com/compare/US/SE.

24. Carina Storrs, "Is Life Expectancy Reduced by a Traumatic Childhood?" *Scientific American*, October 07, 2009, accessed February 23, 2017, https://www.scientificamerican.com/article/childhood-adverse-event-life-expectancy-abuse-mortality/.

Chapter 7

1. "Charts Related to the Latest American Time Use Survey," U.S. Bureau of Labor Statistics, accessed March 27, 2019, https://www.bls.gov/charts/american-time-use/activity-by-parent.htm.

2. Amanda Litvinov, "Our Crumbling Public School Infrastructure," NEA Today, November 05, 2018, accessed February 02, 2019, http://neatoday.org/2018/10/30/our-crumbling-school-infrastructure/.

3. "School-Based Social and Emotional Instruction," What Works for Health, November 13, 2018, accessed March 27, 2019, http://whatworksforhealth.wisc.edu/program.php?t1=20&t2=2&t3=105&id=575.

4. Pamela Garner et al., "Promoting Desirable Outcomes among Culturally and Ethnically Diverse Children in Social Emotional Learning Programs: A Multilevel

Heuristic Model," *Educational Psychology* 26, no. 1 (January 25, 2014): 165–89.

5. Sarah Peterson, "Hurricane Resources," National Child Traumatic Stress Network, April 03, 2018, accessed March 28, 2019, https://www.nctsn.org/what-is-child-trauma/trauma-types/disasters/hurricane-resources.

6. Jessica Lander, "Helping Teachers Manage the Weight of Trauma," Harvard Graduate School of Education, September 26, 2018, accessed January 07, 2019, https://www.gse.harvard.edu/news/uk/18/09/helping-teachers-manage-weight-trauma.

Chapter 8

1. Joseph A. Durlak et al., "The Impact of Enhancing Students' Social and Emotional Learning: A Meta-Analysis of School-Based Universal Interventions," *Child Development* 82, no. 1 (February 2011): 405–432, accessed February 17, 2019, https://onlinelibrary.wiley.com/doi/pdf/10.1111/j.1467-8624.2010.01564.x

2. Dorothy L. Espelage et al., "Clinical Trial of Second Step Middle School Program: Impact on Bullying, Cyberbullying, Homophobic Teasing, and Sexual Harassment Perpetration," *School Psychology Review* 44, no. 4 (December 01, 2015): 464–79, https://doi.org/10.17105/spr-15-0052.1.

3. Roisin P. Corcoran et al., "Effective Universal School–based Social and Emotional Learning Programs for Improving Academic Achievement: A Systematic Review and Meta-Analysis of 50 Years of Research," *Educational Research Review* 25 (January/February 2011): 56–72, https://doi.org/10.1016/j.edurev.2017.12.001.

4. Cherif Boudaba et al., "Increased Tonic Activation of Presynaptic Metabotropic Glutamate Receptors in the Rat Supraoptic Nucleus following Chronic Dehydration," *Journal of Physiology* 551, no. 3 (July 16, 2004): 815–23, https://doi.org/10.1111/j.1469-7793.2003.00815.x.

5. David Benton and Stevens Megan, "The Influence of a Glucose Containing Drink on the Behavior of Children in School," *Biological Psychology* 78, no. 3 (July 2008): 242–45.

6. Betty Lai, "Helping Children Recover from the Trauma of Disaster," CNN.com, September 01, 2017, accessed November

22, 2018, https://www.cnn.com/2017/09/01/health/disasters-children-recover-trauma-partner/index.html.

7. Karyn Hall, "Create a Sense of Belonging," *Psychology Today* (blog), March 24, 2014, accessed February 02, 2019, https://www.psychologytoday.com/us/blog/pieces-mind/201403/ create-sense-belonging.

8. Gary Portnoy, "Where Everybody Knows Your Name" (theme song), *Cheers* (television program), 1983–1992.

9. Youki Terada, "Welcoming Students with a Smile," Edutopia, September 11, 2018, accessed January 11, 2019, https://www.edutopia.org/article/welcoming-students-smile.

10. Ernest Izard, *Teaching Children from Poverty and Trauma*, a report published by the National Education Association, June 2016, https://www.nea.org/assets/docs/20200_Poverty%20Handbook_flat.pdf.

11. "The Importance of Voice in Releasing Trauma," Yoga Calm, January 12, 2019, accessed March 27, 2019, https://www.yogacalm.org/the-importance-of-voice-in-releasing-trauma/.

12. Eric Jensen, *Teaching with Poverty in Mind: What Being Poor Does to Kids' Brains and What Schools Can Do About It* (Alexandria, VA: Association for Supervision & Curriculum Development, 2009).

13. R. Allan Allday and Kerri Pakurar, "Effects of Teacher Greetings on Student On-Task Behavior," *Journal of Applied Behavior Analysis* 40, no. 2 (summer 2007): 317–320, accessed March 27, 2019, https://www.ncbi.nlm.nih.gov/pmc/articles/PMC1885415/.

14. Graham Collier, "What Is the Effect of Music on the Listener?" *Psychology Today*, March 09, 2017, accessed February 11, 2019, https://www.psychologytoday.com/us/blog/the-consciousness-question/201703/what-is-the-effect-music-the-listener.

15. "Mind-Body Exercises to Calm Your Students When They're Stressed," WeAreTeachers, April 02, 2018, accessed March 27, 2019, https://www.weareteachers.com/mind-body-skills/.

16. Holly Matto, Jessica Strolin-Goltzman, and Michelle Ballan, eds., *Neuroscience for Social Work: Current Research and Practices* (New York: Springer, 2014).

17. Julie Crandall, "Poll: Most Approve of Spanking Kids," ABC News, accessed January 02, 2019, https://abcnews.go.com/U.S./story?id=90406&page=1.

18. "Learned Helplessness: Seligman's Theory of Depression (Cure)," Positive Psychology Program, August 23, 2018, https://positivepsychologyprogram.com/learned-helplessness-seligman-theory-depression-cure/.

19. Izard, *Teaching Children from Poverty and Trauma*.

20. *Impact of Student Choice and Personalized Learning*, a report from Hanover Research, 2014, https://www.gssaweb.org/wp-content/uploads/2015/04/Impact-of-Student-Choice-and-Personalized-Learning-1.pdf.

21. Izard, *Teaching Children from Poverty and Trauma*.

22. "Introduction and Frequently Asked Questions," Positive Behavioral Interventions and Supports (PBIS), accessed March 01, 2019, https://assets.website-files.com/5d3725188825e071f1670246/5d7bd792f-6de3210d90755a6_what%20is%20pbis%20q%26a%2030%20june%202018.pdf.

23. Alycia Ernst, "Self-disclosure as Therapy: The Benefits of Expressive Writing," MDedge Psychiatry, December 11, 2018, accessed March 28, 2019, https://www.mdedge.com/psychiatry/article/147848/self-disclosure-therapy-benefits-expressive-writing.

24. K.A. Baikie, L. Geerligs, and K. Wilhelm, "Expressive Writing and Positive Writing for Participants with Mood Disorders: An Online Randomized Controlled Trial," *Journal of Affective Disorders* 136, no. 3 (December 30, 2011): 310–319, accessed March 28, 2019, https://www.sciencedirect.com/science/article/pii/S016503271100749X.

25. Robert Coles and Margaret Sartor, *Their Eyes Meeting the World: The Drawings and Paintings of Children* (Boston: Houghton Mifflin, 1992).

26. "Expressive Drawing: An Interview with Robert Coles," telephone interview by author. May 21, 2005.

27. Jason S. Wrench et al. *Stand Up, Speak Out: The Practice and Ethics of Public Speaking* (Boston: FlatWorld, 2017).

Chapter 9

1. Michael Thomsen, "Get Rid of Grades," Slate, May 01, 2013, accessed March 11, 2019, https://slate.com/human-interest/2013/05/

the-case-against-grades-they-lower-self-esteem-discourage-creativity-and-reinforce-the-class-divide.html.

2. James Wiggins, Elizabeth Schatz, and Richard West, "The Relationship of Self-Esteem to Grades, Achievement Scores, and Other Factors Critical to School Success," *School Counselor* 41, no. 4 (1994): 239–244, accessed November 28, 2017, https://www.jstor.org/stable/23900414.

3. Cynthia Vinney, "Understanding Maslow's Theory of Self-Actualization," ThoughtCo., September 21, 2018, accessed February 28, 2018, https://www.thoughtco.com/maslow-theory-self-actualization-4169662.

4. Saul McLeod, "Maslow's Hierarchy of Needs," Simply Psychology, May 21, 2018, accessed June 28, 2018, https://www.simplypsychology.org/maslow.html.

5. Julia Jacobs, "When Report Cards Go Out on Fridays, Child Abuse Increases on Saturdays, Study Finds," *New York Times*, December 17, 2018, accessed March 28, 2019, https://www.nytimes.com/2018/12/17/health/child-abuse-report-cards-florida.html.

6. *Multi-Tier System of Supports (MTSS): Fact Sheet*, National Center for Learning Disabilities, February 2018, https://nceln.fpg.unc.edu/sites/nceln.fpg.unc.edu/files/resources/NCMTSSFactsheetpost.pdf.

Chapter 10

1. "Core SEL Competencies," Collaborative for Academic, Social and Emotional Learning (CASEL), 2019, accessed March 28, 2019, https://casel.org/core-competencies/.

2. Nicholas Yoder, *Teaching the Whole Child: Instructional Practices That Support Social and Emotional Learning in Three Teacher Evaluation Frameworks,* brief, American Institutes for Research Center on Great Teachers and Leaders, January 2014, accessed May 25, 2020, https://gtlcenter.org/sites/default/files/TeachingtheWholeChild.pdf.

3. Yoder, *Teaching the Whole Child.*

Chapter 11

1. Paul Gorski, "Unlearning Deficit Ideology and the Scornful Gaze: Thoughts on Authenticating the Class Discourse in Education." EdChange.org, December 2010, accessed May 25, 2020, http://www.edchange.org/publications/deficit-ideology-scornful-gaze.pdf.

2. Jane Nelsen and Kelly Gfroerer, *Positive Discipline Tools for Teachers: Effective Classroom Management for Social, Emotional, and Academic Success* (New York: Harmony Books, 2017).

3. Maura McInerney and Amy McKlindon, *Unlocking the Door to Learning: Trauma-Informed Classrooms & Transformational Schools,* Education Law Center, June 2015, accessed May 29, 2020, https://www.elc-pa.org/wp-content/uploads/2015/06/Trauma-Informed-in-Schools-Classrooms-FINAL-December2014-2.pdf.

4. Jessica Swain-Bradway et al., *What Are the Economic Costs of Implementing SWPBIS in Comparison to the Benefits from Reducing Suspensions?,* a brief, U.S. Department of Education, Office of Special Education Programs (OSEP), November 2017, accessed June 3, 2020, https://assets.website-files.com/5d3725188825e071f1670246/5d76c00cb9339d5f3f267ee7_economiccostsswpbis.pdf.

Chapter 12

1. Audry Breen, "UVA Research Finds Suspending Students, in or out of School, Is Problematic," UVA Today, October 12, 2017, https://news.virginia.edu/content/uva-research-finds-suspending-students-or-out-school-problematic.

2. "How School Suspensions Affect Student Achievement," FutureEd, September 19, 2018, https://www.future-ed.org/how-school-suspensions-affect-student-achievement/.

3. "School Bus," Amalgamated Transit Union, accessed May 24, 2019, https://www.atu.org/work/school.

4. Sherri Gordon, "Both Parents and Students Can Prevent Bullying on School Buses," Verywell Family, accessed April 27, 2019, https://www.verywellfamily.com/how-to-make-school-buses-bully-proof-460731.

5. "Trauma-Sensitive School Training Package," National Center on Safe Supportive Learning Environments, accessed May 28, 2020, https://safesupportivelearning.ed.gov/trauma-sensitive-schools-training-package.

6. Tina Nazerian, "'Rocket Fuel': How Schools Can Create a Positive, SEL-Friendly School Culture," EdSurge, June 11, 2018, accessed December 27, 2018, https://www.edsurge.com/news/2018-06-11-rocket-fuel-how-schools-can-create-a-positive-sel-friendly-school-culture.

7. "What Are the Differences Between a School Counselor and a School Social Worker?" OnlineEducation.com, accessed May 28, 2020, https://www.onlineeducation.com/counseling/faqs/school-counselor-vs-school-social-worker.

8. "Shortages in School Psychology: Challenges to Meeting the Growing Needs of U.S. Students and Schools," research summary, National Association of School Psychologists, 2017, accessed May 28, 2020, https://www.nasponline.org/Documents/Resources%20and%20publications/Resources/School_Psychology_Shortage_2017.pdf.

9. Jennifer Crocker, "Self-Esteem That's Based on External Sources Has Mental Health Consequences, Study Says," *Monitor on Psychology* 33, no. 11 (December 2002): 16, accessed May 28, 2020, https://www.apa.org/monitor/dec02/selfesteem.

Chapter 13

1. *Field of Dreams* (1989), DVD, directed by Phil Alden Robinson (Universal City, CA: Universal Pictures, 1998).

2. *Field of Dreams.*

3. *Field of Dreams.*

4. *Field of Dreams.*

5. *Field of Dreams.*

6. *Field of Dreams.*

7. John Payton et al., *The Positive Impact of Social-Emotional Learning for Kindergarten through Eighth Grade Students*, executive summary (Chicago: Collaborative for Academic, Social, and Emotional Learning, 2018), accessed May 28, 2020, https://www.casel.org/wp-content/uploads/2016/08/PDF-4-the-positive-impact-of-social-and-emotional-learning-for-kindergarten-to-eighth-grade-students-executive-summary.pdf.

8. "2017 Meta-Analysis," CASEL, July 2017, accessed May 28, 2020, https://casel.org/2017-meta-analysis/. The full article: Rebecca D. Taylor et al., "Promoting Positive Youth Development Through School-Based Social and Emotional Learning Interventions: A Meta-Analysis of Follow-Up Effects," *Child Development* 88, no. 4 (July/August 2017): 1156–1171.

9. "2017 Meta-Analysis."

10. Sandra Bloom and Sarah Sreedhar, "The Sanctuary Model of Trauma-Informed Organizational Change," *Reclaiming Children and Youth* 17, no. 3 (Fall 2008): 53.

11. Erin Balsa, "5 Marketing Strategies for Schools in the Age of School Choice," School Leaders Now, May 14, 2018, accessed May 28, 2020, https://schoolleadersnow.weareteachers.com/school-marketing-strategies/.

Bibliography

"About the CDC-Kaiser ACE Study Error Processing SSI File." 2016. Centers for Disease Control and Prevention. June 14, 2016. Accessed March 22, 2019. https://www.cdc.gov/violenceprevention/childabuseandneglect/acestudy/about.html.

"Adverse Childhood Experiences (ACEs)." Centers for Disease Control and Prevention. April 01, 2016. Accessed March 08, 2019. https://www.cdc.gov/violenceprevention/childabuseandneglect/acestudy/index.html?CDC_AA_refVal=https://www.cdc.gov/violenceprevention/acestudy/index.html.

Afifi, Tracie O., Derek Ford, Elizabeth T. Gershoff, Melissa Merrick, Andrew Grogan-Kaylor, Katie A. Ports, Harriet L. Macmillan, George W. Holden, Catherine A. Taylor, Shawna J. Lee, and Robbyn Peters Bennett. "Spanking and Adult Mental Health Impairment: The Case for the Designation of Spanking as an Adverse Childhood Experience." *Child Abuse & Neglect* 71 (September 2017): 24–31. https://doi.org/10.1016/j.chiabu.2017.01.014.

Allday, R. Allan, and Kerri Pakurar. "Effects of Teacher Greetings on Student On-task Behavior." *Journal of Applied Behavior Analysis* 40, no. 2 (summer 2007): 317–320. Accessed March 27, 2019. https://www.ncbi.nlm.nih.gov/pmc/articles/PMC1885415/.

"America's Children: Key National Indicators of Well-Being, 2017." Table POP 1. Accessed March 08, 2019. https://www.childstats.gov/americaschildren/tables/pop1.asp.

"Anti-Bullying Help, Facts, and More." Bullying Statistics. Accessed March 09, 2019. http://www.bullyingstatistics.org/.

"Assault and Battery in North Carolina." Waypoint Legal. February 15, 2011. Accessed March 19, 2019. https://www.waypointlegal.com/index.php/topics/view/assault-and-battery.

Baggaley, Kate. "How Being Bullied Affects Your Adulthood." *Medical Examiner* (blog). Slate. Last modified June 20, 2016. Accessed December 12, 2017. https://slate.com/technology/2016/06/the-lasting-effects-of-childhood-bullying-are-surprisingly-not-all-detrimental-in-adulthood.html.

Baikie, KA, L. Geerligs, and K. Wilhelm. "Expressive Writing and Positive Writing for Participants with Mood Disorders: An Online Randomized Controlled Trial." *Journal of Affective Disorders* 136, no. 3 (December 30, 2011): 310–319. December 30, 2011. Accessed March 28, 2019. https://www.sciencedirect.com/science/article/pii/S0165032711100749X.

Balsa, Erin. "5 Marketing Strategies for Schools in the Age of School Choice." School Leaders Now. Last modified May 14, 2018. https://schoolleadersnow.weareteachers.com/school-marketing-strategies/.

Benton, David, and Stevens Megan. "The Influence of a Glucose Containing Drink on the Behavior of Children in School." *Biological Psychology* 78, no. 3 (July 2008): 242–45.

"Bill of Rights." Bill of Rights Institute. Accessed March 19, 2019. https://billofrightsin stitute. org/founding-documents/bill-of-rights/.

Bloom, Sandra, and Sarah Sreedhar. "The Sanctuary Model of Trauma-Informed Organizational Change." *Reclaiming Children and Youth* 17, no. 3 (Fall, 2008): 53.

Boudaba, Cherif, David M. Linn, Katalin Cs. Halmos, and Jeffrey G. Tasker. 2004. "Increased Tonic Activation of Presynaptic Metabotropic Glutamate Receptors in the Rat Supraoptic Nucleus following Chronic Dehydration." *Journal of Physiology* 551, no. 3 (July 16, 2004): 815–23. https://doi.org/10.1111/j.1469-7793.2003.00815.x

Breen, Audrey. 2017. "UVA Research Finds Suspending Students, in or out of School, Is Problematic." UVA Today. Last modified October 12, 2017. Accessed May 28, 2020. https://news.virginia.edu/content/uva-research-finds-suspending—students-or-out-school-problematic.

Brockie, Teresa, Jessica Gill, and Morgan Hienzelmann. "A Framework to Examine the Role of Epigenetics in Health Disparities Among Native Americans." *Nursing Research and Practice* (2013): e 410395. https://doi.org/10.1155/2013/410395.

"Bronfenbrenner's Bioecological Model of Development (Bronfenbrenner)." Learning Theories. May 15, 2017. https://www.learning-theories.com/bronfenbrenners-bioeco logical-model—bronfenbrenner.html.

"Bullying Statistics." National Bullying Prevention Center. Accessed March 09, 2019. https://www.pacer.org/bullying/resources/stats.asp.

"Charts Related to the Latest American Time Use Survey." News Release. U.S. Bureau of Labor Statistics. Accessed March 27, 2019. https://www.bls.gov/charts/ameri can-time-use/activity-by-parent.htm.

"Child Abuse in North Carolina." Waypoint Legal. Accessed January 19, 2019. http://www. waypointlegal.com/index.php/topics/view/child-abuse.

"Child Abuse Stories." Child Abuse Stories. May 07, 2012. Accessed March 08, 2019. http://www. childabusestories.org/factss/2005–2009-congress-cut-federal-funding-states-treat-and-protect-abused-and-neglected-children.

Child Maltreatment 2014. Report issued by the Children's Bureau, Administration for Children and Families. Accessed March 08, 2019. https://www.acf.hhs.gov/cb/resource/child-maltreatment-2014.

Coleman, Doriane Lambelet, Kenneth A. Dodge, and Sarah Keeton Campbell. "Where and How to Draw the Line Between Reasonable Corporal Punishment and Abuse." *Law and Contemporary Problems* 73, no. 2 (spring 2010): 107–166.

Coles, Robert, and Margaret Sartor. *Their Eyes Meeting the World: the Drawings and Paintings of Children.* Boston: Houghton Mifflin, 1992.

Colino, Stacey. "Bully-Proof Your Child: How to Deal with Bullies." Parents.com. Accessed December 11, 2017. https://www.parents.com/kids/problems/bullying/bully-proof-your-child-how-to-deal-with-bullies/.

Collier, Graham. "What Is the Effect of Music on the Listener?" *Psychology Today,* March 09, 2017. Accessed February 11, 2019. https://www.psychologytoday.com/us/blog/the-consciousness-question/201703/what-is-the-effect-music-the-listener.

"Compare the U.S. to Sweden." IfItWereMyHome.com. Accessed February 22, 2018. http://www.ifitweremyhome.com/compare/US/SE.

"Convention on the Rights of the Child." Office of the High Commissioner for Human Rights (HCHR). Adopted September 2, 1990. Accessed March 20, 2019. https://www.ohchr.org/EN/ProfessionalInterest/Pages/CRC.aspx.

"Convention on the Rights of the Child." Global Initiative to End All Corporal Punishment of Children. Accessed March 20, 2019. https://endcorporalpunishment.org/human-rights-law/crc/.

Corcoran, Roisin P., Alan C.K. Cheung, Elizabeth Kim, and Chen Xie. "Effective Universal School-Based Social and Emotional Learning Programs for Improving Academic

Achievement: A Systematic Review and Meta-Analysis of 50 years of Research." *Educational Research Review* 25 (January/February 2011): 56–72. https://doi.org/10.1016/j.edurev.2017.12.001.

Crocker, Jennifer. "Self-Esteem That's Based on External Sources Has Mental Health Consequences, Study Says." *Monitor on Psychology* 33, no. 11 (December 2002): 16. https://www.apa.org/monitor/dec02/selfesteem.

"Cruelty to Animals" (NC Gen. Stat. §14-360). North Carolina General Assembly. Accessed August 29, 2017. https://www.ncleg.net/enactedlegislation/statutes/html/bysection/chapter_14/gs_14–360.html.

Dalesio, Emery P. "NC Supreme Court Weighs Corporal Punishment vs. Child Abuse." *Hendersonville Times-News*, April 18, 2018. https://www. blueridgenow.com/news/2018 0418/nc-supreme-court-weighs-corporal-punishment-vs-child-abuse.

Dohrenwent, Bruce P., Thomas J. Yeager, Melanie M. Wall, and Ben G. Adams. "The Roles of Combat Exposure, Personal Vulnerability, and Involvement in Harm to Civilians or Prisoners in Vietnam-War–Related Posttraumatics Stress Disorder," *Clinical Psychological Science*, 1, no. 3 (February 2013): 223–238.

"Domestic Violence Rampant Among Native Americans." DomesticShelters.org. March 13, 2017. Accessed June 10, 2019. https://www.domesticshelters.org/articles/statistics/domestic-violence-rampant-among-native-americans.

"Dopamine." 2019. *Psychology Today*. Accessed May 05, 2019. https://www.psychology today.com/us/basics/dopamine.

Douglas, Davison M. "God and the Executioner: The Influence of Western Religion on the Use of the Death Penalty." *William & Mary Bill of Rights Journal*, 7th ser., 9, no. 1 (2000): 137–70. Accessed December 24, 2017. https://scholarship.law.wm.edu/wmborj/vol9/iss1/7.

Durlak, Joseph A., Roger P. Weissberg, Allison B. Dymnicki, Rebecca D. Taylor, and Kriston B. Schellinger. "The Impact of Enhancing Students' Social and Emotional Learning: A Meta-Analysis of School-Based Universal Interventions." *Child Development* 83, no. 1 (February 2011): 405–432. Accessed February 17, 2019. https://onlinelibrary.wiley.com/doi/pdf/10.1111/j.1467-8624.2010.01564.x.

Durrant, Joan, and Ron Ensom. "Physical Punishment of Children: Lessons from 20 Years of Research." *CMAJ* 184, no. 12 (September 2012): 1373–1377. Accessed March 08, 2019. http://www.cmaj.ca/content/184/12/1373.

Ernst, Alycia. "Self-disclosure as Therapy: The Benefits of Expressive Writing." M. Dedge Psychiatry. December 11, 2018. Accessed March 28, 2019. https://www.mdedge.com/psychiatry/article/147848/self-disclosure-therapy-benefits-expressive-writing.

Esmaili, Tala. "First Amendment." Legal Information Institute, Cornell Law School. Accessed May 28, 2020. https://www.law.cornell.edu/constitution/first_amendment.

"Expressive Drawing: An Interview with Robert Coles." Telephone interview by author. May 21, 2005.

Fang, Xiangming, Derek S. Brown, Curtis S. Florence, and James A. Mercy. "The Economic Burden of Child Maltreatment in the United States and Implications for Prevention." *Child Abuse & Neglect* 36, no. 2 (February 2012): 156–65. Accessed January 01, 2019. https://ac.els-cdn.com/S0145213411003140/1-s2.0-S0145213411003140-main.pdf?_tid=664e640d-7f9e-43f6-a6fa-45ca8f526e4f&acdnat=1552056161_0575a31869b750f000816a97cd477f7c.

Felitti, VIncent J., Robert F. Anda, Dale Nordenberg, David F. Williamson, Allison M. Spitz, Valerie Edwards, Mary P. Koss, and James S. Marks. "Relationship of Childhood Abuse and Household Dysfunction to Many of the Leading Causes of Death in Adults." *American Journal of Preventive Medicine* 14, no. 4 (May 1998): 245–58.

"Few Consider Spanking Child Abuse." Rasmussen Reports. November 15, 2018. Accessed March 22, 2019. http://www.rasmussenreports.com/public_content/lifestyle/general_lifestyle/november_2018/few_consider_spanking_child_abuse.

"14th Amendment." History.com. November 09, 2009. Accessed January 19, 2019. https://www.history.com/topics/black-history/fourteenth-amendment.

Franc, Dianne. "How Does Religion Affect Parenting? Here Are the 3 Most Important Things You Should Know." Parent Herald. May 5, 2016. Accessed May 29, 2020. https://www.parentherald.com/articles/41487/20160505/religion-affects-parenting-here-3-important-things-know.htm.

Fredén, Jonas. 2018. "Smacking Children Banned." Sweden.se. Last updated January 9, 2020. Accessed August 12, 2018. https://sweden.se/society/smacking-banned-since-1979/.

Garner, Pamela, Duhita Mahatmya, Elizabeth Brown, and Colleen Vesely. "Promoting Desirable Outcomes among Culturally and Ethnically Diverse Children in Social Emotional Learning Programs: A Multilevel Heuristic Model." *Educational Psychology* 26, no. 1 (January 25, 2014): 165–89.

Gershoff, Elizabeth T., and Andrew Grogan-Kaylor. "Spanking and Child Outcomes: Old Controversies and New Meta-analyses." *Journal of Family Psychology* 30, no. 4 (2016): 453–69. Accessed March 17, 2019. https://doi.org/10.1037/fam0000191.

Gorski, Paul. "Unlearning Deficit Ideology and the Scornful Gaze: Thoughts on Authenticating the Class Discourse in Education." EdChange.org. December 2010, accessed May 25, 2020. http://www.edchange.org/publications/deficit-ideology-scornful-gaze.pdf.

____. "Poverty and the ideological imperative: A call to unhook from deficit and grit ideology and to strive for structural ideology in teacher education." *Journal of Education for Teaching* 42, no. 4 (August 2016): 378–386. https://doi.org/10.1080/0260747 6.2016.1215546.

Graham, Edward. "'A Nation at Risk' Turns 30: Where Did It Take Us?" NEA Today. October 26, 2015. Accessed June 10, 2018. http://neatoday.org/2013/04/25/a-nation-at-risk-turns-30-where-did-it-take-us-2/.

Gray, Peter. "The Decline of Play and Rise in Children's Mental Disorders." *Psychology Today*, January 26, 2010. Accessed March 09, 2018. https://www.psychologytoday.com/us/blog/freedom-learn/201001/the-decline-play-and-rise-in-childrens-mental-disorders.

Greenberg, Zoe. "Is the 'Heat Day' the New Snow Day?" *New York Times*, September 06, 2018.

Hall, Karyn. "Create a Sense of Belonging." *Psychology Today*, March 24, 2014. Accessed February 02, 2019. https://www.psychologytoday.com/us/blog/pieces-mind/201403/create-sense-belonging.

Harris, Nadine Burke. "How Childhood Trauma Affects Health across a Lifetime." TED video. 2014. Accessed May 05, 2019. https://www.ted.com/talks/nadine_burke_harris_how_childhood_trauma_affects_health_across_a_lifetime#t-430498.

Heath, Melissa Allen, Katherine Ryan, Brenda Dean, and Rebecka Bingham. "History of School Safety and Psychological First Aid for Children." *Brief Treatment and Crisis Intervention* 7, no. 3 (August 2007): 206–23. https://doi.org/10.1093/brief-treatment/mhm011.

"Here Are 50 of the Dumbest Laws in Every State." *Reader's Digest*. Accessed March 17, 2019. https://www.rd.com/funny-stuff/dumbest-laws-america/.

The Holy Bible: Containing the Old and New Testaments. London: Trinitarian Bible Society, 2010.

"How School Suspensions Affect Student Achievement." Future Ed. September 19, 2018. Accessed May 29, 2020. https://www.future-ed.org/how-school-suspensions-affect-student-achievement/.

"The Importance of Voice in Releasing Trauma." 2019. Yoga Calm. January 12, 2019. Accessed March 27, 2019. https://www.yogacalm.org/the-importance-of-voice-in-releasing-trauma/.

"Interpreting Scripture—Religion in America: U.S. Religious Data, Demographics and Statistics." Charts by Pew Research Center's Religion & Public Life Project. May 11,

2015. Accessed May 29, 2020. https://www.pewforum.org/religious-landscape-study/interpreting-scripture/.

Izard, Ernest. 2016. *Teaching Children from Poverty and Trauma.* A report published by the National Education Association, June 2016. Washington, D.C.: National Education Association, June 2016. https://www.nea.org/assets/docs/20200_Poverty%20Handbook_flat.pdf.

Jacobs, Julia. 2018. "When Report Cards Go Out on Fridays, Child Abuse Increases on Saturdays, Study Finds." *New York Times,* December 17, 2018. Accessed March 28, 2019. https://www.nytimes.com/2018/12/17/health/child-abuse-report-cards-florida.html.

Jensen, Eric. *Teaching with Poverty in Mind: What Being Poor Does to Kids' Brains and What Schools Can Do About It.* Alexandria, VA: Association for Supervision & Curriculum Development, 2009.

Lai, Betty. "Helping Children Recover from the Trauma of Disaster." CNN.com, September 01, 2017. CNN. Accessed November 22, 2018. https://www.cnn.com/2017/09/01/health/disasters-children-recover-trauma-partner/index.html.

Lander, Jessica. "Helping Teachers Manage the Weight of Trauma." Harvard Graduate School of Education. September 26, 2018. Accessed January 07, 2019. https://www.gse.harvard.edu/news/uk/18/09/helping-teachers-manage-weight-trauma.

Layton, Lyndsey. "Majority of U.S. Public School Students Are in Poverty." *Washington Post,* January 16, 2015. Accessed June 09, 2019. https://www.washingtonpost.com/local/education/majority-of-us-public-school-students-are-in-poverty/2015/01/15/df7171d0–9ce9–11e4-a7ee-526210d665b4_story.html?utm_term=.b24785fab703.

"Learned Helplessness: Seligman's Theory of Depression (Cure)." Positive Psychology Program. August 23, 2018. Accessed May 29, 2020. https://positivepsychologyprogram.com/learned-helplessness-seligman-theory-depression-cure/.

Litvinov, Amanda. 2018. "Our Crumbling Public School Infrastructure." NEA Today. November 05, 2018. Accessed February 02, 2019. http://neatoday.org/2018/10/30/our-crumbling-school-infrastructure/.

Madeline. "Bronfenbrenner's Bioecological Model of Development (Bronfenbrenner)." *Learning Theories.* May 15, 2017. Accessed May 29, 2020. https://www.learning-theories.com/bronfenbrenners-bioecological-model-bronfenbrenner.html.

Maslow, Abraham. *Motivation and Personality.* New York: Harper & Row, 1970.

Matto, Holly, Jessica Strolin-Goltzman, and Michelle Ballan, eds. *Neuroscience for Social Work: Current Research and Practices.* New York: Springer Publishing, 2014.

Mavridis, I. 2015, "The Role of the Nucleus Accumbens in Psychiatric Disorders." *Psychiatrike,* October 25, 2015. Accessed May 05, 2019. https://www.ncbi.nlm.nih.gov/pubmed/26709994.

May, Cindi. "Bullies Hurt Themselves." *Scientific American,* April 16, 2013. Accessed March 27, 2019. https://www.scientificamerican.com/article/bullies-hurt-themselves/.

McEvoy, Alan. "Abuse of Power." *Teaching Tolerance* 48 (Fall 2014): 51–53. Accessed December 12, 2017. https://www.tolerance org/magazine/fall-2014/abuse-of-power.

____. "Teachers Who Bully Students: Patterns and Policy Implications." Paper presented at the Hamilton Fish Institute's Persistently Safe Schools Conference, Philadelphia, September 11–14, 2005. Accessed December 13, 2017. http://nospank.net/mcevoy.htm.

McInerney, Maura, and Amy McKlindon. *Unlocking the Door to Learning: Trauma-Informed Classrooms & Transformational Schools.* Pittsburgh, PA: Education Law Center, June 2015. Accessed May 29, 2020. https://www.elc-pa.org/wp-content/uploads/2015/06/Trauma-Informed-in-Schools-Classrooms-FINAL-December2014-2.pdf.

McLeod, Saul. "Maslow's Hierarchy of Needs." Simply Psychology. May 21, 2018. Accessed June 28, 2018. https://www.simplypsychology.org/maslow.html.

"Memory, Learning, and Emotion: The Hippocampus." Psych Education. December 2014.

Accessed March 09, 2019. https://psycheducation.org/brain-tours/memory-learning-and-emotion-the-hippocampus/.

"Mind-Body Exercises to Calm Your Students When They're Stressed." WeAreTeachers. April 02, 2018. Accessed March 27, 2019. https://www.weareteachers.com/mind-body-skills/.

Mitchell, Travis, "The Links Between Religious Upbringing, Current Religious Identity." Pew Research Center's Religion & Public Life Project. November 01, 2016. Accessed February 17, 2018. http://www.pewforum.org/2016/10/26/links-between-childhood-religious-upbringing-and-current-religious-identity/.

Multi-Tier System of Supports (MTSS): Fact Sheet. PDF. Washington, D.C.: National Center for Learning Disabilities, February 2018. https://nceln.fpg.unc.edu/sites/nceln.fpg.unc.edu/files/resources/NCMTSSFactsheetpost.pdf.

National Association of School Psychologists. "Shortages in School Psychology: Challenges to Meeting the Growing Needs of U.S. Students and Schools." Research summary. Accessed May 28, 2020. https://www.nasponline.org/Documents/Resources%20and%20publications/Resources/School_Psychology_Shortage_2017.pdf

National Center for Injury Prevention and Control. *The Relationship Between Bullying and Suicide: What We Know and What It Means for Schools.* Chamblee, GA: Centers for Disease Control and Prevention (CDC), 2014. https://www.cdc.gov/violenceprevention/pdf/bullying-suicide-translation-final-a.pdf .

"National School Lunch Program (NSLP)." Food and Nutrition Service. December 19, 2018. Accessed February 09, 2019. https://www.fns.usda.gov/nslp/national-school-lunch-program-nslp.

Nazerian, Tina. "'Rocket Fuel': How Schools Can Create a Positive, SEL-Friendly School Culture." EdSurge. Accessed December 27, 2018. https://www.edsurge.com/news/2018-06-11-rocket-fuel-how-schools-can-create-a-positive-sel-friendly-school-culture.

Neal, Gerald Wade. *Quiet Desperation: The Effects of Competition in School on Abused and Neglected Children.* Lanham, MD: Hamilton Books, 2008.

"Nearly Half of American Children Living Near Poverty Line." Columbia University, Mailman School of Public Health. March 02, 2016. Accessed May 28, 2019. https://www.publichealth.columbia.edu/public-health-now/news/nearly-half-american-children-living-near-poverty-line.

Nelsen, Jane, and Kelly Gfroerer. *Positive Discipline Tools for Teachers: Effective Classroom Management for Social, Emotional, and Academic Success.* New York: Harmony Books, 2017.

Otterstrom, Kristina. "The Legal Rights and Responsibilities of a Parent." Lawyers.com. Accessed February 18, 2019. https://www.lawyers.com/legal—info/family-law/children/the-legal-rights-and-responsibilities-of-a-parent.html.

Park, Jisung. "Temperature, Test Scores, and Human Capital Production," *Harvard Education.* February 26. 2017. Accessed December 02, 2018. http://scholar.harvard.edu/files/jisungpark/files/temperature_test_scores_and_human_capital_production_-_j_park_-_2–26–17.pdf.

Payton, John, Roger P. Weissberg, Joseph A. Durlak, Allison B. Dymnick, Rebecca D. Taylor, Kriston B. Schellinger, and Molly Pachan. "The Positive Impact of Social-Emotional Learning for Kindergarten Through Eighth Grade Students." Executive Summaary. Chicago: Collaborative for Academic, Social, and Emotional Learning (CASEL), 2018. Accessed May 28, 2020. https://www.casel.org/wp-content/uploads/2016/08/PDF-4-the-positive-impact-of-social-and-emotional-learning-for-kindergarten-to-eighth-grade-students-executive-summary.pdf

Perry, Bruce. *Incubated in Terror: Neurodevelopmental Factors in the 'Cycle of Violence' In: Children in a Violent Society.* New York, NY: Guilford Press, 1997.

___. "Traumatized Children: How Childhood Trauma Influences Brain Development." *The Journal of the California Alliance for the Mentally Ill* 11, no. 1 (2000): 48–51.

Perry, Bruce, and Ronnie Pollard. "Altered Brain Development Following Global Neglect in Early Childhood." *Society for Neuroscience: Proceedings from the Annual Meeting,* New Orleans. 1997.

Pert, Karen M. "Bullying-Suicide Link Explored in New Study by Researchers at Yale." Yale News. December 21, 2017. Accessed December 11, 2017. https://news.yale.edu/ 2008/07/16/bullying-suicide-link-explored-new-study-researchers-yale.

Peterson, Sarah. "Hurricane Resources." National Child Traumatic Stress Network. April 03, 2018. Accessed March 28, 2019. https://www.nctsn.org/what-is-child-trauma/trauma-types/disasters/hurricane-resources.

Portnoy, Gary. "Where Everybody Knows Your Name." Theme song. *Cheers* (television program), 1983–1992.

"Positive Behavioral and Supports: Brief Introduction and Frequently Asked Questions." Accessed March 01, 2019. https://assets.website-files.com/5d3725188825e071f1670246 /5d7bd792f6de3210d90755a6_what%20is%20pbis%20q%26a%2030%20june%202018. pdf.

Press, Bill. "Bush Cuts Children's Health to Pay for Tax Cut." CNN.com. April 06, 2001. Accessed March 08, 2018. http://edition.cnn.com/2001/ALLPOLITICS/04/06/press. column/.

"Religion in America: U.S. Religious Data, Demographics and Statistics." 2015. Pew Research Center's Religion & Public Life Project. May 11, 2015. Accessed January 17, 2018. http://www.pewforum.org/religious-landscape-study/.

"Religion in America: U.S. Religious Data, Demographics and Statistics." Pew Research Center's Religion & Public Life Project. May 11, 2015. Accessed March 14, 2018. http:// www.pewforum.org/religious-landscape-study/belief-in-absolute-standards-for-right-and-wrong/.

Robinson, Phil Alden, dir. *Field of Dreams.* 1989; Universal City, CA: Universal Pictures, 1998. DVD.

"Same-Sex Marriage Fast Facts." CNN.com. May 25, 2019. Accessed June 3, 2020. https:// www.cnn.com/2013/05/28/us/same-sex-marriage-fast-facts/index.html.

Schlesinger, Arthur, Jr. "Mark Twain, or the Ambiguities." *Atlantic* Monthly. August 01, 1966. Accessed March 19, 2019. https://www.theatlantic.com/magazine/archive/1966/08/ mark-twain-or-the-ambiguities/305730/.

Schlumpf, Heidi. "Spare the Spanking, Respect the Child." *National Catholic Reporter,* October 7, 2014. Accessed June 3, 2020. https://www.ncronline.org/news/people/spare-spanking-respect-child.

"School-Based Social and Emotional Instruction." What Works for Health. November 19, 2018. Accessed March 27, 2019. http://whatworksforhealth.wisc.edu/program. php?t1=20&t2=2&t3=105&id=575.

"School Bus." Amalgamated Transit Union. Accessed May 24, 2019. https://www.atu. org/work/school.

Shakespeare, William. *Romeo and Juliet.* Edited by Barbara A. Mowat and Paul Werstine. Washington: Folger Shakespeare Library, n.d. Accessed September 17, 2020. https:// shakespeare.folger.edu/shakespeares-works/romeo-and-juliet.

___. *Hamlet.* Edited by Barbara A. Mowat and Paul Werstine. Washington: Folger Shakespeare Library, n.d. Accessed September 17, 2020. https://shakespeare.folger. edu/shakespeares-works/hamlet.

___. *Julius Caesar.* Edited by Barbara A. Mowat and Paul Werstine. Washington: Folger Shakespeare Library, n.d. Accessed September 17, 2020. https://shakespeare.folger.edu/ shakespeares-works/julius-caesar.

___. *King Lear.* Edited by Barbara A. Mowat and Paul Werstine. Washington: Folger

Shakespeare Library, n.d. Accessed September 17, 2020. https://shakespeare.folger.edu/shakespeares-works/king-lear.

_____. *Macbeth*. Edited by Barbara A. Mowat and Paul Werstine. Washington: Folger Shakespeare Library, n.d. Accessed September 17, 2020. https://shakespeare.folger.edu/shakespeares-works/macbeth.

_____. *Measure for Measure*. Edited by Barbara A. Mowat and Paul Werstine. Washington: Folger Shakespeare Library, n.d. Accessed September 17, 2020. https://shakespeare.folger.edu/shakespeares-works/measure-for-measure.

_____. *The Merchant of Venice*. Edited by Barbara A. Mowat and Paul Werstine. Washington: Folger Shakespeare Library, n.d. Accessed September 17, 2020. https://shakespeare.folger.edu/shakespeares-works/the-merchant-of-venice.

_____. *A Midsummer Night's Dream*. Edited by Barbara A. Mowat, Paul Werstine, Michael Poston, Rebecca Niles. Washington: Folger Shakespeare Library, n.d. Accessed September 17, 2020. https://shakespeare.folger.edu/shakespeares-works/a-midsummer-nights-dream.

_____. *Othello*. Edited by Barbara A. Mowat and Paul Werstine. Washington: Folger Shakespeare Library, n.d. Accessed September 17, 2020. https://shakespeare.folger.edu/shakespeares-works/othello.

_____. *The Tempest*. Edited by Barbara A. Mowat and Paul Werstine. Washington: Folger Shakespeare Library, n.d. Accessed September 17, 2020. https://shakespeare.folger.edu/shakespeares-works/the-tempest.

_____. *Twelfth Night*. Edited by Barbara A. Mowat and Paul Werstine. Washington: Folger Shakespeare Library, n.d. Accessed September 17, 2020. https://shakespeare.folger.edu/shakespeares-works/twelfth-night.

Soard, Lori. "Bullying Statistics." LoveToKnow.com. Accessed December 12, 2017. https://teens.lovetoknow.com/Bullying_Statistics.

Storrs, Carina. "Is Life Expectancy Reduced by a Traumatic Childhood?" *Scientific American*, October 07, 2009. Accessed February 23, 2017. https://www.scientificamerican.com/article/childhood-adverse-event-life-expectancy-abuse-mortality/.

Swain-Bradway, Jessica, Sarah Lindstrom Johnson, Catherine Bradshaw, and Kent McIntosh. 2017. *What Are the Economic Costs of Implementing SWPBIS in Comparison to the Benefits from Reducing Suspensions?* A brief. Washington, D.C.: U.S. Department of Education, Office of Special Education Programs (OSEP), November 2017. Accessed June 3, 2020. https://assets.website-files.com/5d3725188825e071f1670246/5d76c00cb9339d5f3f267ee7_economiccostsswpbis.pdf

Tarico, Valerie. "Does the Bible Sanction Child Abuse?" Salon.com. October 22, 2013. Accessed December 07, 2018. https://www.salon.com/2013/10/23/does_the_bible_sanction_child _abuse_partner/.

"10 Components of a Successful Education Marketing Plan (Part 1)." Caylor Solutions. February 1, 2018. Accessed June 3, 2020. https://www.caylor-solutions.com/10-components-education-marketing-plan-part-1/.

Terada, Youki. "Welcoming Students with a Smile." Edutopia. September 11, 2018. Accessed January 11, 2019. https://www.edutopia.org/article/welcoming-students-smile.

Thomsen, Michael. 2013. "Get Rid of Grades." Slate. May 01, 2013. Accessed March 11, 2019. https://slate.com/human-interest/2013/05/the-case-against-grades-they-lower-self-esteem-discourage-creativity-and-reinforce-the-class-divide.html.

"Trauma-Sensitive School Training Package." National Center on Safe Supportive Learning Environments. Accessed May 28, 2020, https://safesupportivelearning.ed.gov/trauma-sensitive-schools-training-package.

"Trends in Party Affiliation Among Demographic Groups." Pew Research Center for the People and the Press. September 18, 2018. Accessed April 15, 2019. https://www.people-press.org/2018/03/20/1-trends-in-party-affiliation-among-demographic-groups/.

Twenge, Jean M. "Americans Reporting Increased Symptoms of Depression." News Center, San Diego State University. September 30, 2014. Accessed July 09, 2018. http://newscenter.sdsu.edu/sdsu_newscenter/news_story.aspx?sid=75201.

"2017 Meta-Analysis." Collaborative for Academic, Social and Emotional Learning (CASEL). July 2017. Accessed May 28, 2020. https://casel.org/2017-meta-analysis/.

U.S. Department of Health and Human Services. *Child Maltreatment 2012.* Washington, DC: Administration for Children and Families (ACF), 2013. Accessed June 3, 2020. http://www.acf.hhs.gov/sites/default/files/cb/cm2012.pdf.

"U.S. Supreme Court: Parents' Rights Are Fundamental (Review of Troxel v. Granville)." Home School Legal Defense Association (HSLDA). August 17, 2001. Accessed March 19, 2018. https://hslda.org/content/docs/nche/000010/20011210.asp.

Vinney, Cynthia. "Understanding Maslow's Theory of Self-Actualization." Thought Co. September 21, 2018. Accessed February 28, 2018. https://www.thoughtco.com/maslow-theory-self-actualization-4169662.

"Violence in the Home Leads to Higher Rates of Childhood Bullying." University of Washington News. Accessed December 13, 2017. http://www.washington.edu/news/2006/09/12/violence-in-the-home-leads-to-higher-rates-of-childhood-bullying/.

"What Are the Differences Between a School Counselor and a School Social Worker?" Online Education.com. Accessed May 28, 2020. https://www.onlineeducation.com/counseling/faqs/school-counselor-vs-school-social-worker.

"What Is SEL?" Collaborative for Social and Emotional Learning (CASEL). Accessed March 03, 2019. https://casel.org/what-is-sel/.

"Why Some Soldiers Develop PTSD While Others Don't." Association for Psychological Science. Accessed March 27, 2019. https://www.psychologicalscience.org/news/releases/why-some—soldiers-develop-ptsd-while-others-dont.html.

Wiggins, James, Elizabeth Schatz, and Richard West. "The Relationship of Self-Esteem to Grades, Achievement Scores, and Other Factors Critical to School Success." *School Counselor* 41, no. 4 (March 1994): 239–244. Accessed November 28, 2017. https://psycnet.apa.org/record/1994-47010-001.

Wrench, Jason S., Anne Goding, Danette Ifert Johnson, and Bernardo Attias. *Stand Up, Speak Out: The Practice and Ethics of Public Speaking.* Boston, MA: FlatWorld, 2017.

Yoder, Nicholas. *Teaching the Whole Child: Instructional Practices That Support Social and Emotional Learning in Three Teacher Evaluation Frameworks.* Washington, D.C.: American Institutes for Research Center on Great Teachers and Leaders, 2014. Accessed May 25, 2020. https://gtlcenter.org/sites/default/files/TeachingtheWholeChild.pdf.

Index

www.ingramcontent.com/pod-product-compliance
Lightning Source LLC
Chambersburg PA
CBHW031133270326
41929CB00011B/1607